Fighting for Life

Fighting for Life

CONTEST, SEXUALITY, AND CONSCIOUSNESS

Walter J. Ong

WIPF & STOCK · Eugene, Oregon

Wipf and Stock Publishers
199 W 8th Ave, Suite 3
Eugene, OR 97401

Fighting for Life
Contest, Sexuality, and Consciousness
By Ong, Walter J., SJ
Copyright©1981 Cornell University Press
ISBN 13: 978-1-61097-830-9
Publication date 11/15/2011
Previously published by Cornell University Press, 1981

Copyright © 1981 by Cornell University
This is a reprint edition authorized by the original publisher, Cornell University Press.

*For Kathleen Kemp Forrest
and William Craig Forrest
and their children,
Ted, Kathryn, and Sara*

The trilling wire in the blood
Sings below inveterate scars
And reconciles forgotten wars.
   —T. S. Eliot, *Burnt Norton*

Contents

Preface   9

PART ONE. BACKGROUNDS

1. *Contest and Other Adversatives*   15
    Adversativeness   15
    Origins of the Present Work   24
    Procedures: Understanding and Asymmetric Opposition   29
    Contest, Language, and Thought   34
    Some Differentiations: Contest and Alternative Concepts   37

PART TWO. PATTERNS OF ADVERSATIVENESS

2. *Contest and Sexual Identity*   51
    The Sexes and the Adversative   51
    The Expendable Sex   52
    Combat between Conspecific Males   56
    Ritual Combat   59
    Combat, Stress, and Masculine Identity   64
    Male Fights Male   76
    Bonding Patterns and Loners   80
    All-Male Secrets and Woman's Secret   89
    Vicarious Contest   91

3. *Separation and Self-Giving: Pietà and Quixote*   97
    Externality of Masculinity   97
    Self-Giving, Feminine and Masculine   99
    Maximizing Male Risk   103
    Vocal and Physical Bravado   107
    Masculinity, Contest, Differentiation   112

Contents

PART THREE. PAST, PRESENT, AND FUTURE

4. *Academic and Intellectual Arenas*   *118*
   The Agonistic Heritage of Academia   118
   The Oral Roots of Agonistic Noetic   122
   Residual Orality in Academia   125
   The Latin Connection   129
   From Agonistic to Coeducation: The In-Depth Revolution   134
   Realignment of Agonistic Structures   139
   The New Setting   144

5. *Some Present Issues*   *149*
   Spectator Sports   152
   Politics   158
   Business   163
   Christian Life and Worship   167

6. *Contest and Interiorization*   *184*
   The Variable Settings of Contest   184
   From Violence to Inwardness in Narrative   187
   Contest and the Inward Turn of Scholarship   190
   Contest, Consciousness, and the Self   193
   Adversativeness in the Service of the Person   199

References   211

Index   223

Preface

From antiquity the human being has been considered the "microcosm," the "little world" in which all of the forces and all of the reality of the entire great world, the universe or macrocosm, are represented. Sometimes the human being was thought of as a kind of mirror of all else in the universe. Today we are even more taken by the connections between the human being and the rest of the cosmos than the ancients were, but we cannot be content with such a simplified representation of the connections. Earlier views of the individual as a microcosm tended to be atemporal and generalized. Our present understanding of our complex relationship to the rest of the universe is largely temporal, based on a knowledge of the evolutionary and historical past in relation to the present, and it tends to be quite circumstantial and concerned with details of human behavior.

Humankind has a long past, and it is all present, for, like all beings in history, we are where we are, inevitably, because of where we came from. Even though free choice is partly responsible for our present situation, free choice itself cannot be exercised groundlessly. Any choice is made at a given time in a given situation and thus depends on the options that the time and situation provide, that is, the options that the past has brought into being.

We have become increasingly aware of the biological base of some of these options. Sociobiology, understood in Edward O.

Preface

Wilson's sense (1975:595) as "the systematic study of the biological basis of all social behavior," and variously identified as a new synthesis and as a fad, is in either case very much in the news today. Some people think of it as reductionist, as it can well be, eliminating anything distinctively human by making it out to be purely biological. But sociobiology need not be reductionist. Thought and human free choice can be dependent on biological activity, particularly on neurophysiological activity (serious brain damage makes thought and decision impossible), without being the same thing as biological activity.

This book has grown out of the study of intellectual, literary, and cultural history—in short, of the history of consciousness. At certain points such study is inevitably driven back into biology. The biological side of our nature is nothing to be ashamed of. Human consciousness has always a biological grounding or complement. And biological activity makes little if any sense apart from its evolutionary history. The complexities of biological evolution that we now know thus make an investigation of consciousness a task more complex than ever before.

But in the end we come to an impasse. For what is most distinctive of human beings, male and female, is human self-consciousness. Human self-consciousness is biologically unprocessable because it is genetically free-floating. The "I" that I utter is distinct from and totally cut off from all else, directly accessible only to itself and from its own inside: no one else can know the taste of self (to use Gerard Manley Hopkins's expression) which I experience when I say "I" or when I am simply aware of my own presence to myself. My body resembles the bodies of my parents and earlier ancestors. But my own self, what I refer to when I say "I," is no more related to my parents than to anyone else. It has no genetic constitution. And even though it is embedded in a particular culture, which provides it with its characteristic ways of relating to others, to the world, and even to itself, it still floats free of its culture. The "I" that I say is as completely different from any other self in my own culture as it

Preface

is from any other self in any other culture, real or imaginable. I am simply not you, no matter who or how close you are.

But the human biological organism, in which self-consciousness is nested, does not float free as self-consciousness does. It has a past of millions of years of biological evolution, not to mention a much longer inorganic past. Biological evolution underlies social structures in the infrahuman world and in the human world as well: patterns of aggression and appeasement, of hierarchy, dominance, and submission, of group formation, of sexual drives, and much else. Knowledge of the genetic heritage, far from destroying human freedom, enables us better to understand and exercise freedom, for it provides understanding of the fields in which freedom operates. Exponents of sociobiology have not always been clear on this point, it is true, and the discussion of freedom has been perhaps more muddled than clarified by diversion into discussion of altruism, which already in the eighteenth-century West had proved an intellectual dead end.

This book goes a bit farther than sociobiology ordinarily does. Indeed, if the term is properly understood, what it deals with might be called "noobiology," the study of the biological setting of mental activity (Greek *nous, noos*, mind). Intellect does not sit on the biological organism like a rider on a horse in a Cartesian or Platonic superdualistic world. Thought itself operates out of genetic as well as intellectual history. It has neurophysiological support or grounding. If a human being is truly a microcosm, as he or she is in an even deeper sense than the ancients could have been conscious of, he or she will bring together the extremes of existence: the genetic heritage, which reaches back into the inorganic world, and the biologically unprocessable, genetically free-floating self-consciousness which is the only situs of human intelligence and of its dialectical complement human freedom. (There is no knowledge or human freedom outside of individual, personal consciousnesses.)

This book is an exploration of the cosmology of the "little

Preface

world," the human being, the microcosm, in some of its rich complexity. There are of course many ways into this complexity. The one taken here is through the study of adversativeness as focused in a special kind of adversativeness, contest. My reasons for taking this way in will, I hope, appear in the text that follows.

Abridgments of the six chapters in this book constituted the six Messenger Lectures delivered at Cornell University in October and November 1979. Much of the content of the lectures and of the book was conceived and initially nurtured at the Center for Advanced Studies in the Behavioral Sciences at Stanford, California, when I was a fellow there in 1973-74.

Material from my earlier study "Agonistic Structures in Academia: Past to Present" has been incorporated in this book, mostly in Chapter 4, with some bits in other chapters. The study first appeared in *Interchange* (published by the Ontario Institute for Studies in Education, Toronto), 5, no. 4 (December 1974), pp. 1-12, and in abridged form in *Daedalus: Journal of the American Academy of Arts and Sciences*, Fall 1974, issued as vol. 103, no. 4, of the *Proceedings of the American Academy of Arts and Sciences*, pp. 229-38, copyright Ontario Institute for Studies in Education. This material is used here with the kind permission of the editors of *Interchange* and *Daedalus*.

I am grateful to the many who have put up with me as I worked out some of the thinking here in conversation with them and am especially grateful to the late Charles K. Hofling, M.D., for his counsel and his careful reading of the manuscript of this entire book, and to John C. Hawley, S.J., for his reading of an early draft. As for any errors the book may contain, I shall hope that they are small things but must acknowledge that they are my own.

WALTER J. ONG, S.J.

Saint Louis, Missouri

PART ONE

Backgrounds

I

Contest and Other Adversatives

Adversativeness

Contest is a part of human life everywhere that human life is found. In war and in games, in work and in play, physically, intellectually, and morally, human beings match themselves with or against one another. Struggle appears inseparable from human life, and contest is a particular focus or mode of interpersonal struggle, an opposition that can be hostile but need not be, for certain kinds of contest may serve to sublimate and dissolve hostilities and to build friendship and cooperation.

Contest is one kind of adversativeness, if we understand adversativeness in the ordinary large sense of a relationship in which beings are set against or act against one another. Adversative action, action against, can be destructive, but often it is supportive. If our feet press against the surface we walk on and it does not resist the pressure, we are lost. We all have suffered from dreams in which we feel ourselves plummeting through space. Such dreams can be terrifying, for bodily existence is such that it requires some kind of againstness. Gravity is reassuring; it establishes fields where adversativeness can work and where it functions as a central element in all physical existence.

But adversativeness is significant beyond the physical. It has provided a paradigm for understanding our own existence: in order to know myself, I must know that something else is not me and is (in some measure) set against me, psychologically as well as physically. Erik Erikson (1963:410-11) has discussed the need of the child to find psychic borderlines for guidance—"Stop it! You may not do that!"—and even to locate or imaginatively project some specific enemy—often a "monster"—to free himself or herself from anxieties reaching vaguely into the unknown. Maturity reduces the need to find or project an enemy in order to hold oneself together: psychic organization becomes more interiorized.

Various kinds of adversativeness have been exploited to deal intellectually with the world and with being itself from as far back as we can trace human thought up to the living present. "See now the works of the Most High," we read in Sirach 53:15. "They come in pairs, the one opposite the other." We find adversatives in the all but ubiquitous Mother Earth and Father Sky, the Chinese *li* and *ch'i,* yin and yang, Empedoclean attraction and repulsion, the Platonic dialectic, matter and form, Abelard's *sic et non,* essence and existence, Hegelian dialectic, and countless other binary modes of analysis. These modes proceed by taking one or another sort of adversativeness as an ultimate given and reducing or otherwise referring everything in one way or another to it, thereby satisfying the appetite for understanding, or part of the appetite. Empedocles used adversatives to construct a cosmology, Hobbes to construct a kind of sociology, Hegel to construct a metaphysic of historical change, Charles Darwin and Herbert Spencer to construct a biodynamics of "struggle" for life.

Historians often rest their cases on adversative paradigms. For some two hundred years we have been quite happy with "explanations" of what is going on in history that proceed by selectively grouping elements around opposing poles: what happened in the latter part of the eighteenth century was that something called "romanticism" emerged as a "reaction" to something called "classicism" (or "neoclassicism")—*that* is what happened. Everyone knows that "for every action there is an equal and opposite reaction." Our satisfaction with the zigzag through time that such explanations construct probably owes as much to this adversative paradigm of Newtonian physics as it does to Hegelian theorizing, though it probably owes even more to our muscular experience of adversativeness in the physical world.

In modern times adversativeness has become even more particularized as a tool and object of thought. Binary opposition serves as the foundation of virtually all of modern structuralism, whether linguistic, as in Roman Jakobson's phonemics (Jakobson, Fant, and Halle, 1969), which is related to Ferdinand de Saussure's earlier binary linguistics (Schneidau, 1977:144-45), or anthropological, as in Claude Lévi-Strauss (1969), whose doctrine Morris Freilich sums up: "Everything of importance comes in twos and in conflict" (1977:246). Binary opposition underlies all modern communication theory and computerization. Robert Frost was onto the pattern: "It almost scares / A man the way things come in pairs." But Charles Sanders Peirce is perhaps the most forthright of all authenticators of adversativeness: "A thing without oppositions *ipso facto* does not exist" (1931:I, no. 457).

Recent decades have seen the growth of an immense literature reporting analytic, clinical, and experimental studies concerning specific manifestations of adversativeness ranging from the cataclysmic to the trivial, particularly among living organisms, including the human. Psychologists, psychiatrists, physiologists, endocrinologists, sociologists, biologists and sociobiologists, anthropologists, criminologists, political scientists, jurists, rhetoricians, communications experts, philosophers, theologians, and others have studied innumerable instances and kinds of aggression, conflict, polemic, hostility, confrontation tactics, clashes of personalities, competition, games, contest, and other adversative manifestations. They have canvassed various ways of dealing with or eliminating or circumventing or increasing or reducing or stabilizing these and related adversative phenomena. In Egypt a few years ago I met an itinerant self-styled "conflict engineer" who was roaming the world to accumulate conflict experience before settling down to the permanent practice of conflict engineering in California.

Certain works on adversativeness of various sorts have become classic. Johan Huizinga's wide-ranging *Homo Ludens: A Study of the Play Element in Culture* (1955) has made the present generation aware of the pervasiveness of agonistic activity in the form of play through the entire human lifeworld. Huizinga is concerned chiefly with human beings but makes some references to animal behavior. He suggests that the antagonistic, antithetical structures of archaic societies act out antithetical structures in the cosmos (1955:53-56), but he has also outlined some of the civilizing or consciousness-raising effects of agonistic activity.

Roger Caillois's *Man, Play, and Games* (1961) undertakes to classify all games as based on either competition (*agōn*), chance (*alea*), mimicry (*imitatio* or *ars mimica*), or dizziness or vertigo (*ilinx*), suggesting that the transition to civilization is marked by the reduction of the *imitatio-ilinx* pair and the ascendancy of the *agōn-alea*. His treatment is useful but far narrower than Huizinga's.

Two other widely read semipopular books, *On Aggression* (1966), by the Nobel Prize winner Konrad Lorenz, and *The Territorial Imperative* (1967), by the former free-lance writer Robert Ardrey, have treated animal behavior in greater detail, familiarizing the general educated public with the elaborate agonistic patterns evolved in animal behavior and urging that humankind's evolutionary past has programmed the species genetically for war. Moving from physics through biology to psychology, Pierre Teilhard de Chardin has interpreted the whole of cosmic and human social evolution as a form of conflict resolution (1965a:21, 29, 105; 1965b:21, 71, 147; 1969:105, 108, 134; Heagle, 1973:46-58).

In *The Origins and History of Consciousness* (1954), still a capital summary work that will serve occasionally in the present study as a point of reference, Erich Neumann has brought together in a generally Jungian framework a good deal of thought touching on struggle as an element in both ontogenetic and phylogenetic psychic development. Neumann's first stage is that of the undifferentiated, self-contained whole symbolized by the uroboros (Greek *ouroboros*, tail eater), the snake with its tail in its mouth, seeking to tuck itself inside itself and thus to eliminate from consciousness all external reality. (The thumb-sucking child, regressing into itself from a threatening external world, is engaged in a similar project.) Except for this initial stage (1), a flight from all conflict, all of the stages that Neumann discerns in the development of consciousness through human history are more or less agonistic in constitution: (2) domination by the Great Mother, (3) separation of the world parents, (4) birth of the hero (rise of masculinity and the personalized ego), (5) slaying of the mother and (6) of the father, (7) freeing of the captive, and (8) transformation into self-conscious individualism, symbolized primordially in the Osiris myth but today entering into new personalizing phases. Erik Erikson's *Childhood and Society* (1963), a corresponding Freudian account of development, mostly ontogenetic, treats adversativeness in human personality developments, especially in connection with trust and mistrust and with American identity.

Finally, Edward O. Wilson's massive *Sociobiology: The New Synthesis* (1975) has pulled together a vast amount of work on adversativeness and related subjects now available in sociological, anthropological, psychological, biological, and related literature, and has interpreted the whole in terms of the continuities between animal ethology and human sociology. To avoid multiplication of references, for support of certain statements in the present work I at times cite *Sociobiology* alone without explicit mention of the scattered publications that validate the statement and that the reader can readily trace through Wilson's work. One need not agree entirely—as I by no means agree entirely—with the philosophically couched theories Wilson advances in this book to value and use the comparative data he so generously provides. The book is particularly valuable because of the specificity and range of the research it reports on and synthesizes, and future work not only in sociobiology but also in a great many other fields will always be indebted to Wilson.

Wilson defines sociobiology (1975:595) as "the systematic study of the biological basis of all social behavior." Applied to human beings, such study has great values and certain limits. One of its great values is that it shows real relationships between the highest human intellectual and volitional activities and the permanent biological roots of humanity. Its limits are set by the fact that there are breaks, greater than quantum leaps, between biology and human consciousness, which shapes what is most definitive in human behavior and which sociobiology does not deal with as such. Sociobiology says nothing of the self-consciousness in which human behavior roots itself, the unique "I" that each person utters and that is inaccessible to anyone else in the world. It says nothing about the free decisions that underlie so much of human behavior, nothing of the uniquely human subject-predicate juncture that marks the use of language (Ong, 1967:138-61), and nothing of the observance of incest prohibitions, which, although they have direct biological consequences, appear to be closely tied to the use of language (Wilden, 1972:16, 240-51, 269-73). All of these forms of human behavior, and others, transcend the biological, although they also tie in with it. They involve adversativeness in various ways and are given attention later in this book. Nevertheless, despite its limitations, sociobiology does provide insights into certain continuities, also treated later, between biology and human sociology that make possible a new understanding of human life in relation to nature (*natura*, birth, biological origin) more holistic in many ways than any other available.

Adversativeness in human beings has not only genetic sources but also conscious sources. Adversativeness can be cultivated. In fact, deliberate cultivation of the adversative lies at the deepest roots of intellectual development, particularly in the West. In his seminal work *Polarity and Analogy* (1966), G. E. R. Lloyd has shown that for ancient Greek thought, which has proved absolutely crucial to the development of thought and culture all over the world today, adversativeness was essential (as it is for Lloyd's own thought: polarity itself refers to a form of adversativeness, and it is set up by Lloyd as an "adversative of analogy").

Contest and Other Adversatives

Lloyd has surveyed series of opposites in selected indigenous cultures around the world (South America, Africa, North America) to situate the various ancient Greek series of opposites in a worldwide framework. He finds that the Greek opposites have no salient characteristics that differ from those of the others. The ancient Greeks simply reflected more on their adversatives and gradually reshaped them. The reasons are certainly connected with the effects of writing, which in its fixity shows up disparities in competing accounts that oral reporting tends to gloss over or adjust (Goody, 1968:56, 67-68). Havelock (1978:9-10), quoting Oppenheim (1975) on the inhibiting, noncontrastive world view in ancient Mesopotamian cuneiform writing, attributes the Greeks' predilection for sharp polarization precisely to their use of the alphabet. Cuneiform writing was nonalphabetic, basically pictographic. But other forces were also doubtless at work. Studying the origins of Greek social thought, Alvin W. Gouldner (1965: 43-55) has shown that the ancient Greek way of life was marked by (1) the quest for fame (*fama*, what people say about you, Latin *fari*, to speak—a deep concern of primary oral cultures, which are typically highly agonistic, as will be seen) through (2) personal action in (3) a contest system of operation setting person against person. Gouldner's perspectives show how deep-set the adversative structures were in the Greek ethos.

In one way or another adversativeness may be deep-set in all cultures and personalities. Goody (1977:52-73, 146-62 and *passim*, in places citing Ong, 1958b) has provided a rich cross-cultural account of many of its manifestations and of its effects in the "domestication of the savage mind." But the Greeks seem to have made more careful use of adversativeness than did other cultures, both as an analytic tool and as an operational intellectual procedure. Adversativeness sets the stage for the central Greek development that has changed the world, formal logic and all that goes with it. Formal logic, we know (Bochenski, 1961:10-18, 23-39, 417), did not grow out of a dispassionate or irenic setting such as the concept of logic itself might suggest—what could be more objective, neutral, uninvolved than logic? Rather, it grew

Fighting for Life

out of reflection on disputation, on verbal and intellectual contest, on the question "How is it that what you say demolishes what I say?" Formal logic remains over the ages committed to diaeretic procedures, and it is no accident that formal logicians, past to present, have quite commonly proved to be disputatious people and not infrequently cantankerous (Durand, 1960:191-99, 453-55).

Indian logic, which never developed so far nor had so much global influence as the Greek, is the only formal logic in the world with any claims to have originated independently of Greek logic (Bochenski, 1961:416-17, 430-40), though it came into being so much later than Greek logic that one may have doubts about its total independence. In any event, it, too, arose from analysis of dispute, of adversativeness. By contrast, Chinese culture minimized dispute, thought of rhetoric as serving propriety and harmony, downplayed individual difference in favor of conformity (Oliver, 1971:145-81, esp. 180; cf. Maspero, 1928), and, despite its other stupendous achievements, produced nothing like formal logic at all.

When ancient Greek thought devoted itself to analogies or likenesses rather than to adversatives or contrasts, it proceeded by relentlessly noting differences or contrasts, as well as resemblances, within the analogies themselves. With logic, ancient Greece formalized adversativeness as no other culture had done. In so far as matter could be fully processed in logical format, it was resolvable into a clear-cut yes or no. The principle of the computer had been conceived, nonnegotiable binary opposition. Rhetoric, out of which formal logic grew, proceeds also by opposition, but by contrast with formal logic, rhetoric deals typically with soft oppositions. Rhetorical oppositions are negotiable.

Formal logic begins with analysis of extant thought processes. Mathematics begins with postulates. Of all forms of knowledge, it appears that only mathematics proceeds, at least in principle, without adversativeness. The reason is clear: whatever could be argued about is deactivated in postulates or definitions. "A straight line is the shortest distance between two points." To propose as a mathematical starting point a definition such as this, or a postulate, is to say in effect: Let us agree at the outset on "short" and "distance" and "between." These things we *could* argue about, because in fact they are very difficult, and in some cases impossible, to define adequately. But we *won't* argue or even attempt to define "short" or "distance" or "between." We shall practice what Michael Polanyi (1958, 1966) styles "tacit" agreement or understanding—which means in effect that, although we have not fully articulated what these terms mean and perhaps cannot, for our grasp of them is largely subconscious or unconscious, we shall proceed with the agreement that we do somehow mean the same thing by them.

To put in another way the resulting irenic character of mathematical understanding, we can say that in mathematical thinking there is no dialectic, in a sweeping sense of this term, including the Hegelian dialectic—unless you plunge into the postulates and definitions as you do in studying the foundations of mathematics. But the foundations of mathematics are not entirely mathematical. Certain adversative proofs used in mathematics, too, rest on principles that are not mathematical but philosophical and that can thus be adversative. For example, showing that a theorem is true because its contradictory is false is not a distinctively mathematical operation, however useful in mathematics, but a philosophical ploy.

Lloyd's work is indispensable for an understanding of adversativeness in ancient Greek intellectual life and in human existence generally. But it is only a beginning. Not all of the manifestations of adversativeness in human cultural and intellectual history have been studied, by any means. The present work undertakes examination of a cluster of some such manifestations that cut across the fields of anthropology, sociology, biology, linguistics, psychology, literary and intellectual history, educational history, particularly academic educational history, and Christian ecclesial and theological history. These are diverse fields, although perhaps not quite so diverse as at first they appear. It will be the business of the present work to show some of the deep and intimate connections between certain seemingly unrelated phenomena from these and various other fields, with a view to understanding better the evolution of consciousness. The literature tangential to the present study is enormous, and to try to enter into discussion with all of it would be impossibly distracting. Most of what is not referred to specifically in the text can be traced through citations found in works in the References. The countless popular and semipopular works, particularly on questions of sexual identity, are mostly not attended to here.

Origins of the Present Work

Thought always emerges from its own history, so perhaps it will be helpful here to note how the present lines of investigation developed. They have emerged, not out of biology or the social sciences or psychology as such, but out of long-standing concern with intellectual history in its deeper structures, specifically in the academic world. My work in the 1950s with Peter Ramus and the sixteenth-century milieu brought home the highly programmed contentiousness of Renaissance and earlier academic intellectualism. It soon became apparent that, although academia was the focus of programmed contentiousness, the fabric of the circumambient nonacademic life-style was significantly contentious, too, particularly in its verbal performance. Its contentiousness was continuous with the classical tradition. Concern with rhetoric—and with formal logic, which had grown out of rhetoric—marked the tradition. But rhetoric was as much the consequence as the cause of the agonistic pitch of existence. By contrast with this earlier academic world and the culture that supported it, at least in the West, present-day culture puts very little effort into deliberately creating and living out stress situations. We are unabashed irenicists, so unabashed that we have been unaware how irenic we are by contrast with this earlier world.

In the earlier culture, contest and high-stress operations suggestive of contest marked a wide variety of phenomena at first seemingly unconnected: the dominance of rhetoric and dialectic or logic in curricula, the use of a language other than the mother tongue, acquired (with negligible exceptions) only by males and under stress situations, for all formally intellectual work, the totally male population of academia, the vigorous and often brutal disciplining of pupils, the dominantly agonistic teaching procedures, the constant recycling of all knowledge, even that acquired by reading, through the agora of public oral disputation, the programmatically combative oral testing of knowledge, and much else (Ong, 1954, 1956, 1958a, 1958b).

Further excavation of the old agonistic structures and of the psychic and cultural roots of contest itself brought to light deep connections between all these and other seemingly unrelated phenomena as well. Clues led in many directions: into the evolutionary, biological depths latterly explored by the now popular sociobiology (Edward O. Wilson, 1975) as well as into human academic history and intellectual development. The clues connected at strategic points with old folk wisdom and well-known literary *aperçus*. Problems of sexual identity, particularly male sexual identity, showed in the agonistic patterning, from athletic events to academic teaching and testing (Ong, 1974). The entire mix of issues, deeply involved with the dialectic of the sexes, which figures always as a standard variable in the evolution of consciousness, opened insights into areas of human existence undergoing active evolution today, when, for example, spectator sports build up and focus the agonistic drives around the world in huge regional, national, and global configurations totally unknown before electronic communication. Developments in agonistic patterns relate to the stages of consciousness described by Jung, Erich Neumann (1954), and others. Huizinga's work (1955) with "play" was relevant, but his insights have to be refined and redirected by attention to later work in the behavioral sciences, particularly concerning animal behavior. All in all, for reasons to be indicated later, the data coming my way could be better processed by thinking in terms of "contest" rather than of "play" as such.

Fighting for Life

The fate of agonistic structures is tied in with the history of verbalization, and in particular with the technologizing of the word. Words are essentially oral events. They came into being in sound. They can never be totally disconnected from sound. To realize the meaning of a word, including the written or printed word, one must refer it somehow to the oral world, directly or indirectly, in speech or in imagination. The technologies of writing, print, and electronics convert, or seem to convert, the sound or event that constitutes a real word into a kind of thing, permanent and fixed. The conversion or technologizing of verbal performance gives the word and thought itself marvelous new powers and restructures the psyche. Technologizing of the word by writing made possible the "arts" of rhetoric and dialectic or logic, which with grammar constituted in the West the ancient and long-persistent *artes sermocinales,* arts of discussion or of discourse, or of verbal communication.[1] Without writing, rhetoric could be and was practiced, but no reflective, analytic treatise or "art" explaining its working could be devised.

The later history of these arts in relation to contest is tied to the history of the technologized word. Protracted study has made it clear (Ong, 1958a, 1958b, 1967, 1971, 1977a, and references in these works) that in the West rhetoric as the art of oratory, always highly agonistic, atrophied spectacularly after the advent of print, while dialectic (sometimes styled logic), originally an art governing the agonistic world of public debate, the "art of discourse" (*ars disserendi*), radically social and personal, was reinterpreted in print cultures as an art governing purportedly private and, by implication, more or less wordless, nonagonistic thought. The

---

[1] The term *sermocinalis*, with such cognates as *sermo*, derives ultimately from *sero*, to join or bind together, pleat, interweave (Sanskrit *sarat*, thread; Greek *seira*, rope; cf. Latin *series*, English *series*). Like the Greeks, who thought of the singer of tales as "stitching together songs" (*rhaptein*, to stitch, sew; *rhapsōidein*, to stitch together songs, hence the English *rhapsodize*), the Latins had early conceived of discourse and of thinking itself as a stringing together or assembling of somewhat discrete elements.

romantic cult of solipsistic—and hence in principle irenic—"creativity" is a product of a sensibility shaped by print.

Through study of the noetic economy and its evolution in a variety of cultures (Peristiany, 1966; Goody, 1968; Ong, 1958a, 1958b, 1967, 1971, and references there) it becomes evident that verbal contest is a massive and seemingly universal phenomenon in early cultures across the world, not merely in the West. It is most marked in primary oral cultures, those totally unaffected by writing, and remains in always weakening residue as writing, and particularly alphabetic writing, once invented, is gradually interiorized by the psyche. The greater or lesser persistence of overt verbal contest in fact gives a rough indication of how much pristine orality a given later culture retains (Ong, 1971:23-47).

Further investigation of verbal agonistic behavior (Ong, 1971, 1974), corroborating or at least dovetailing with the massive research on animal behavior such as has been gathered together by Wilson (1975) and Sebeok in *How Animals Communicate* (1977), has revealed many antecedents in the infrahuman animal world, most notably in ceremonial combat among males, an activity that is highly functional in evolutionary selection and that will be discussed in detail in subsequent chapters.

The roots of verbal combat thus prove to be deeper than consciousness and temporally antecedent to the emergence of consciousness. In excavating the roots one is forced to pay attention to the biological and sociological analogues of the agonistic structures in human intellectual and communicative activities. As earlier noted, we can style the present work, which treats these analogies, an essay in "noobiology" (from the Greek *nous,* genitive *noos,* pronounced in two syllables, meaning "mind"). Just as, putting aside Wilson's more sweeping philosophical or ideological claims—which I believe, as do many others (Midgley, 1978:xvii and *passim,*) have less substance and less freshness than his data—we can say that sociobiology is the study of the biological underpinning of social behavior, including human social behavior, so noobiology is the study of the biological underpinning of human mental or intellectual activity. The present essay in noobiology undertakes to examine some of the relationships between intellectual activity and biological activity which are found centered around contest. Contest has been a major factor in organic evolution and it turns out to have been a major, and indeed seemingly essential, factor in intellectual development.

As has been mentioned and will be clarified later, to relate intellectual activity, and thereby the field of free choice, to the biological is by no means to reduce the intellectual and the voluntary to the biological. Relationism is not reductionism. Human intelligence and free choice cannot be reduced to biology, although they cannot be exercised without biological accompaniment.

Since contest is so pervasive in the evolution of consciousness, there appears to be no way to give a full account of all that contest means to the psyche: its roots are too deep for total excavation. The aim of the present study is therefore limited. It is not prescriptive or even diagnostic, but interpretive, undertaking to improve understanding of the force with which contest affects human life from its biological base to its intellectual heights. In particular this study undertakes ultimately to show some of the ways in which struggle, and in particular the kind of struggle we identify as contest, has functioned more or less directly to shape the noetic world itself, and specifically its academic development. Contest operates in many sectors of life—in politics, in sports, in commerce, in the adversary procedures of jurisprudence, to name only a few obvious sectors. The present study concerns itself principally with contest in sectors closer to consciousness as such, that is, with contest as it has entered into the constitution and management of knowledge itself and generated what we know as academic knowledge, that is, knowledge formalized or rendered relatively abstract with the direct or indirect aid of writing and publicly taught, as against what is learned by less verbalized participation or apprenticeship, as in the family, in a trade, or in such other specialized occupations as hunting and fishing.

Contest and Other Adversatives

Contest has figured relatively little in the development of knowledge outside of formal academic settings. It has been less operative, for example, in the learning of one's mother tongue or in the acquisition of a knowledge of mechanics. Although the fact has been almost entirely overlooked in cultural history, the academic world itself has in the past been conspicuously dominated by agonistic activity and structures—from its beginnings in the ancient rhetorical and dialectical tradition in the West and comparable traditions elsewhere through later academic and other educational practices dominant until the advent of the Romantic movement, which reduced or masked the agonistic mind-set in academia but did not eliminate it.

Agonistic activities and structures develop in the noetic world in ways complexly related to their development elsewhere. The romantic abandonment of ceremonial contest as a means (indeed, historically, a basic means) of transmitting conceptualized knowledge from one generation to the next is not unrelated, the present study hopes to show, to women's liberation movements, student demonstrations, pacifism, and the substitution of the existential, noncontesting fugitive hero (Kafka's protagonists in *The Trial* and *The Castle*, who can find nothing real to push against, and John Updike's protagonist in *Rabbit, Run*) in place of the agonistic hero of the older epic and romance. Shifts in agonistic structures within the world of knowledge relate to other major shifts within the noetic world itself: to the shift, for example, from closed-system paradigms to open-system paradigms in Western thinking generally, and to what analytic psychology has described as the breakthrough of the dark side of the psyche in the West, the conscious recognition of the unconscious and the internalizing in the individual psyche of the evil present in the human lifeworld (Ong, 1977a).

Procedures: Understanding and Asymmetric Opposition

Although this work has grown out of the study of cultural and intellectual history, it makes considerable use of anthropological

Fighting for Life

and sociological and psychological as well as biological research—this last largely where tangent to the social sciences. Consequently, something should perhaps be said concerning the relationship between the thought processes here and the methods of the social sciences, particularly since reflection and statement on this subject have been kindly and persuasively urged on me by one of the deans of American sociologists, Robert K. Merton.

The procedure here, like that in virtually all interpretations of historical developments, is to work from hypotheses. These hypotheses are sometimes declared but often simply implied. The hypotheses cannot always be articulated to the full. Not infrequently, in studies of historical developments and in other humanistic studies, hypotheses are far more explicit at the conclusion of the work than at the beginning. The hypotheses may first reveal themselves at the end as "conclusions." The reason for this deferred fuller articulation of hypotheses appears evident enough. The hypotheses in historical and other humanistic studies are usually complex in the sense that they contain a great many interrelated and nuanced details, so that they cannot be adequately stated until a large body of discussion has been assimilated, and also in the sense that they commonly leave generous margins of what has well been called "productive ambiguity." Generally speaking, in such historical interpretations as this book proposes there can be no total verification of the sort that the natural sciences commonly achieve and that the social sciences frequently ambition (but seldom achieve) for the reason that in material of the sort considered here, total verification would mean massive and disastrous fragmentation of observations and data and all but certain trivialization of categories, as well as impossible complications in the conclusions. This is not to say that verification should not be attempted or is not attempted at all—it should be worked out to the absolute maximum practicable. Nor is it to say that massively verified conclusions available from various sciences or quasi-sciences should not be respected, for they are often invaluable and should also be used to the maximum whenever they are relevant, pro or con.

In any investigation, even in the physical sciences or mathematics, the conclusions are always only more or less explicit, more or less totally "clear" in all of their implications. Total explicitness is impossible in human statement—which is not at all the same as to say that we cannot tell whether a statement is true or false, but rather that we cannot at any given moment raise to the level of full consciousness everything that any statement means, every bit of truth the statement involves (including this present statement). Generally speaking, in matters of deep philosophical or cultural import, the more totally explicit a principle or a conclusion is—that is, the more its total meaning is a matter of purely conscious apprehension without proportionate unconscious implications—the more likely it is to be trivial. (This truth is caught—rather inaccurately and defensively—in the popular definition of a Ph.D. as one who knows more and more about less and less.) The truly profound and meaningful principles and conclusions concerning matters of deep philosophical or cultural import are, I believe, invariably aphoristic or gnomic, and paradoxical. Their meaning is both clear and mysterious, and dialectically structured.

By dialectically structured I do not mean containing a contradiction. Speaking of thought as developing by means of contradictions is cheap, overly facile, almost as cheap and facile as Arthur Schnitzler's still amusing statement that if you shake an aphorism (which is often, or even typically, a paradox), a lie falls out and leaves you with a platitude. I mean that the ultimately profound statements are always duplex: they say, at least by implication, two things that are related to one another by asymmetric opposition. "Experience is the best teacher." But experience is also the worst teacher, as Roger Ascham observed in *The Schoolmaster* (1570): too many people die of it, and this is basically why it is a good idea to go to school and learn to some degree vicariously rather than experientially. "Experience is the worst teacher" is not a contradiction of "Experience is the best teacher," for which the contradiction is simply "Experience is *not* the best teacher." To say that experience is the worst teacher is not to say that it is not the best teacher, but only to suggest that if it is the best teacher it is so in a limited way—in such a way that in another way it is also the worst teacher. The concept "best" here is not a simple concept but is in fact duplex, containing an implicit qualification. The opposition between the two statements is not symmetrical (is-is not) but asymmetrical (is-but). When you look carefully at the one statement, the somewhat askew qualification buried within it shows, revealing that the statement is really duplex. And when it is stated in duplex form, at least one of the two resulting contrasted statements will have new duplicities within it.

The ultimate paradigm or model for dialectical relationships is not a flat contradiction of formal logic but something from the personal, human lifeworld, conversation itself, dialogue about a particular matter, in which each statement by one interlocutor needs qualification from the other interlocutor's statement in order to move toward fuller truth. Dialogue entails a certain negativity, for there is always at least some subtle negative element in any articulated dialogic response. Even a "yes" means "Yes, I do agree, as you were *not* sure I did before I said yes—which is why you cast your positive question negatively, as 'You do agree, *don't* you?' " This negative element is a response to the limitations of the original statement. And the response requires further qualification from the first interlocutor. There is opposition here but no head-on collision, which stops dialogue. (Of course, sometimes dialogue has to be stopped, but that is another story.)

The duplex condition of human statement is hardly surprising. For humans, embodied consciousnesses, are essentially duplex beings. My body is both inside me ("Stop kicking *me*," not "Stop kicking my body") and outside me (I feel myself somehow inside my body, which is a frontier between the "I" that I know and all other things in the world, including even my body itself). For such duplex beings, it is inevitable that statements touching the depths would have a duplex structure, without which there would be no human resonance or truth. There is no way to say something philosophically worthwhile in monist form. Serious philosophical statement deeply involves not only consciousness but also the unconscious (more "bodily," less freed than consciousness).

The dialectical structure of truth in depth does not mean that we cannot tell truth from falsehood. For we can make statements that are absolutely true in the sense that their contradiction is false. "The human being is a speaking animal." It is false to say that the human being is not a speaking animal. We know our assertion is true, but we are not fully aware of all that it says. We are not fully aware of the size of the truth we have uttered. It is impossible to explain fully, to make totally explicit all that "speaking" means. We cannot establish its exact bounds. Dialogue enables us to begin to establish the bounds of this as of other meanings.

The dialectical structure of deep truth suggests why adversativeness has proved so crucial in the development of knowledge and of consciousness itself. As Hegel well knew, the inner structure of truth as we receive it and conceive it is adversative. *Die Wahrheit ist symphonisch*, Hans Urs von Balthasar announces in the title of one of his books (1972): truth is symphonic. A symphony involves many instruments or voices struggling against or with one another—in a contest, "against" and "with" come to the same thing. Like contest, as will be seen, the adversative structures of truth are not lethal or even hostile, but life-giving, though at some cost.

The dialectical structure of deep truth also makes clear—though of course not totally clear—why total explicitness, total clarity, total explanation is impossible. Nevertheless, for reasoned understanding it is commonly advisable to maximize explicitness. Explain all you can. But recognize the built-in limitations of the undertaking. In a study such as this, while demonstrations and conclusions are as explicit as I can make them in my present state of enlightenment, they are also charged with subconsciously or unconsciously apprehended significance, more conspicuously, though hardly more really, than conclusions in the hard-nosed sciences. This is one of the principal reasons that history, philosophy, literary analysis and theory, and other subjects subsumed under the term "humanities" are enjoyable. They always say more than they mean because they mean more than they say. I trust that this is true of the present work.

Contest, Language, and Thought

Historically, some of the most conspicuous manifestations of adversativeness in the human lifeworld across the globe have been in speech itself. In distant ages, speech, together with thought, was a highly combative activity, especially in its more public manifestations—much more combative than we in our present-day technological world are likely to assume or are even willing to believe. Lloyd's work cited above (1966) suggests the fascination of the Greeks with the adversativeness—or, to use Lloyd's term, "polarity"—they could discover in any and all phenomena, including especially language and thought themselves. The ancient Greeks' fascination with the adversativeness of language and thought shows in their abundant works on rhetoric and dialectic and, as noted above, ultimately in formal logic, which grew out of dispute and polarized "yes" and "no" as never before. The Greek fascination with the agonistic structures of speech and thought spread and continued through the West, not only in the study of rhetoric, dialectic, and logic, but in a myriad of other less immediately conspicuous ways.

But if the concern with adversativeness or polarity growing out of ancient Greece has been in some ways more intense in the West than elsewhere, dispute or verbal struggle of one sort or another has been curiously integral to the noetic economy of humankind everywhere. Robert T. Oliver's *Communication and Culture in Ancient India and China* (1971), with its lengthy bibliography, shows comparable structures in the Far East (see especially pp. 91-99), though the agonistic thrust was managed quite differently there, was in fact deliberately suppressed, with the

Contest and Other Adversatives

result that in ancient China, as already noted, formal logic (the ultimate in adversativeness: yes, no) was never developed at all.

Comparable agonistic verbal performance in subsaharan Africa is by now abundantly evident in the novels of Chinua Achebe, Camara Laye, Elechi Amadi, and others. Such studies as those anthologized by Arthur L. Smith in *Language, Communication, and Rhetoric in Black America* (1972) reveal similar agonistic structures, noetic and linguistic, in black culture in the United States. Roger Abrahams (1968a, 1972) has pointed out that proverbs and riddles, essential to oral cultures as means of storing and retrieving and advancing knowledge, find some of their commonest uses in verbal combat, in attempts to top another's utterance, to put the other person down, and has described how performances of "men of words" in black communities are essentially shows of masculine strength (1972). Frank E. Manning (1973:62-72, 115-45) reports the highly combative life-style of a culture largely centered on oral verbal exchange and other kinds of "gaming," a culture that explicitly as well as implicitly places high value on the "man of words." The spectacularly combative verbal stance of a particular "man of words" seen by his associates as a somewhat dangerous person, given to attacking others verbally quite at random, and therefore downgraded by them as "mad," has been described in detail by Peter J. Wilson in his "Oscar: An Inquiry into Madness" (1974), although Wilson has not noted that many agonistic features of Oscar's personality structure are quite representative of oral cultures generally across the globe.

The study of the adversative stance in the noetic world, the world of knowledge, involves us not only with the far-distant past but simultaneously with the present and future. In *The Double Helix* (1968; see also Merton, 1968), James D. Watson has given an exciting account of the extremely agonistic atmosphere in which he and others labored to discover the structure of DNA. In a more spectacular way, it has long been evident, even from the news media alone, how much the moon shot and the space race generally have been dependent on an agonistic state of affairs. Had there not been a contest between the two great powers, the United States and the USSR, it appears most unlikely that either could have managed to divert to the space projects the tremendous amount of psychic, intellectual, and physical energy they required. The competitive sense fostering mobilization of the vast resources demanded for space exploration appears to have depended not entirely or even chiefly on military threat. Military threat was and is much more real at the lower level—in a quite physical sense of the term "level"—of aircraft lanes, intercontinental ballistic missiles, and the like. More important for the space race as such was simply the feel of a contest. In a report to the American Academy of Arts and Sciences, Hans Mark (1975:19) notes that "no important *fundamental* or unexpected discovery has been uncovered in our exploration of space." The exploration of outer space was quite as romantic as it was scientific, unavoidably challenging, massive, and agonistic in import: the people of the United States of America could perhaps really put men on the moon, and so they had better work at the project now, and hard, because otherwise someone else could very well beat them to it. Really, that was why.

It should be clear that in attending to the agonistic structures of language and thought, I do not mean to imply that these are the only structures, and that in noting the connections of these structures particularly with male ceremonial combat, I am not suggesting that such contest completely controls language. Women talk and think as much as men do, and with few exceptions we all, whether we are male or female, learn to talk and think in the first instance largely from women, usually and predominantly our mothers. Our first tongue is called our "mother tongue" in English and in many other languages, and perhaps in all languages is designated by direct or indirect reference to mother. There are no father tongues—a truth that calls for deeper reflection than it commonly commands (Ong, 1977a:22-34).[2] But the agonistic

---

[2] Since this 1977 publication, it has been called to my attention that classical Latin uses an adjective derivative from *pater*, father, in connection with speech

procedures in the use of language and its connection with male ceremonial combat, which will be examined later, here need attention because they are so conspicuous and have not at all adequately been reckoned with.

Some Differentiations:
Contest and Alternative Concepts

The present study of what I have called the "adversative stance" is focused on the notion of contest. To suggest the reasons for this particular focus, it will be well initially to examine at least some of the terms related to "contest" and to note how we use them to structure our knowledge and its reference to actuality. As already intimated, recent literature, especially in psychology and ethology, has activated a great many of these related terms, sometimes in highly specialized contexts and often in contexts not very carefully controlled. Any linguistic term is adaptable to uses beyond those to which it is put at any given time. But the

---

in the expression *patrius sermo,* but this expression does not mean "father tongue": *patrius* yields such terms as "patriotic," "patrimony," not "paternal," and *patrius sermo* (not *lingua*) means the national speech or language, the language coming down the line of one's ancestors (not simply from one's father), something inherited, as land is, an external possession, almost a commodity. It refers to a line of conveyance, not to personal origins. *Lingua materna,* which occurs by medieval times, is a quite different term, being formed with the suffix *-no-,* which indicates origin: provided by, formed out of, mother. The masculine counterpart is *paternus. Patrius* goes with *sermo,* conversation, discourse, for which the Proto-Indo-European root is *ser,* meaning to line up. *Materna* goes with *lingua,* for which the Proto-Indo-European root is *dnghu,* meaning tongue (the physical organ). Mother tongue, father lineup. Adjectives referring to fatherhood do not accrue to *lingua.* The expression **patria lingua,* "father tongue," does not occur, nor does **paterna lingua. Patrius,* which does accrue to *sermo,* as has been seen, is in fact a much later formation than *maternus,* and is not personal but legalistic: there is no form **matrius* because legal inheritance in classical Roman times was not through the female line. In sum, *patrius sermo* means the national speech bequeathed by ancestors who held it as a kind of property, whereas *lingua materna* means quite simply "mother tongue," the tongue you interiorized as it came to you from your mother (or a mother figure). The contrast is between legally inherited speech and "natural" speech (Spitzer, 1968: 25-29).

possible adaptations are always determined to some extent by the current uses of related terms, so that we can get a better sense of the direction of the present study and of the bearing, actual and potential, of the term "contest" by examining the constellation of terms in which it is positioned.

Of the terms related to "contest," the one perhaps most agitated in recent times is "aggression." Konrad Lorenz's book *On Aggression* (1966) has ridden the crest of the wave of research and writing which has given this term its present currency. "Aggression" is used in a variety of ways, but most, and perhaps all, appear more or less actively related to its initial, etymological meaning. Etymologically, "aggression" means walking or stepping toward: *ad* (toward, to) plus *gradi* (to step, walk). "Aggression" is thus in a basic way a territorial term connected with bodily existence and the consequent occupation of space: it signals moving out of one's own space and invading another's. The sense of one's own space is centered on what we may call body space, that space occupied by and immediately adjacent to one's body which others generally keep out of. A sense of body space pervades the animal kingdom (Wynne-Edwards, 1962; Ardrey, 1967). Among most mammals, birds, reptiles, and many lower organisms, each individual carries around with itself a kind of psychological buffer zone called individual distance or social distance (Edward O. Wilson, 1975:257): any other individual approaching so closely as to invade this zone is immediately attacked, except under certain specific conditions (Edward O. Wilson, 1975:257-59). This is true even of gregarious animal species (Eibl-Eibesfeldt, 1970:120; Edward O. Wilson, 1975:257). The elaborate billing and cooing of nesting pairs of many species of birds is devised to neutralize the buffer zone or sense of body space so that the pair can tolerate close contact with one another while breeding (Edward O. Wilson, 1975:216, 224-25). Other individuals coming too close to either of the pair are immediately driven off.

How far actual body space extends among human beings is partly conventional and varies from culture to culture. It has frequently been pointed out that in conversing, a person from the United States normally stands at a greater distance from the person he or she is talking to than does a person from at least some Latin American countries. Misunderstandings result: if a Latino and an American converse, the Latino will think the American cold and withdrawn (as he always suspected), and the American will think the Latino overvoluble and pushy (as he also always suspected). Body space is extended by "territory," the total space in my environs or in the universe in which I am free to move and act as I will. Today a vast ethological and psychological literature treats the territoriality of individuals in various animal species in its manifold implications (Wynne-Edwards, 1962; Ardrey, 1967; Carthy and Ebeling, 1964, and later works of contributors therein).

"Aggression" also refers to other activities readily likened metaphorically to territorial invasion, and consequently implying attack of some sort. For John Paul Scott the term "simply refers to fighting and means the act of initiating an attack" (1958:1). This is a quite specialized and even idiosyncratic use of the term. "Aggression" as used by other speakers and writers often does not refer to fighting at all, though it may occasion fighting. In *Frustration and Aggression* (1939:1) John Dollard and others advance the hypothesis that "aggression is always a consequence of frustration." With or without this hypothesis, aggression does appear always to involve volunteer impingement on another's person or possessions, intrusional initiative, physical or psychological. An "aggressive" speaker is a speaker who moves into psychological or noetic areas that he knows, or should know, are regarded by his interlocutors as somehow their preserves. Territory is of itself inactive, so that here as elsewhere it appears that aggression implies an action ("walking in") impinging on some relative inaction (of territory as such). Defense can be as hostile and as vigorous as aggression, but it is not aggression because it does not initiate action, but waits for and responds to attack.

Two bodies cannot occupy the same space, and in the case of

movable bodies on the surface of our globe, intrusion of one mobile being on another is thus from time to time likely or inevitable. Moreover, the extent of one's body space, and a fortiori one's territory, physical or psychological, is variable and often negotiable. Hence aggression—in either its basic sense of invasion of another's body space or territory or its various metaphorical senses—is to be expected in life and in certain ways is desirable and indeed indispensable, physically and also psychologically, as Joost A. M. Meerlo explains in *The Difficult Peace* (1961).

In *On Aggression* (p. 43) Konrad Lorenz notes three ways in which aggression serves the good of a species: (1) "balanced distribution of animals of the same species over the available environment" (among the resulting advantages is the maximum utilization of the scattered food supply), (2) selection of the strongest individuals for propagation of the species, and (3) protection of the young.

In accord with Anthony Storr's *Human Aggression* (1968), the psychiatrist William W. Meissner, in "Toward a Theology of Human Aggression" (1971:325-26), points out that in human affairs aggression need not be simply destructive of individuals, as Freud seemed to think, but can also be constructive. For proper channeling of human aggression, interaction with a loving, protecting, and supporting maternal figure in infancy is essential. A mother seems to absorb aggression, allowing the child to direct some aggression against her but at the same time identifying so closely with the child that the otherness of the object of aggression is virtually obliterated and any threat from the object minimized: the child feels "at home" in invading what is outside and beyond his or her own body, what belongs to someone else—namely, the body space or person of the nurturing mother. One reason is that the infant does not initially regard the maternal figure as other than himself or herself but has to learn that the maternal figure is another by the processes of separation and individuation so beautifully described by Margaret Mahler (1965 and 1971; also Mahler and Furer, 1963). Treading on another's territory is thus not necessarily resented by the other: there are times when it is desired and welcomed.

The nurturing of a mother or mother substitute is a necessity not only for human beings but also for many subhuman animals, particularly higher forms. The permanent damage to behavior when various subhuman primates are deprived of a living, nurturing, reactive mother has been studied in great detail (Harlow and Harlow, 1962; Denenberg, 1969). Sharing one's own interior body space with another to communicate assurance and strength is of course a feminine prerogative, of which the paradigmatic examples are found in human sexual intercourse and pregnancy. Anatomically males are not fitted for this creative absorption of aggression and its transformation into life.

In a certain sense aggression may be an expression of weakness more basically than of strength: it calls for the use of strength, but because of a lack, a need—for example, a need to annex adjacent space for security that one's unbuffered body does not ensure. The predominance of aggression in males, while associated with males' greater physical prowess, is also one of the many indicators of male insecurity. As the Chinese proverb has it, "The female always overcomes because of her quietness." (Quietness is of course not the same as pure passivity: quietness can be actively chosen as a course of action.)

Aggression can of course run wild and become destructive. Gregory Rochlin, in *Man's Aggression: The Defense of the Self* (1973), shows the connection that specifically human aggression can have with human narcissism: able to be aware of himself as self, the human being gives a distinctive psychological, more interiorized setting to what we have here called his bodily situation: instead of merely acting as though "my body needs some room," which is true, he may act as though "there is nobody in the world but me, I am the universe"—which is not true.

So much for the term and concept of aggression. Another term related to "contest" is "polemic," which comes from the Greek word for war (*polemos,* a word of uncertain origin). Not all contest is war as such, though war is clearly at least related to contest and though it often, and probably always, includes elements of contest. Polemic or war differs from contest in that it implies a direct attempt to inflict real harm, whereas contest refers directly, though not exclusively, to the infliction of ceremonial or symbolic harm. A sports event is a contest as much as war is, but it is not war. Ceremonial harm, however, can of course have real effects, too. Victory or defeat in an amateur game can affect an individual's nonludic life. But it does so indirectly, as by producing elation or dejection. Winning a war can directly affect one's food supply, as winning a basketball game does not—unless the basketball game is played by professionals for hire, in which case it is less purely a game. (The paradigm for sports is amateur sports, disengaged from "real life" issues.)

"Combat" (etymologically, "striking together") and even more "fight" (Proto-Indo-European *pek-*, to pull the hair out of, pluck) are like "polemic" in implying an attempt to inflict real harm and thus a kind of unqualified hostility. "Fight," however, has a more generalized sense: to put forth an effort against odds. "He is fighting hard to win the game." This is the sense chiefly implied in the title of the present work, which the subtitle further specifies.

Still another related term is "struggle" (from the Middle English *struglen,* also of obscure origin). Struggle is less personal than contest: struggle can be person-with-person but it need not be. A wrestler can struggle against another wrestler, but a swimmer can also struggle against the current or a mountain climber against the forces of gravity. "Contest" works differently. If we think of the swimmer or the mountain climber as being engaged in a contest with the current or with gravity, our conceptual apparatus turns metaphorical. We go a bit out of our way to imagine the sea or gravity as a person or at least a living being, somehow conscious of an opponent, against whom it knowingly pits itself.

Another possible term related to contest is "conflict," which comes from the Latin *conflictus,* a striking together (*cum* or *con,* together; *fligere,* to strike—Proto-Indo-European *bhlīg,* to strike). "Conflict" is close to "contest," but is slanted to refer to action less animate and less personal. Abstractions, such as "interests" or "tendencies," can be in conflict with one another, but, again unless we turn metaphorical, not so readily in "contest" with one another. "Contest" tends to imply active give-and-take between conscious beings. When "conflict" is applied to human beings, because of its historical roots in the concept of striking, exchanging blows, which means treating another like an object, the term suggests a state of trouble or unhappiness, as "contest" does not necessarily.

"Competition" lies closer to "contest" than "conflict" does, since it also suggests interaction between conscious beings. But it is more specialized in meaning because it involves acquisition of something in addition to mere victory, generally of something more or less tangible. Competition is more like work, ordered to something definite outside itself, whereas contest is more like play, which has its own justification. One competes "for" something, but one need not contest "for" something: what is essentially at stake is simple success in the contest, "winning." Still, these terms, "competition" and "contest," are close.

"Contention" (etymologically, "stretching," "straining") suggests interpersonal action, sometimes for acquisition of a prize, and thus is close to "competition." But it is farther than this latter term from "contest" because it can readily imply real hostility.

Still another term, Greek *agōnia*, comes near to being a quite adequate alternative for "contest," as we are using the latter term here. Indeed, *agōnia* is pretty well the ancient Greek word for what we mean by "contest" in English. It comes from the Greek *agōn*, which means an assembly, an arena, an action at law, a contest, and which in turn comes from *agein*, meaning to lead, bring, drive, weigh, celebrate (a festival or the like). The fact that the term for an assembly in ancient Greece meant also an action at law or a contest calls attention to the terrain we are on. For in the litigious Greek world, as commonly enough in early human cultures generally, an assembly, a getting together to discourse, was rather essentially a mobilization for contest. The assembly came together to debate, to match pros and cons, to struggle, not fatally, but seriously and in dead earnest, man against man. A legislative body was, and still is, an organization for productive struggle.

The Greek *agōnia* can be used in this special technical sense, but it has entered the English language at a somewhat different pitch, as "agony," a term normally meaning not contest but only one of the things that contest commonly—and other actions also—may involve, the undergoing of pain or distress, even without struggle. Hence *agōnia* and its cognates are likely to be distracting for present purposes, though they will be used, and particularly the term "agonistic," in settings deemed adequately controlled.

Play, treated so well by Johan Huizinga, is clearly allied to contest. Play is often, if not always, agonistic, as in basketball or soccer. But "play" is a narrower term than "contest." It hardly includes, for example, such things as the fighting of stags—which is contest that is nonludic though at the same time nonlethal (save by accident). Contest can be ceremonial, which is not the same as to say ludic. Ceremony is less formally distinct from work or the world of direct existential involvement that play as such is. The ceremony of inaugurating a president is not a game: it has special rules distinguishing it from ordinary life, as do games, but ceremony normally has an immediate direct effect in ordinary life, as games do not: after the ceremony of inauguration, the inauguree is really president. A game does not of itself change real life. After the tennis game, the subordinate who beat his superior at tennis is still an inferior off the court.

For the purposes of this study, the foregoing and all other terms ultimately yield to "contest" as a center of focus. We can understand contest, in a way consonant with its ordinary usage, as a struggle, earnest, possibly but not at all necessarily lethal or even unfriendly, between sentient beings, and at peak between reflectively conscious intelligent beings, that is, human beings, entered into to determine dominance of one or another sort. The dominance can be purely ludic, as in a game of amateur sport, or existentially real, as in a lawcase or in war.

Huizinga (1955:31) insists on the "underlying identity of contest and play." Whatever this underlying identity may consist in, the present treatment of contest attends to matter not attended to, or not much attended to, by Huizinga, notably territoriality, biological evolution, the achievement of masculine identity, the effects of shifts in the so-called media of communication on agonistic tensions in the psyche and in society, and what we may call the undercover history of academia. For, although Huizinga states (1955:156) perceptively that "all knowledge—and this includes philosophy—is polemical by nature," he does not treat in any detail the historical role of agonistic procedures in academic educational practice. Moreover, his quite overt hostility to "modern life" and his indifference to depth psychology precludes effective treatment of the evolution of consciousness, with which he is really and at times quite evidently concerned. For all this, *Homo Ludens* remains a pioneering pivotal and permanent resource for any work on agonistic structures and activities, a book for which Huizinga deserves deep and abiding gratitude.

The present sense of the term "contest" reflects and refracts its fascinating etymology, which reveals why the term exquisitely suits the present study. "Contest" comes from the Old French *conteste*, which in turn derives from the Latin *contestari*. *Testis* means a witness and derives from the Proto-Indo-European root *trei* (three) compounded with *stā* (stand), to yield the form (unattested in extant literature but pointed to by phonological patternings) *tri-st-i*, meaning a third person standing by, as in a dispute between two others. Thus a *testis* or witness, a "third stander," implies an agonistic situation between two persons which the *testis* or third person reports from outside.

The term "contest" intensifies the meaning of *testis* by a kind of reduplication. "Contest" comes, through the French *conteste*, from joining the Latin *con-*, a combining form of *cum* (together), and *testari* (to attest). *Conteste* was at first a legal term. It referred to bringing together witnesses for the contending sides in a lawsuit. One *testis* or third stander viewing an altercation from outside is set against another *testis* or third stander also viewing the altercation from outside. The *conteste* between opposing witnesses is adjudicated by still another third person, the judge, who views the *conteste* itself from outside. "Contest" is thus etymologically not only very human (it confronts person with person) but also nicely disinvolving and objective; as a legal term it refers to action based on deliberation and reason, not to violent physical action. The term "contest" thus from the start belongs in a setting of fairness and humaneness, as "struggle" and "aggression" do not always. Little wonder that "contest" is not of itself a negative or hostile term, even when applied to activities far removed from its original legal frame of reference. It suggests a certain dispassionate distance, achieved and controlled by rules, either explicitly enunciated or tacitly assumed. Confrontation, yes, but in the interest of arriving at truth.

The usage of terms often registers their etymologies with startling permanence and finesse. It is noteworthy that the term "contest" today tends to apply only to living things and indeed more satisfactorily to human persons than to brute animals. It can, of course, at times be applied to brute animals: two stags battling it out in the autumn woods can be said to be engaged in a contest. But it applies not quite so readily to such stags as to two cocks in a cockpit surrounded by a tense group of Balinese men, so well described by Clifford Geertz (1972). The cocks are not just engaging in ordinary male ceremonial combat: they are set against one another, "pitted" against one another, by men, who are conscious of themselves, of their opposition, and of deep human issues here darkly at stake. The action of such "pitted" cocks seems more of a contest, though not more of a struggle or conflict, than does that of the battling stags, because of human involvement. A struggle between two human beings is a contest most of all. A witness (*testis*) has to be a person, a conscious, self-possessed human being. To have a full-fledged, maximal "con-test," or bringing together of two third persons, you should have human beings struggling against one another for some kind

Contest and Other Adversatives

of dominance (which does not at all mean struggling with lethal intent). Such contest is what this study is centrally about.

In its paradigmatic form, a struggle between persons, contest simply cannot be reduced to impersonal structures, which ultimately means that it cannot be completely pictured or diagrammed or quantified. What contest is about is buried within the interiors of two interior consciousnesses. It cannot be computerized, for its basis is not a binary opposition: it is an opposition whose terms are never fully stated, for the terms themselves are included in what is being negotiated. Geertz (1972) has shown the obscure, deep, inarticulate, unconscious human struggles involved in cockfights. There are of course structural elements in contest, as is well known to those who watch football games, especially on television, with the analytic playbacks from various angles. Indeed, although it does not consist of structures, contest generates and thrives on structures. Even more, if the conclusions of this book are correct, it generates intellectual structures, the structures that make science itself.

But at its heart contest involves more than patterns or a play of patterns. "Structuralism," even so deft as that of Lévi-Strauss or Lacan or Piaget, does not of itself account for ultimates: what underlies linguistic and social structure is not structures or systems, but persons, who are assimilable to both closed and open systems, but in the last analysis are neither. An *I* for an *I* and a *du* for a *du*. No model can represent what we are here concerned with, though models can be of peripheral assistance. Besides, not everything in communications and social life can be shown to be in fact structured.

For a human being who takes part in contest, the activity is desperately personal: his or her whole being is involved. "How do you feel when you lose?" a television interviewer a few years ago asked the St. Louis Cardinals' pitcher Bob Gibson. The interviewer hung on Gibson's reply, eager for an inspiring answer along the lines of "He marks—not that you won or lost—but how you played the game." "When I lose, I feel terrible," Gibson answered. "I hate to lose. I want to win."

Contest does not develop independently of other social activities and structures. For example, the child-rearing practices described by Philippe Ariès (1962) and David Hunt (1970) have a great deal to do with the incidence and styles of contest in the societies they treat. Hence what is here said about contest has its limitations. Nevertheless, what is here noted is significant because it affects more of life than one might at first imagine. If contest is conditioned by child-rearing practices and other social institutions, these factors in turn are conditioned by the psychodynamics and history of contest. Reciprocal causalities here soon become too complex for complete analysis.

Although this book hinges on discussion of contest as such, it is not and cannot be restricted to the study of contest alone. The other terms just surveyed here and still further related terms will in the natural course of discussion come into play. It is hoped that this preliminary review will simply help to keep the lines of discourse relatively clear.

PART TWO

Patterns of Adversativeness

2

Contest and Sexual Identity

The Sexes and the Adversative

Need for the adversative is common to all human beings, male and female. But by and large through the entire animal kingdom, among infrahuman as well as the human species, conspicuous or expressed adversativeness is a larger element in the lives of males than of females, for reasons relating both to the development of individual males and to the evolution of species. Male combativeness is more marked among vertebrates than among invertebrates: it reaches its higher pitches higher in the evolutionary scale (Scott, 1958:69-70; see also Ewer, 1968, esp. Bibliography, pp. 371-92). It appears therefore as an advanced rather than a primitive form of behavior. When human consciousness appears, both sexes contribute to its growth, but the male contribution is effected largely through a kind of ritual contest. Females can also be highly competitive. But their competitiveness seldom if ever shows in the conspicuous, all-out, one-to-one ritual or ceremonial contest found among conspecific males, such as the intensive, protracted battles of stags or rams or of male Siamese fighting fish, *Betta splendens*. Paradoxically, intraspecific male fighting becomes more ritual or ceremonial at the same time that it becomes more strenuous.

In treating of differences, adversative and other, in the behavior of the two sexes, it is well to keep in mind that, among human beings at least, probably no concrete act is determined by sex alone. Sex always works through and with a given culture. This is not to say that sexual differences can never be identified as truly sexual differences or that they can be reduced to cultural differences, but only that sexual determinants of behavior cannot manifest themselves in isolation from other determinants. This situation has many analogies. Roman Catholics are distinguishable from non-Christians and even from other Christians by certain profound differences in belief and practice. And yet there are no "pure" Roman Catholics, in the sense that Catholic beliefs are always incarnated in a specifically differentiated culture, so that one finds only French Catholics or West African Catholics or United States Catholics or Brazilian Catholics or Vietnamese Catholics, never simply a culture-free, disengaged Catholic. The situation is somewhat similar with sex and culture. Males as a class everywhere tend to be significantly and even spectacularly more boisterous than females. Boisterousness is biologically determined. Rough play is distinctive of males in infrahuman species, too. But boisterousness expresses itself in certain ways in Eskimo culture, in other ways in Ewondo culture, in other ways in Austrian culture. It can be encouraged or repressed or variously conditioned. There is no abstract expression of pure boisterousness that is not contoured by a specific heritage, already operative in infants. Yet, though we never get it pure, we know very well what boisterousness is, and we know that it is connected in some special way with masculinity. However treated, it cannot be ignored. Boys will be boys. Sexually determined behavior is always mingled with other things. But it is still sexually determined behavior.

The Expendable Sex

Elaborate psychological studies have confirmed in detail, which is sometimes highly informative and sometimes utterly trivial, what stock breeders have in effect known for centuries: male hormones produce combative behavior. Early stock breeders may not have known what hormones were, but they were quite aware that an ox was less dangerous than a bull and a gelding more docile than a stallion. Capons could not be induced to fight as cocks could.

Agonistic behavior can be interspecific (between individuals of different species) or intraspecific (between individuals of the same species). In both cases male and female behavior commonly differ. Among many vertebrate species, the male or males in a close-knit group are typically the most active in warding off predators (Edward O. Wilson, 1975:46, 121-22). They are larger and often equipped with special weapons, such as tusks, and thus more effective. But their strength is a by-product of their uselessness. Evolutionary selection makes it advantageous that males rather than females develop the size, strength, and aggressiveness that successful fighting demands. One reason is that fighters are the individuals most likely to be killed, and a species can more easily survive the loss of males than the loss of females. A colony of one surviving male and twenty females can in most species reproduce itself with a proficiency that cannot be matched by a colony of one surviving female and twenty males. Paradoxically, males, at least in many instances, have become big and strong in part—for there are also other evolutionary pressures—so as to serve as the chief extraspecific defense fighters, because for the other individuals and for the species itself they do not count so much as the so-called "weaker" sex does. Even when males are not larger and stronger than females, they are often the ones assigned to lethal risk situations. Male dung beetles of the family Scarabaeidae regularly do the work at the surface of dung piles and outside of their burrows and thus are eaten in fantastic numbers by predators while the females work safely within the burrow under cover (Heinrich and Bartholomew, 1979:148, 151).

Indeed, in not a few species of animals, males can sometimes be dispensed with altogether: even among some species of lower vertebrates (fishes, amphibians, lizards) parthenogenetic populations have been recorded, and among invertebrates such populations occur regularly (Edward O. Wilson, 1975:315; Shull, 1965:338-41). Aphids, for example, can reproduce parthenogenetically for generations, in some species apparently without limit, unfertilized females giving birth to other females. The females of certain mites can also reproduce parthenogenetically. Over two dozen species of lizards have populations consisting totally of females that reproduce generation after generation without mating: their offspring, always females, are in effect clones (Cole, 1978). There is no way for a species to reproduce only with males.

Praying mantis females commonly eat the male during copulation with no harm to the species (and with considerable nutritional profit to themselves and their offspring). John Alcock considers this connubial cannibalism so significant that he uses as a cover illustration and a frontispiece for his college textbook *Animal Behavior* (1975) an actual photograph of a female starting to bite to pieces and consume the head of her spouse *in copula* with her. In some vigorously predatory flies of the family Empididae, the female might eat the male even before copulation had not a preventive behavior been evolved: the male will catch another kind of fly and present it to the female, copulating with her in safety while she eats his substitute for himself and making his getaway before she turns from consuming his gift to consuming him (Edward O. Wilson, 1975:157, 227; this explanation of the gift has not been universally accepted—see Ewing, 1977:405). If, conversely, the male ate the female, soon there would be no more mantises or Empididae.

The archetypal image of the devouring mother has a biological base: what mother eats is, or at one point was, good for you—if only she doesn't make a mistake and eat you, too. Mother is a reservoir for the species in a way that father is not, for she harbors the larger of the reproductive cells or gametes. Indeed, females are defined as the sex that produces the larger gamete, the ovum; males as the sex that produces the smaller, the sperm (Edward O. Wilson, 1975:324, 578). Isogamous reproduction, in which two cells of the same size combine, is not unknown among some extremely low forms of plant life—green algae of the phylum Chlorophyta (Chapman, 1974:490, 496)—but anisogamy, or differentiation of reproductive cells, is the rule among higher forms of life (and exists as an alternative form of reproduction even among the Chlorophyta). Anisogamy can confer tremendous power on the female regarding not only the future of the species but also the future of individual males, as we shall see.

The greater specialization of males in fighting equipment evolves not merely because of its advantage for defense against predators of other species, but also, and much more, because of its advantage in contest between conspecific males. Evolutionary processes favor polygyny if there are no special countervailing forces (as there very often are). For males that are genetically programmed to copulate with large numbers of females have more progeny than less promiscuous males, and thus a greater influence on the gene pool, producing a larger and larger number of males programmed to mate with many females, whereas (normally—there are exceptions, as we shall see) females that copulate with a large number of males do not have more progeny than less promiscuous females (the Bateman effect or principle; see Edward O. Wilson, 1975:325, 327). Mating with a large number of females means staving off other males bent on mating, an activity that takes strength and aggressiveness. Hence in many animal species a pattern has evolved in which male ceremonial contest eliminates from breeding activity all but a very few males—the larger and stronger and more vigorous—who then become the sole male progenitors of the next generations.

The case of seals and other pinnipeds is well known: here the polygynous males fight one another for territory, a few of the larger and stronger or more aggressive preempting that territory where the oestrous females congregate or are kept congregated by the males. Most male pinnipeds ("fin feet," such as seals, sea lions, walruses) succeed in mating seldom, if ever. The males of such gallinaceous birds as the sage grouse (*Centrocercus urophasianus*), using a lek system of mating, do not directly fight among themselves but rather compete by elaborate courting displays, each in his own territory—which is secured, however, by displays of aggression. The strongest and usually most mature

Fighting for Life

cocks secure the best territories. There each struts or otherwise displays his feathers and other ornaments in competition with other nearby males doing the same thing. Normally a very few males succeed in attracting almost all of the females; the other males are simply kept out of the gene pool. (Edward O. Wilson, 1975:332-33; Wiley, 1978:114-25).

This kind of intraspecific or conspecific elimination is effected not by killing—as is the elimination of males through extraspecific combat—but simply by exclusion from reproductive action. This system does not reduce the population of the species in the next generation: there are as many young as there would have been if more males had mated. Most males just do not count very much as individuals, though the ones that do count count far more than any female, since they have far more offspring and thus far more effect on the gene pool. In other words, variance in a gene pool is likely to be achieved more through males than through females (Bateman's principle—Edward O. Wilson, 1975:324-30). If variance were to be achieved by exclusion of large numbers of females rather than of males, the population might quickly drop below the critical level and the species would disappear.

Seen in these perspectives, as in many others, masculinity is a high-risk condition: all or nothing. Femininity, by contrast, is stable: in many hundreds of species, especially among higher animals, almost all females have offspring, almost all males do not (Edward O. Wilson, 1975:125-26, 324-30). Males are the expendable sex, and not only for evolutionary development: in a culture that raises domestic animals for consumption, most of the meat consumed, mammalian or avian, is the meat of young males, often of castrated young males. At the same time, masculinity also means differentiation, here as in so many other places, for it is through the ceremonial struggle of males and its consequences that the gene pool is most altered.

Combat between Conspecific Males

The situation of the male vis-à-vis conspecific males is not the same as the situation of the male regarding enemies outside the species. Males of the same species fighting among themselves for dominance or territory perform differently from males fighting other species. Typically, they do not fight to the death (Eibl-Eibesfeldt, 1970:315-25). They fight to stand off one another, physically or psychologically or both. In many species, fighting between males is most immediately for territory, only more remotely for females. This is not to say that infrahuman animals never kill other members of their species, for they occasionally do, and not just by accident (Edward O. Wilson, 1975:247). For example, a male lion that becomes the new mate of a female will kill her cubs sired earlier by another male. But the ordinary ceremonial fighting of male against male is another thing entirely, ordinarily not at all lethal.

As Eibl-Eibesfeldt reports (1970:314ff., with abundant illustrations; see also Hediger, 1955:33, 69-72, 129-45), an oryx antelope buck, which uses its horns to gore a lion, will not use them to gore another oryx buck, but will fight its conspecifics in a ritualized, nonlethal pattern. The male giraffe uses its hoofs, which can prove fatal, against predators, but uses its short, nonlethal horns to fight rival males. Male snakes of the same species do not strike at one another but beat one another with their heads in a kind of wrestling bout that, if they were not snakes, might be described as shoulder to shoulder. Some male fish and some male lizards spar with one another with their heads or tails. Male Norway rats may engage in some brief biting to grip each other, but not to kill each other.

In nearly all cases, a defeated rival male of a given species has a way of falling into a behavior pattern that completely "turns off" his opponent, releasing nonaggressive and even friendly behavior. A male wolf defeated by another rolls onto his back like a puppy—a behavior pattern that brings the victor to lick his erstwhile enemy's belly. Often the pattern that inhibits further aggression resembles behavior patterns typical of females or young of the species. Or, in any number of species, a defeated male simply flees. Flight of a vanquished male can be an inhibitory signal for the other male contestant. Victorious males do not normally pursue the vanquished male for any great distance;

they do often pursue fleeing females persistently and ardently, as among many artiodactyls, such as deer and some bovid species (Walther, 1977:701). Flight of a female can be a stimulant to a male rather than an inhibitory signal. A male will chase another male only so far; he will chase a female indefinitely.

One usual result—although not a universal result—of fighting among conspecific males is in one way or another the spacing out of the individuals of a species, as Wynne-Edwards (1962) reports in detail. This spacing out is one of the advantageous results responsible in part for the evolution of male combative patterns. If, for example, male American robins have evolved—as they indeed have—a genetically built-in mechanism for staking out territory (largely by song, which they deliver at regularly established singing posts around the territory's borders) and for fighting off other male robins that may intrude in their purlieus, each robin breeding pair is likely to have enough territory to ensure food for its young. If the males were more irenic and the pairs nested too close together because of the absence of such an agonistic mechanism for dispersal, they all might have to forage so far away for food that none would succeed in raising a brood.

It has already been mentioned that a fight between two males of the same species can sometimes prove fatal. In the wild, such deaths are normally accidental, but in captivity they can be common enough. Combative males artificially confined together in a small space and thus prevented from following the dispersal pattern in which intraspecific male ceremonial combat normally terminates may well fight to the death. Sometimes, but rarely, confinement of combative males has evolved naturally. The fig wasp, *Blastophaga psenes,* hatches and breeds within the fruit of the wild fig, and the hatched males, unable to flee one another, practice natural selection by fierce fighting followed by execution and dismemberment of the losers. After insemination by the winners, the females leave the fig in which they and their mates hatched and fly to lay their eggs in another young fig, setting the stage for the next carnage (Hrdy and Bennett, 1979:26-29).

In confinement, fighting is often more savage, if not lethal, when one male has established an antecedent claim to the confined space. If a half-dozen male rats are deposited in a new cage all at once, they normally will not fight. If one is put in the cage first and allowed to have it to himself for a day or so, the next male or males introduced into the cage are normally in for much trouble.

Ritual Combat

Intraspecific male ritual combat, even in subhuman species, often has a certain abstractness about it in the sense that though it is between individuals of the species, it is not always focused simply on relations between individuals, but on territory. In many species, as we have just noted, each male stakes out a territory—either the one in which nesting and foraging for food will later take place (as in the case of many songbirds) or an area in a lek or communal display and mating arena apart from feeding grounds (as in the case of many grouse species and open-country antelope species such as the Uganda kob). In either system, the male mates with females that come to his territory (Edward O. Wilson, 1975:331-35). If in a lek the female moves to the contiguous area of a rival male, the first male will simply relinquish her. The boundaries of the separately held territories are set up by ritual combat between males, so that wandering into another male's territory is aggressive and would touch off an attack. But the point here is that the direct focus of male ritual combat is the territory, not the female or females. Similarly, male rats share the females (and females the males) but fight vigorously over territory (Barnett, 1963:84-85).

Among subhuman animals, females of the same species also of course do some ritual, nonlethal fighting with one another for dominance. There is a pecking order among hens. But the fighting is generally far more perfunctory among females. Watts and Stokes (1971:112-18) report that in the semiarid grasslands of southeastern Texas, winter flocks of male turkey sibling groups are formed, in each of which the individual tom must fight to find his place in the order of dominance. Once these sibling groups are interiorly structured by internal combat, they set out to fight others, group against group, to establish their collective order of dominance. The fights between individual males in each group are nonlethal but they are also extremely arduous: they may last more than two hours and end in the complete exhaustion of one or both birds. The turkey hens also form into winter flocks, where they fight for rank, but perfunctorily, with none of the ferocity of the toms and without forming the sibling groups of fighting "gangs" characteristic of the males. The females work out dominance more efficiently and get down to business. The behavior of this one particular species is obviously not matched exactly in all other animal species, but it is thoroughly typical of male-female differences in behavior.

At the infrahuman level the behavior of groups such as these bands of male turkeys anticipates the human ability to form combative teams, to which mature human males will commit themselves passionately as relatively few mature women will.

In the exceptional cases of some animal species whose males have taken on the greater share of parental care (certain species of seahorses and other pipefishes, certain "poison-arrow" frogs, phalaropes and some eight other species of birds), females develop a special competitiveness for males, who will take care of their eggs and young (Edward O. Wilson, 1975:324-29). Through evolutionary selection the females of these exceptional species have often developed competitive breeding display equipment and behavior to attract males at the expense of other females, but apparently in no cases have the females evolved the strenuous ritual fighting among themselves that marks male behavior quite generally in higher animal species. Indeed, in many species whose males take on all of the postpartal parental care, such as the sticklebacks and the Siamese fighting fish, *Betta splendens,* or phalaropes, the males remain fiercely competitive for their own territory and thus in effect for females, who come to the male's territory to mate and lay their eggs. When female competitiveness is maximized, it is thus still not agonistic in the way in which male competitiveness is.

Contest and Sexual Identity

In many animal species without sexual dimorphism, the male recognizes the female largely by her lack of interest in rough male ceremonial combat. He attacks all members of his species more or less indiscriminately. When the individual attacked responds with weak agonistic behavior or none and yet does not flee, as a defeated male would do, or flees and returns nonagonistically, unruffled, simply disregarding defeat, he shifts to mating behavior. When the agonistic behavior has been reduced to virtually none, mating can take place (Eibl-Eifesfeldt, 1970:129-30). Among the artiodactyls (even-toed ungulates such as swine, camels, antelopes, bovines) the male courtship displays, which are "basically aggressive" toward females, frequently involve real threats toward females and fighting with them until the agonistic behavior of the females ultimately subsides, although in some antelope and bovid species the aggression has become ritualized into something like a dance or even a static display such as a blocking posture (Walther, 1977:701). Males often combine aggression toward females with appeasement behavior—nuzzling, licking (Walther, 1977:707-8).

Females, of course, including human females, are aggressive, in some ways as much as or more so than males, but their pattern of aggression is different. Rough bodily contact is far less common, and human females are likely to use intermediaries (girls will get a powerful adult to intervene for them), "verbal slings and arrows, and subtle interpersonal rejection frequently masked as solicitous caring" (Bardwick, 1971:126-27). The sexual differentiations here are certainly reinforced or deemphasized by culture, but they are basically independent of culture, biological (largely endocrinological) at root, the human differentiations paralleled by those in subhuman animals (Bardwick, 1971:84-113, 126-34). Moreover, females can and do fight physically and violently on occasion, but the occasions are likely to be more realistic and less ceremonial or ritualized, likely to concern more immediately vital issues—for example, defense of the young against a potential predator. Evolutionary development has consequently equipped females generally with fewer of the controls that normally turn off intraspecific male ceremonial combat at a certain threshold—a fact that led Margaret Mead (1967) to argue against involving women as combatants in aggressive military action, which among males seems to have a ritualized component that normally exercises a minimal kind of control. Defensive military action is different, all-out, and women have engaged in it throughout history.

The folkloric and literary treatment of woman as unconcerned with "fair play" (that is, combat behavior governed by gaming rules) is in line with Mead's recommendations here. Margaret Hennig and Anne Jardim in *The Managerial Woman* (1977) put very pointedly what countless proverbs, folktales, and literary works express about the human experience of male and female agonistic attitudes across the world: "Men see risk as loss or gain; winning or losing; danger or opportunity," while women "see risk as entirely negative. It is loss, danger, injury, ruin, hurt. One avoids it as best one can" (p. 27). Women often have little sense of "a game being played, of a temporary adoption of a different style for reasons of self-interest. It is all for real" (p. 31). Successful women M.B.A.s from Harvard regularly report that their involvement in their work is less ego-defensive and less competitive regarding monetary stakes (the "game" of business) than that of their male colleagues (Robertson, 1978:50-60)—though, as will be seen, this lesser competitiveness does not itself indicate that they are less successful than males. They are more likely to regard or at least to report on their work in terms of self-improvement opportunities. Among males in certain cultures, even war can be a kind of game, perhaps seasonal, in which killing is an objective only halfheartedly or incidentally achieved. The ancient Greeks called off their wars for the Olympic Games and resumed them again immediately afterward: psychologically, the wars and the games were somewhat equivalent.

In his profoundly comic *Spotted Horses*, William Faulkner (1954:367-439) catches with exquisite finesse the differing relationship of male and female to risk taking and ritual combat. A pair of ne'er-do-well Texans, traipsing into a small Mississippi town with a herd of broncos so wild that they have been strung together with barbed wire, succeeds in luring the men of the town into bidding against one another for the horses (symbols of power in the subconscious and throughout literature—and, for that matter, also in real-world mechanics, which measures in "horsepower"). When each townsman has bought himself one of the horses, by now untied and running loose in a crude corral, the men cannot of course catch their animals (ineffectiveness of males in dealing with their own masculinity—the male clown figure, the limp phallus), and some of the horses break loose. One of them bolts into the home of a Mrs. Littlejohn, who with magnificent womanly indignation snatches up a washboard and smashes it into the animal's face—the stupid male, boys-will-be-boys game playing is tearing up her home.

Faulkner's superb sense of the feminine critique of masculine preoccupation with bravado and dominance, often pointless and poignant at the same time (the Don Quixote syndrome), is matched elsewhere by his equally superb sense of the male's resentment that females are not inclined to take the risks that males, in their chronic and restless insecurity, simply feel compelled to take. Women simply know without having to find out: "She already knows more than I with all the man-listening in camps," Isaac McCaslin thinks to himself glumly in *The Bear* (Faulkner, 1954:347). "They are born already bored with what a boy approaches only at fourteen and fifteen with blundering and aghast trembling."

Certain admonitions to young girls seem to be based often on a sense of deserved feminine security as contrasted with masculine insecurity or induced-stress activity. Mothers and other tutelary female figures will frequently condemn as "unladylike" in young girls forms of conduct that they tolerate—not without amused annoyance—in boys and indeed in men, such as rough-and-tumble fighting, boisterous shouting, openly aggressive language, and other actions here identified as typical of male ceremonial contest. The message conveyed to the girl appears often, if not always, to be, at least in part: As a female you do not need to do these things that boys and men need to do to hold themselves together. You have "got it all together" already. Just stay with it. The pitying resignation shown by the Kabyle women regarding their men's constant obligatory risk taking in the highly macho Kabyle society, commented on in Chapter 3, is significant here.

Combat, Stress, and Masculine Identity

Combat among human males, as registered in literature and in real life, is not exactly the same as among subhuman animals, but it is not entirely different either. Like subhuman males, human males tend to fight one another more vigorously than do human females, but at the same time more ceremonially or ritually. This tendency has shown markedly in the past throughout the noetic world—in verbal performance, in academic life, and in intellectual activity generally. But before contest in these fields is discussed, it will be well to reflect on what is known of the deeper biological and psychological roots of the disposition to contest in the human male, with occasional reference to subhuman analogues.

From the beginning of an individual mammalian male's life, his masculinity involves living in a state of adversity, in an environment which, despite its supportiveness and his utter dependence on it, is nevertheless to a degree permanently hostile. As Judith M. Bardwick reports in her *Psychology of Women* (1971:97-98), the male embryo must at a very early stage of its development begin to manufacture testosterone from its own gonads "to produce masculinity and to offset the possible effect of circulating maternal hormones," hormones that do the female embryo no harm, but good. The formation of the female genital tract "occurs essentially without hormonal differentiation," whereas the orderly development of male anatomical characteristics, including the modification in males of the hypothalamic region of the brain, which controls the function of the pituitary gland, depends on the excretion of androgens by the male embryo and fetus (Talalay, 1978:21). The male mammalian organism must from the start react against its environment. Thus masculinity has a certain resistance to being nurtured: for a male, being nurtured has special dangers. At its biological and historical source, the male's vocation is not acceptance but change. Again, masculinity means differentiation.

The uncomfortable-dependency situation might have no great consequences if it were confined to uterine life, but it continues after birth for human males (and males of higher mammals generally): the male still needs a feminine environment for development in early postuterine life. This poses psychological problems. From carefully analyzed case histories Robert Stoller has concluded that contrary to "Freud's position that masculinity is the natural state" of which femininity is a modification, the male child has "a task in developing his gender identity [sense of masculinity as against simple biological sex] that does not burden" the female (Stoller, 1968:263-64; see also 265-68). Stoller distinguishes *sex,* which is determined by an algebraic sum of chromosomes, external genitalia, internal genitalia (uterus, prostate), gonads, hormonal states, and secondary sex characteristics, to which in the future brain systems will very likely be added, from *gender,* "the amount of masculinity or femininity found in a person" (p. 9). "Sex we refer to as male and female, gender as masculine and feminine" (p. 9). The young human male is very feminine in significant ways, and necessarily so, because of his earliest maternal environment. After initial identification with the feminine, the boy must grow away from "the feminine [gender] identification that resulted from his first encounter with his mother's female body [sex] and feminine qualities [gender]" (p. 264).

Interference with the necessary separation from mother, often together with other patterns of behavior in both parents, produces transsexualism or transvestism (neither of which is the same as homosexuality; see Stoller, 1968:159). Transsexualism, in Stoller's careful, clinically grounded analysis, is the feeling not merely of behaving in ways considered appropriate to the gender opposite to one's biological sex but also of being of the biological sex opposite to one's actual biological sex. (Transsexuals are typically not just interested in their surgical sex transformation but will make almost any sacrifice to effect it.) Transsexualism is very rare among females, being estimated to occur at most one-third and perhaps even only one-eighth as frequently in females as in males (p. 197). Stoller states that transvestism, so far as he can discover, has not been found in any females at all, though some women may have transvestic tendencies (p. 197). Stoller defines transvestism as fetishistic, intermittent cross-dressing [wearing of women's clothing] in a biologically normal man who does not question that he is a male—that is, the possessor of a penis (p. 176; cf. pp. 89-92, 132, 159). Such a person's gender role (sense of masculinity) at times conflicts with his clear-cut sexual identity. Stoller knows of no case of a woman with such a conflict. The occurrence of both transsexualism and transvestism in males is due in various ways to failure to achieve "separation" of the male infant from his experience of his mother's body (see Mahler and Furer, 1963, and Mahler, 1965) because of her possessive and permissive behavior and to concomitant deficiencies in the father's masculine role. Such failure to achieve separation from mother can affect female infants adversely, too, but does not confuse their sexual or gender identity. When transsexualism does occur in females, its causes differ from those that operate in males' transsexualism (Stoller, 1968:194-205). The male's problem here again is one of differentiation. He must come to feel that he is not what was at first closest to him—woman, usually his mother.

Bardwick (1971:106-8) reviews some of the abundant literature showing the greater strain under which boys operate and mature as compared to girls. This strain is common knowledge to parents and has long been the object of literary humor, as in George W. Peck's popular *Peck's Bad Boy and His Pa* (1883) and the earlier work by the Brothers (Henry and Athol) Mayhew, *The Image of His Father: or, One Boy Is More Trouble than a Dozen Girls* (1848). It has been shown that, given the same choices, in composing sentences males use significantly more overtly hostile verbs (e.g., "stabbed") than neutral verbs by comparison with females (Gilley and Summers, 1970)—not a surprising finding at all. Males are driven to create stress situations: Evel Knievel is a paragon of masculinity, become a caricature of itself. Robin Lakoff's account (1977) of the quite significant differences in women's and men's use of language points out women's greater adherence to "correct" grammar and careful articulation, which men tend to fight against. The stress situation for the male, begun in the womb, comes to a peak in the mature male with sexual intercourse itself, in which the difference between the sexes reaches its maximum and which is always a test of the male's, not the female's, physical ability to perform, to achieve intromission.

Humor relieves psychological strain, especially hostilities, and, as Martin Grotjahn has noted (1957:54–66, 83–118, 139–74), humor relates diversely to the male and female psyche. Humor lies closer to the male world, especially gross and boisterous humor, for it relieves conflict, particularly as caught in father-son relationships, which focus the young male's struggle for his masculine identity. There have been few female clowns, though a few are now appearing in circuses. Clowns have normally been disabled father figures, who can be funny as disabled mother figures cannot be.

Unlike Charlie Chaplin, such female comic figures as Carol Burnett and the columnist Erma Bombeck tend not to be hapless victims. They often talk about themselves as victims, calling attention to the chaos around them, but they are seldom as much at the mercy of the chaos as is the Chaplinesque male. Quite the contrary, they are often subtly in charge, amused at themselves in their plight, advertising feminine viability even amid utter chaos, unflappable, nurturing mothers, centers of stability in a world of infantile (and often regressive adult male) turbulence. The situation around Erma Bombeck is what is amusing. Mrs. Bombeck herself is not so much amusing as entertaining: she herself is amused. The comedian and the comedienne typically operate quite differently: psychoanatomically, Grotjahn maintains, the clown or other male comic figure often directly suggests in behavior and accoutrements the limp phallus, total ineffectiveness. The phallus can be mocked, as the womb cannot be (Grotjahn, 1957:103). Carol Burnett laughs comfortably at herself, for she is really charming the audience into laughing with her at others. Charlie Chaplin is laughable, but he himself only mourns. Some male comedians operate like Carol Burnett, but there seem to be no female Charlie Chaplins. Women loners are not funny.

If stress or insecurity means an uneasy or unstable relationship with one's environment, males are insecure because they are in more constant and complex conflict with their environments than are females—clinical data show this to be true from the age of two, at least, and most likely true from birth, as, in the way just explained, it is even before birth. Boys refuse more often to obey, precipitate more fights, refuse more frequently and steadfastly to learn in school (most pupils held back to repeat grades are boys), and stutter (a sign of conflict) in four times as many cases as do girls and more severely, and so on (Bardwick, 1971:106-8). Gambling, which can result from and temporarily alleviate insecurity—if I take a great risk and win, I sense for a euphoric and vertiginous moment that I am absolutely invulnerable—is commoner among men than among women, and especially illegal gambling.

Everywhere and at all times for which figures are available, the number of male criminals is many times the number of female criminals—commonly 8 to 12 males to 1 female in all crimes combined, but, as of a few years ago, in burglary 79 to 1 and in shopbreaking 243 to 1 (Hibbert, 1963, esp. pp. 234-35). In *Women and Crime* (1975) Rita James Simon provides more detailed and more recent figures, variously broken down. With women more active extradomestically today, the proportion of female criminals is increasing significantly only in economic crimes (forgery, embezzlement, larceny), as it has increased in earlier periods of economic hardship. The increase in these economic crimes today appears to be due in part to the increased number of women functioning as heads of households, that is, to increased domestic pressures. Crimes committed by women continue to be typically nonviolent—women perform 85 percent of the acts of shoplifting in the United States (Mitre Corporation, 1979)—and often "victimless," with no overall significant change toward violence, though sentences for women criminals now tend to be rather more severe than in the past (Rans, 1977). The few spectacularly violent women criminals, such as Patty Hearst and members of the Baader-Meinhof group, are only partial exceptions, for they have all operated in concert with violent males. Male violent criminals do not typically operate with violent females, though they sometimes do.

It has often been pointed out (Hibbert, 1963:234) that women may be more involved in crime than these figures might suggest, since many crimes are committed by males at the instigation, overt or tacit, of women. This observation brings home once more the point earlier made, that males are readier risk takers for a species because they have been so programmed evolutionarily, as the more expendable sex.

In *Of Love and Lust,* Theodor Reik (1957:422) suggests that "the more urgent and, in its manifestations, immediate sexual drive of the male is perhaps an expression of his weaker biological nature, of his *Lebenshunger,* which would explain his restlessness." Whereas women are "more self-satisfied," men are "restless and dissatisfied," and thus are more likely to be agents of change—though even for this assertion of masculinity the man must rely on confidence derived from the feminine, mother or wife or muse, Jung's *anima.*

The sexual identity crisis of woman, pointed to in women's liberation movements today, can be real enough, but it is preceded ontogenetically and phylogenetically, it would seem, and to a great extent brought on, by the abiding sexual identity crisis of the male, which registers throughout early history in the various kinds of antifeminism. Antifeminism, overt and covert (the downgrading of specifically feminine values), is endemic in both sexes and probably arises largely as a defense or reaction against the total control a mother exercises over her young child (Lerner, 1974)—the umbilical cord protracted postnatally as the apron strings—a control extending now by express law in many places to the power to decide arbitrarily whether or not to allow the unborn child to live or have the child killed: more total power over another is unthinkable.

But antifeminism is often most virulent among males. It is intimately associated with verbal performance, oral and literary, and with intellectual and academic activity, and is tied into male insecurity. This insecurity has a rather obvious psychological source, related to the biological base just described. The human male is beset with the psychological as well as physical problems of proving his masculinity, which means in effect proving he is not female. His share in human nature is male. Yet we conceive of nature, rightly, as typically female—"Mother Nature." "Nature" itself in its original Latin (*natura*) means birth (as its correlative *physis*—whence the word "physics"—does in Greek). To ask the "nature" of something is to ask how it was born, which is to say basically how it relates to the feminine.

Though they may resist acknowledging the fact openly, human males find themselves in stress situations not only because of their biological insecurity but also because psychologically they must set themselves off from a backdrop of femininity that has not had to establish itself but is simply there, a given. As a boy, the young human male must "prove himself a man," differentiate himself from this given ambience in which he finds himself. He must prove he is not a "sissy" (sister, girl). It is assumed that he is unless he proves the contrary. Anatomical differences do not suffice, since the fact is that all boys started out in the feminine world. How are they to be psychologically sure, consciously or unconsciously, that they have really ever left that world, that they have really achieved the differentiation that it is every male's business to achieve? They must cut girls out of their lives, scorn feminine sources of comfort and safety, do things that they hope their mothers and sisters cannot do. They have to "fight it"—"it" being anything that seems easy. They must discover or invent risks. Accusations of "effeminacy" normally strike the male heart with terror: you have not had the strength to become yourself. Although penis envy can indicate a degree of insecurity among females vis-à-vis males, this insecurity is based on a felt lack of something belonging to the other sex and thus is quite the opposite to insecurity deriving from fear of absorption into the other sex. Masculinity does not hold the same fears for women that femininity holds for men. Stoller (1968:265) comments on "the fear of effeminacy in so many men and the relative lack of a corresponding fear of being masculine in most women."

One reason for woman's lesser fear would seem to be a certain dominance over masculinity due to the fact that male children are born of women just as female children are. Females carry males as well as females in their own bodies and nurse and nurture male as well as female infants. Women know that male children in infancy and for some years after need to be surrounded by femininity. From their physical and psychological envelopment of males women know all about males—in a sense more than the males themselves do. (It should be superfluous to note that saying that masculinity does not hold certain fears for females is not at all saying that individual males cannot or do not brutalize individual females.)

Women regularly appropriate masculine accoutrements in many if not all cultures with no threat to their feminine identity. Although strong addiction to masculine-styled clothing can indicate gender confusion in a woman (Stoller, 1968:197-205), widespread styles for women generally, including women supremely secure in their gender role, are often intentionally and openly vaunted adaptations of male clothing: masculine styling can render clothing chic and detract not at all from the wearer's femininity, for in these cases when something masculine enters the feminine world, it is immediately subjected to that world. (Cf. Stoller, 1968, on sex and gender, and the early pages of this present section.) The feminine simply takes over the masculine style, subtly feminizing it and thereby expropriating and appropriating it.

So, too, females can and do appropriate without embarrassment common nouns initially used only for males. "Guy" (originally referring to an effigy of Guy Fawkes and subsequently to any male regarded more or less unceremoniously) was once a restrictively masculine noun, as in the title of Damon Runyan's *Guys and Dolls* (1932). In recent years, girls and women have come to use it quite commonly for themselves (as well as for men or, in the plural, for mixed groups). "Dolls" can hardly be correspondingly extended by males to include themselves. Masculinity, it seems, cannot psychologically assimilate the feminine form and survive. The psychodynamics in play here would appear to govern certain deployments of masculine and feminine gender forms in languages where those forms contrast. Thus in the French, *ils sont orgueilleux* (they are proud), though pronoun and adjective are masculine in form, they can also express common gender (including both females and males) when the context warrants. The form *elles sont orgueilleuses,* where the pronoun and adjective are feminine in form, will not work to include males. It is the only alternative: there are no separate common gender forms in French. Overspecialization in masculine forms as common gender forms (such as "he" in English for both sexes) can be distasteful and needs to be counteracted. But the psychodynamics with which one is working in making adjustments here have a life and pattern of their own, not unconnected with male insecurity, of which both females and males are at least unconsciously aware.

Women's given names in many if not all cultures can be feminized names of men: Johanna, Jeanne, Thomasina, Bernadette, Caroline, Michelle. Such names are as feminine as other names of different provenience. It would endanger the ego structure of most males to take an adapted name of a woman: they cannot appropriate a woman's name to the male world. Femininity is too powerful. In Latin and some other cultures, it is true, devotion to the Virgin Mary leads occasionally to the conferring of her name on boys, but seemingly always as an auxiliary name, as in José María or Jean-Marie, which is seldom if ever used with its masculine counterpart in addressing its bearer and is frequently dropped or reduced to an initial.

In many cultures a married woman "takes" her husband's name with no threat to her own identity at all, and typically with strengthening of ego structures. Note the term: taking is an aggressive action. It is true, as explained in Chapter 1, that aggression may indicate a weakness, but it is still also a show of strength. A woman's taking of her husband's name can of course be viewed as an indication of her subjection to him, but it can be viewed otherwise, too.

Names, which situate individual human beings in their own history, are commonly given by others rather than adopted at their bearers' own choice. In a pattern common in the West and elsewhere, one receives the name of one's family at birth and is given by parents a personal name that is often that of a relative or friend or of some revered person, such as a saint. Sometimes a name is given because of a particular achievement: Publius Cornelius Scipio was surnamed Africanus by the ancient Romans because of his conquest of Africa. In those Roman Catholic religious orders whose members change their names upon entering, the new religious name is commonly given by superiors, not "taken," though the individual's preference may at times be honored. Gratuitously "taking" a name, at least in Western cultures, commonly advertises ego strength or the need to believe one has strength. Such writers as Voltaire and Etiemble take names seemingly to cope with the strains on ego structures imposed by writing. Other writers take a noms de plume as shields to protect them from the strains. Some United States blacks have taken African or Muslim names by way of self-assertiveness in establishing personal identity. Dictators—for example, Stalin and Tito—take names, often rather defensive names, asserting strength (Stalin means "steel"). Pope John II (533-535), whose given name, Mercury, the name of a pagan god, seemed singularly inappropriate for a pope, began the practice, followed by all of his successors to this day, of taking a new name upon election. Such a practice is at least an assertive action, suggesting a kind of summoning together of the powers of the papacy.

All of these instances show the "taking" of a name to be a sign of strength. But they are all exceptional practices, at least in the West. The most widespread name acquisition in Western culture thought of as the "taking" of a name is the bride's "taking" of her husband's name. There is plenty of literature, much of it highly defensive, edgy humor, making clear that the "taking" of her husband's name can come across as an act of possession, a taking possession of him: she has "got" her man.

Woman in recent Western culture has normally had the ego strength needed to "take" her husband's name and build more ego strength with the taking, both because of the sturdiness of her biological and psychological femininity (as seen in the feminine appropriation of masculine styles of dress and of males' given names) and because of the additional support that cultural mores provide, although the cultural supports have been weakening or at least shifting in recent years. Far from being a threat to her femininity or her security, taking a husband's name has typically advertised and can still advertise a certain distinctively feminine strength: the man was, after all, the one who came asking her. Hers, not his, was the ultimate decision. All women being wooed are in the position of women in the courtly love tradition that comes out of the European Middle Ages, having power over a suitor abject at their feet. The courtly love tradition was, among other things, the apotheosis of the wooed woman, and as such tremendously humanizing, if at times erratically so, a true raising of consciousness, for it was thereby an apotheosis of freedom, of woman's free consent, though that is not all it was.

The precariousness of the male's claim to his own children can establish a permanent, if not always conscious, stress situation for the human male by contrast with the female. On the basis of gross biological evidence, a father has a much harder time proving that he is a given child's father than a mother has in proving that she is the mother: the child emerged from her uterus, but how can the man prove that his sperm was the only sperm she received? Her chastity is his only assurance. Social institutions sometimes reinforce the mother's claim and make it total, to the exclusion of the father's. Among the Banyanga (the Nyanga people) of eastern Zaire, for example, a polygamous man may have wives of two sorts: those to whom he is joined in the classic form of marriage, by payment of the so-called bride price to the family of the bride, and "spirit wives," for whom he has paid no bride price. The children of the first sort of wives are recognized as his own children, on whom he has a claim. To his children by his spirit wives he has no claim at all: they are related to the mother and her family only, being aligned with the agnatic descent group consisting of her father, brothers, and paternal uncles, with no acknowledged family relationship to their biological father (Biebuyck and Mateene, 1971:8). Far from being simply a way of "purchasing" a bride (with the possible implication of feminine insecurity, of the reduction of the woman to a mere object), the so-called bride price here is an indication of the male's insecurity: it is the male's only means of obtaining a right to have his own children acknowledged as his.

Out of the stress situation of the male, however, assurance can eventually develop. Constant testing of oneself against an opponent, as Thomas J. Farrell of St. Louis Community College at Forest Park has suggested to me, can result in an acquired confidence that coexists with insecurity in order to counter it. This is probably a typical male state of mind. A confident male gains the assurance that he can handle risk situations by constantly facing or even creating them. Male performance tends to proceed by establishing stresses, not only in the physical world but also in the world of discourse and of the mind. As reported in an article by Farrell (1979:909-10), Sarah D'Eloia of the City College of the City University of New York has noted that, in her own experience, men characteristically (not always, of course) develop a rhetorical argument by beginning with something like their final conclusion, whereas women characteristically (not always) begin with the expectation that they must pull their audiences around to their point of view by "indirection." The characteristic male approach here (1) risks attack from the first ("Here is where I stand") and (2) shows a certain playfulness, which is to say takes a kind of ceremonial or gaming, stress-inviting stance ("I dare you to try to knock me over").

The procedure identified by D'Eloia as characteristically masculine is in fact that of the public classical oration (statement of position followed by proof, with refutation of adversaries), which belonged to the exclusively male world. The indirection that she finds in feminine persuasive discourse fits private conversational exchange, which can readily develop by, first, provisional statements, followed by reactions of the listener, which in turn lead to adjustments and additional provisional statements. A similar indirection is congenial to the writing process, which can work tentatively—with erasures, cuts, emendations, insertions—as an oration cannot, for what an orator has spoken he has spoken. These tentative, indirect, nonstress characteristics have close affinities with those identified by another woman linguist as marking feminine use of language (Lakoff, 1977:77–80). "Characteristically" feminine of course does not mean exclusively feminine: it refers to tendencies that need not define every case. Women, who earlier had been, and still are, typically more powerful determinants of private life than men, came increasingly into public life as writing and print affected noetic processes more and as electronic amplification altered oratorical style from the older, often bellowing, ceremonially combative male polemic to the tête-à-tête conversational oratory common on television and also gave women's voices for the first time a physical volume equal to men's. These shifts are further discussed in Chapter 4.

Male Fights Male

Two kinds of behavior connected with human male insecurity can be noted here. The first is the need felt by males, particularly young boys, to fight each other. The second is the tendency of males to be "loners" more than females are, and the somewhat paradoxically related tendency of males to form all-male groups, the male "bonding pattern" (Tiger, 1969).

The adversary relationship with the environment, which has been seen to go back to the biological situation of the male embryo and fetus in the womb, would appear to serve as one basis for the male's psychological tendency to fight. Human males tend to feel an environment, including other individuals of the species, as a kind of againstness, something to be fought with and altered. Environment is feminine, and women typically find they can rely on it as it is or comes to them. The received symbol for woman, Venus's mirror (♀), adopted by feminists apparently everywhere, signifies self-possession, gazing at oneself as projected into the outside world or environment and reflected back into the self from there, whole. The received symbol for man, Mars's spear (♂), signifies conflict, change, stress, dissection, division.

In numerous well-known psychological experiments, human males regularly break up a field where females regularly do not, but keep it whole—a difference correlating with males' greater proclivity for analysis (fractioning), and related to other differences in cognitive styles regularly marking the two sexes in the most diversified cultures (Witkin, 1967:111-13). To this tendency in field breaking there are of course individual exceptions, though not enough to alter the general pattern significantly (Bardwick, 1971:110-12). Sex differentiation in field breaking has been reported on in a vast variety of cultures across the world, including the United States (varied educational and social backgrounds), Western Europe (England, Holland, France, Italy, and other countries), Israel, Hong Kong, and Sierra Leone, with the Eskimos as a curiously isolated exception (Witkin, 1967:111-13). (It appears here again that present-day concern with ecology and preservation of environment, holism as against fractioning, represents a feminine input in the history of consciousness. Ecology seems to have less appeal in cultures where masculinity is notably more insecure—machismo cultures—and thus inhospitable to this further feminine input.)

Behavioral studies of apes and other infrahuman species have documented a matter of otherwise commonplace informal observation: groups of young males playing together interact with high aggression and rough bodily contact; groups of young females are vigorous in their play but more gentle, often avoiding bodily contact almost totally (Bardwick, 1971:85; Van Lawick-Goodall and Hamburg, 1974). As this pattern is found in groups reared in isolation, the learning of such behavior patterns may be ruled out. The same difference is found in young human beings, beginning with infancy. Various cultures may minimize or maximize this and other sexual differences in behavior, but it is always there, and strong. Males like rough fighting.

But why the predilection of males for fighting other males in particular? In the case of human beings, what sort of psychological satisfaction is achieved by a young boy who succeeds in standing up against another boy? For the only adversary who can enable one to establish male identity is another male. It will not do to beat up even a seemingly much stronger, older girl. If he is to free himself of the accusation, and the deep suspicion in his own mind, that he is a sissy, if he is not to be a woman, a boy must venture into the all-male world. This is to say, in effect, that he must face the threat of masculinity within himself by facing it in others like himself. To be a man, the male must be able to face insecurity, for that is what maleness implies—existence in an environment that is both needed and hostile. The male carries this insecurity within himself. So does the other male, who is thus a surrogate for himself: if the boy can stand off the male restlessness, the adversativeness of the other, he can live with his own built-in uneasiness.

Standing off physical female might has no attraction for males, and in fact repels them. It is very difficult psychologically for a man deliberately to fight a woman (attacking a woman in a blind fit of anger is another thing). Woman is a threat psychologically already, and to own by fighting her that she is also a physical threat would devastate the male ego, which is supported by the fact that woman is physically "the weaker sex" and which must keep asserting defensively that she is. In other words, human males typically fear competing with women, for they can achieve their masculinity only by establishing independence of the initially all-enveloping feminine. If a male is overcome by a female, he is back where he started. His worst fears about himself are realized and his ego, unless monumentally sturdy, is likely to be demolished.

Combined with these fears, the male's reverence for mother and by extension all of her sex makes fighting women extremely distasteful to men. Reverence involves fear. A soldier connected with the U.N. Truce Commission dealing with Arab-Israeli hostilities of a few years ago reported that when Israeli women were sent out on guerrilla raids and were recognized as women, their male opponents simply retreated or surrendered (Tiger, 1969:81). (It is very rare, across the world, for women to serve in front-line military attack, but not uncommon for them to serve in defensive operations, or in behind-the-lines support functions.)

Masculine identity among higher animals often entails intensive distancing of one individual from another, and, in the case of reflective human beings, of personal self from personal self. The typical fight between conspecific males, in subhuman species as well as among human beings, is a standoff or face-off operation: it does not eliminate the opponent but rather establishes and maintains distance from him and thus, in the case of human beings, since the opponent is a surrogate for oneself, distance from self—whence the drive to male asceticism, as will be seen (Eibl-Eibesfeldt, 1970:314-25).

An informative and amusing example of the distancing theorem is the series of duels, or the protracted duel, fought over a period of nineteen years, beginning in 1794, by the two French officers Fournier and Dupont, who, following an initial engagement in which Fournier was wounded and claimed a second bout on recovery, agreed that every time they were within 100 miles of one another they would fight (Baldick, 1965:165-68). When Dupont managed to get himself engaged, he and Fournier dueled again in a match that they agreed would be the last, so that if he survived, Dupont could marry with some assurance of viability. Dupont refused to press his advantage when Fournier had emptied his own pistol, thereby advertising the basically playful attitudes underlying their desperate attempts to kill each other. They separated, agreeing to keep at least 100 miles apart forever after.

The often ridiculously elaborate codes for the duel (Baldick, 1965) suggest the curiously formal quality of male-with-male combat. Such combat is typically not simply a murderous action, however much the males may like to pretend it is and however much it may really hurt. Mortal enemies or warring nations commonly have or develop rules that bind more stringently than the effort to kill—the point here being not that such rules are violated or sometimes fail to develop but that they normally do tend to develop. What is important for the male is that the contest be formally competitive (and thus, at one level, abstractly analytic) and of high intensity. Male viewers of television sports like the instant replays, which enable them to analyze the formal structure of the intense agonistic activity.

Distancing by combat occurs between females also, but by and large, as has been seen above, without the spectacular combative procedures common among males throughout the higher animal kingdom. The fact that the females typically achieve comparable results with less effort and bloodshed shows once more the short-term redundancy and waste typical of male behavior. It also shows that the results of combat between females and between males, while comparable, are not the same. The relation of female to female is not the same as that of male to male. Something could perhaps be made here of the suggestion offered by Anthony Wilden, in "Piaget and the Structure of Law and Order" (1972:90), that "redundancy and enormous 'waste' of effort ... are the concomitants of long-range stability."

Bonding Patterns and Loners

The curious male bonding pattern, well studied in psychological and sociological research, has been brought to popular attention by Lionel Tiger in his book *Men in Groups* (1969). Some male bonding patterns of a sort can be found among infrahuman animals, as in the winter flocks of turkeys mentioned earlier (Watts and Stokes, 1971). But it is particularly obvious among human males that the support from the other achieved by distancing him (that is, in effect, distancing or standing off oneself) can be enhanced by grouping. The bonding pattern in male groups is well known: it consists of closeness and distancing simultaneously. It includes banter, "ribbing," constant psychological pushing, shoving, swatting (among young males, the pushing, shoving, swatting are physical as well). Thus each assures himself that everybody is a friend though at the same time everybody is on his own and keeping everybody else at arm's length—an admiring arm's length, in a kind of diffuse communal narcissism.

Male bonding groups are associations of loners. The male values a companion whom he can stand up against and who can stand up against him: each receives assurance from the other's decently adversative stance, for it reminds him of his own needs and resources. This masculine intense friendly aggression is foreign to most women's experience. Clinical work by W. G. King (1970) has shown that, generally speaking, human males and females judge friendly and unfriendly behavior of the opposite sex rather well, except that females' judgment of the violent, jokingly hostile friendly behavior common among males is notably restricted. One can hypothesize that the agonistic understructure is difficult for females to interpret: to women such exchanges of violence normally seem truly hostile in intent. (See also Hennig and Jardim, 1977:31.)

Among human beings male bonding is often effected by shared hardships. "Forsan et haec olim meminisse iuvabit," Virgil has Aeneas say (*Aeneid* i.203) to his companions when the going is rough: "Perhaps someday it will be enjoyable to remember these things." Women, too, experience ties of this sort, but not so exclusively in this fashion with other women. The war party, where this sort of bonding functions in anticipation of action as well as in retrospect, is a typically male phenomenon. And in male clubrooms and bars around the world the most casual companions can often establish immediate bonding by recalling the hardships that all men share, namely, the threats that woman poses to man—one of the constant themes of "bull sessions" (note the term: there are no "cow sessions" or "heifer sessions" or prepubertal "calf sessions"). A bull session seems to generate corporately a kind of psychological testosterone to ensure protection against the female environment—or just against environment in general, for many of the problems arising from other surroundings can be projected onto women. All environment is enveloping, womblike. The male craves freedom, and for many males the symbolic independence of all environment which one establishes by setting up as a loner, with occasional participation in a bonded gang of loners, is the ultimate accomplishment and happiness.

Shared hardships can encourage the male bonding pattern even though the hardships may have been undergone from opposing sides of a battlefield. The "dear enemy" phenomenon has evolved in territorial distancing even among infrahuman species (birds, for example; see Edward O. Wilson, 1975:274-75). And among humans, there may even be quite frequently camaraderie, often of a wry, good-humored sort. Hostile terms for males can readily carry a load of grudging affection, for the hostility normally has at least a covert gaming quality. "The old bastard is a pretty decent guy."

The predisposition to individual psychological distancing evinced by males even when closely bound in groups is paralleled by a male predisposition to leave the group entirely and to become a "loner." The male loner is a far more common phenomenon than the female loner, certainly among human beings and very widely among infrahuman animals. Almost all adolescent male chimpanzees in the wild spend "long periods—hours or even days—completely out of sight and often out of earshot of other chimpanzees" (Van Lawick-Goodall, 1962:57-64). This behavior is part of the male chimpanzee's problem of breaking away from his mother, who has been his constant companion into adolescence. (Again, masculinity means differentiation.) During his period as a loner, the adolescent chimpanzee is perforce choosing between his mother and the agonistic companionship of adult males who both attract and terrify him (Van Lawick-Goodall and Hamburg, 1974:47).

In certain species otherwise gregarious the adult males are all loners—African elephants, for example. A herd is led by a mature female elephant and consists only of immature and mature females and immature males. When a male becomes sexually mature, he leaves herd life for good, managing on his own, casually friendly with other males he meets and taking up with a female only to mate when she is estrous (Edward O. Wilson, 1975:494–98). As a general pattern, groups of animals headed by an adult female do not have permanent adult male members, although rarely they do, as among zebras (Eibl-Eibesfeldt, 1970:358, quoting H. Klingel).

Among human beings, somewhat similar patterns exist. It appears that there have never been any matriarchal societies in the sense of societies in which women have normally been the chief political or military leaders, although many societies have occasionally been headed politically by a woman, generally surrounded by male ministers. (Even in the mythical realm of the Amazons these imagined female warriors ran a completely feminine, not a bisexual, society. Strabo, in his *Geography*, xi, 5, 1, has them mating with males of other peoples and retaining only their female children. Male children were returned to their fathers. The Amazon story is very likely an instance of the recurring tale of a distant land where everything is the reverse of normal, so that women are the warriors.) There have been and still are matrilineal and matrifocal societies, in which descent and inheritance and, largely, prestige are through the female line. In these societies, however, the maternal uncle is of major importance, for a young male must connect with the male political and military world through his mother's line, so that her brother is his closest male kin, outranking his own father—is, in fact, a kind of matriarchal father. Traces of such matrifocal social organization can be seen in the West as late as the Middle

Ages. In the Arthurian stories, for example, Modred (or Mordred), who is identified specifically as Arthur's "sister's son," ultimately becomes his adversary, to produce a maximally tragic situation: a son at odds with his matriarchal father, who in some versions is also his biological father, Arthur having produced Modred by incestuous union with his own sister.

But only naively macho thought would believe that political rulers and military leaders are the principal forces in human life, holding society or the individual psyche together. A history focused on politics and war is not a very profound history of humankind. Existence may be influenced by politics and war, but it is rooted in more enduring realities. Edward O. Wilson (1975:19) has pointed out that societies of the higher animals—vertebrates and especially mammals—are marked by "close mutual affiliation of females." Males "may come and go, but females typically endure." Here again, validated in sociobiology, we find the "fey" male, isolated and doomed to die, like the Marine fighter pilot Bull Meecham in Pat Conroy's *The Great Santini*, contrasting with *das ewige Weib*, the enduring or eternal woman of folklore and the unconscious. At the conclusion of Faulkner's great saga of Yoknapatawpha County, the dynasty of male Compsons has perished, but of Dilsey and her indomitable and indeed unflappable feminine world Faulkner quietly remarks, "They endured" (Faulkner, 1954:756). In the long run, the female component outweighs and outperforms the male component in holding society and individuals together. The male's usefulness, biologically grounded, for effecting distance and divergence and change ultimately wastes the male.

The convergence typically effected by females and the divergence typically effected by males accords with the distancing function of male ceremonial contest. At the human level mother and daughter tend to merge symbolically and socially (whence the worldwide stock of mother-in-law jokes), father and son to diverge, to distance themselves from one another. Nancy Friday's recent popular work, *My Mother / My Self* (1978) rehearses the many patterns in which the permanent mother-daughter merger asserts itself. Contest often advertises the distancing of son and father. Across the world, in literature and in life, sons do battle with fathers, and quite commonly with fathers not known to be such—hence superlatively distanced. Such fathers turn up everywhere, from *Oedipus Rex* to *Sohrab and Rustum* on down to the popular Johnny Cash ballad "A Boy Named Sue," whose father, in abandoning (distancing) him, had given him a name that would assure his son masculinity. Sue, of necessity, learned to fight. His father would not have had thus to put Sue on the spot if he himself had remained at home so that his son could have fought against him, at least in play. In fact, Sue's father does show up at the close of the ballad, and the son finally engages him in battle. At first Sue does not know who his opponent is, and when he finds out, the battle modulates from a lethal into a more ceremonial contest, which seals the father-son relationship at last and brings matters back to normality, to the proximity-distance relationship that strengthens males.

In real life across the world, ceremonial physical contest between father and son—wrestling, boxing, dueling—helps to bring sons to normal maturity, establishing the friendly agonistic distancing the male psyche needs. Daughters do not normally engage in ceremonial physical contest at all with their mothers. Such contest is distancing, and mothers are permanently too close to invite or to bring about distancing. If a young girl engages in such contest with a parent, as many do at times, it is likely to be with father and it has its limits—tennis, fencing perhaps, for rougher sports would risk either overmasculinization or perhaps incest. (Even boys of course engage in no comparable physical contests with their mothers.) Woman's typical program for maturity does not involve distancing in the same way: "I want to be *me,* to realize what is in me," not "I want an adversary to keep at bay so as to give me confidence in what I can do." (See Hennig and Jardim, 1977:14 and *passim.*)

The male loner pattern contrasts with the female fear of being alone, of abandonment, of being left (a version of the fear of being left empty), which Erik Erikson (1963:410-11) discusses and which Shakespeare and others whose noetic possessions and structures had emerged from folklore and the commonplace tradition knew very well. "Hell hath no fury like a woman scorned." The man may want to be abandoned: his male identity is related to distancing. The female wants to be pursued. If the male does not pursue, the female loses interest, and at times may sulk or rage.

Some of the problems among human females regarding competition with males (Matina Horner, unpublished paper reported in Bardwick, 1971:179-83; Hennig and Jardim, 1977:14, 27, 31, and *passim*) seem to lodge here. Competition of the sort that males typically and passionately have practiced, in business, politics, academia, and elsewhere, is based in great part on gaming to stand off others. When a woman enters into this game, she may play it very well, but in it she must put aside the wish to be pursued—which of course is not at all her total being—and work for a dynamic distance situation instead.

One cannot, however, assume that high competitiveness correlates with success, as early studies of women active in once exclusively male arenas have perhaps tended to do. Studies recently reported (Duncan, Featherman, and Spence, 1979), to be discussed later here, suggest that, although in every factor tested men are significantly more competitive than women, the most successful women and men in science and business are significantly low in competitiveness. They are high in "work competence"—that is, they do their jobs extraordinarily well (hardly a surprising discovery). Only among the least successful does greater competitiveness lead to greater (very modest) success. Among the most successful, high competitiveness means less great success. The implications of this pattern as women move more and more into business and science—and other areas in which studies are not complete—will have to be seen. In many places, the male loner's show of standoff contest may be quite irrelevant and even a disability.

However irrelevant to success, the male loner pattern shows starkly in the appeal of loner's games to men, especially when the games are territorial. Chess is an apropos example here.

Contest and Sexual Identity

Chess is a contest between conspicuously lone loners, whom the press and the popular imagination like to isolate even more by decorating them with real or imaginary idiosyncrasies. There are no ties between individual players in chess other than those that bond opponent to opponent in combat. Chess contrasts here, for example, with bridge. Bridge is a comparably intellectual contest, in which the male's strictly physical advantages—larger size, longer reach, greater upper-body strength, and so on—are no advantages at all, but it is more socialized than chess, not merely in setting twosomes rather than singles against one another but also in honoring social structures not formally part of the game. Often and typically, bridge partners consist of a male and a female: this kind of pairing shows that the game has a sociosexual dynamism extending beyond that of its formal game rules.

Chess contrasts with bridge in being a territorial game, played, as bridge is not, on a "board," of which each opponent sets out to gain total possession. In chess there is no chance whatsoever other than that of human error. This fact makes chess more "formal" or "abstract" than bridge. It is concerned with one element only, occupied and occupiable territory in itself, not territory as determined by something uncontrollable and nonterritorial, such as chance distribution of cards. Chance would introduce an issue other than the purely territorial and in that sense make the game less formal or abstract. Ritual contest, as has been seen, typically isolates not only individuals but also issues, and chess qualifies superlatively as ritual contest. A game of chess is an arabesque worked out in a network of rules involving territory and territorial dominance (pawns have least territorial dominance, knights and bishops more, and so on). One wins the game by eliminating the opponent's territorial hierarchy of "men" one by one from positions on a field to which each opponent and each of the "men" has certain claims. Moreover, the common practice in which one master chess player takes on a number of competitors in separate but concurrent games curiously resembles the practice in territorial contest among species of animals, such as some grouse and some antelopes, that use the lek system for breeding, a system that fosters some of the most high-stress territorial behavior in the animal kingdom (Edward O. Wilson, 1975:331–34). On the lek the most powerful male must defend the quite limited prime territory he occupies not merely against one rival but against any number of surrounding claimants, moving from one front to another as the master chess player does. However utterly intellectual chess may be, it generates behavior patterns that curiously suggest the biological past.

This totally territorial loner's game appears to have an overwhelmingly greater appeal to the male than to the female psyche. This is not to say that it does not have considerable appeal to some women. But, despite the fact that the male's strictly biological advantages are no advantages at all, top chess competition is entirely between males. The 1978 *Guinness Book of World Records* lists only two women's names for chess, the winner and the runner-up in matches restricted to women—that is, matches from which males are excluded. Females are not excluded from the open matches that males regularly win. Women are simply not so intensely concerned with chess. Readers of *Chess Life and Review*, published by the United States Chess Federation, find themselves in a virtually all-male world. Vigorous promotion of chess among females produces comparatively minuscule results, as reported in the December 1977 issue (p. 639) by Betty Trahim, the only woman author to be found in hundreds of pages of this periodical. In the same issue, the "Top 50" list, which is open to women, includes none. To compensate for this situation, there is a "Top 50 Women" list, but the highest rating in this list is well below the lowest in the "Top 50" open but in fact all-male list. Indeed, the ratings of the "Top 50 Women" have a range lower than the "Top 50 under 16 [years of age]," which is also open but in which all those qualifying are males. The seven highest ratings in the "Top 50 under 13" (again open to girls, but in fact consisting only of boys) are higher than the lower ratings of the "Top 50 Women." It should be remembered that at this age girls are in verbal and academic achievement well ahead of boys. The

September 1977 issue features a cover story on the National Scholastic Chess Tournament team from Vaux Junior High School in Philadelphia, and the cover photograph shows them as all black and all male. Since the intellectual ability of females matches that of males, it seems reasonable to conclude simply that across the globe the intense one-to-one territorial competition of chess is seldom so interesting and never so utterly compelling to the feminine psyche as it can be to the masculine. Some may believe that the pattern may one day change, but thus far women who are interested in chess seem to have in the last analysis other, more overriding concerns as well.

All-Male Secrets and Woman's Secret

Seemingly always and everywhere men have formed groups whose mystique is based on the exclusion of women, from men's clubhouses in primitive societies to the myriad fraternal organizations founded in the eighteenth-, nineteenth-, and twentieth-century United States. These groups may perform very specific extramural functions, providing life insurance, support for children's hospitals, or serving other benevolent purposes. But intramurally they have been resolutely male. At other times all-male groups are formed to serve ordinary, commonplace purposes but in an all-male setting. McSorley's bar and grill in Manhattan for years drew a huge clientele by serving only men. Now, of course, it is open by court decision to both sexes, for as the threat from femininity has lessened in recent years in both the male and the female psyche (see Chapter 6), women have succeeded in making their way into more and more of the doggedly male enclaves. Males, of course, have no corresponding drive to invade women's societies, for reasons earlier suggested: born of women, reared as young children in a feminine setting, dominated necessarily—and for their own masculine psychological health—by a mother or mother equivalent, their masculinity is tied to moving away from the feminine, to a kind of escape.

Where they will find refuge from the feminine now remains a question, discussed though not at all entirely answered in Chapters 4, 5, and 6.

Women congregate with women, but secret societies (lodges, sororities) for women have normally been less grandiloquent and less defensive replicas of preexistent male originals: the urgency is not there for females. First, as earlier noted, not only human society but societies of the higher animals generally are marked by "close mutual affiliation of females" (Edward O. Wilson, 1975:19). There is no need for special organizations to secure what society as a whole enforces. Second, as just noted, each woman is her own secret society: this is what makes women attractive to men. The internality of the female sexual organs is crucial here, biologically and psychologically. Woman's body is a mystery, for what is most distinctively feminine about it, its reproductive equipment, is largely invisible. Hence exploitation of women's sexual attractiveness—in fan dancing, striptease, or simply scanty costume generally—is based on the promise of disclosing more and more, which of course is never enough. By contrast, efforts to exploit male sexuality in this way have limited appeal and to most persons appear simply ludicrous. Male sexual organs are not secret and mysterious: they are external, for everyone to see—and to make fun of, often enough. The phallus and testicles are regularly the subjects of jokes, female sexual organs more rarely and the womb almost never (Grotjahn, 1957:103). When female sexual organs figure in jokes, they do so commonly as threats to males from the biting, devouring, castrating female, so that again the male and not the female is the object of ridicule.

In a profound sense, by contrast to man, woman is interiority, self-possession. She relates to herself interiorly, and others relate to her interiorly—her lovers, her children. The virgin is permanently a symbol and realization of this interiority and self-possession, and of its tremendous power: the inviolate secret interior, self-possessed, which the virgin knows and draws strength from in full freedom. The bonded male group has its secrets, too, but they are weak and even ludicrous by comparison. They are manufactured secrets, imitations of women's natural secrets, calculated to establish males as distinct from women and able to compete with women (Murphy, 1959). The contrived male secrets are parlayed into an unreal mystique: the bull-roarers, once you know how they work, are not terrifying at all. But the women give birth to real children. In the typical male mystique, women, who know too much about secrets already—as Faulkner's characters protest over and over again—must be kept away from the strictly masculine affairs so that the confected male secrets can be protected from disclosure and ridicule. For, deep down, the men know that they have no real secrets at all and, to make it worse, suspect that the women know it too.

Vicarious Contest

Human males often practice vicarious combat, using animals of various species as surrogates for themselves. Here one's human opponent is not physically injured at all, but nevertheless is forced to concede victory. In many cultures, birds are favorite surrogates for males in combative action. Clifford Geertz (1972) has shown in exquisite depth and detail how totally macho the cockfights are in Bali and how they catch up in their felt dynamism the typical masculine anxieties concerning sexual prowess, public prestige, combat effectiveness, courage to take maximum risks, ability to bear pain, and the like. Cockfights in most if not all cultures would appear to have the same symbolic force. Roosters commonly strut enough to strike all human beings as singularly macho, and, as Geertz makes clear, Balinese males identify their masculinity totally at almost every conceivable level with their own fighting birds. The same identification obtains among cockfighters ("handlers") in the United States, I have been informed by frequenters of the fights who have read Geertz's article.

Horse racing can under some conditions also function to tie an owner-rider's masculine self-image to the prowess of an animal surrogate, but not so powerfully as cockfighting can. In Faulkner's *The Reivers* and in some Western movies, winning or losing a horse race can affect a male owner's masculine self-image. High commercialization of horse racing, however, readily distances owner from mount and compromises close identification. Jockeys interpose themselves as third parties. They are at first male ("jockey" is a diminutive of the masculine name Jack or Jock), but a few women jockeys are now appearing. And of course women own race horses. The horse race is not directly rooted in biology as the cockfight is. Cocks fight under their own power. Horses do not race unless a human being guides them. The contest does not spring out of the tensions between intraspecific males and its appeal to the human male psyche is proportionately tenuous and variable.

The earlier and cruder sports of bullbaiting and bearbaiting are macho in cast, too, but they seem to belong to another class of male activities related in psychic history less to intraspecific male combat than to the slaying of the dragon, that is, to the young man's achievement of masculinity by the slaying of the Great and Terrible Mother, the archaic female figure "with masculine, but not paternal, features" (Neumann, 1954:155).

Bullfighting is a special case. It is lone male against lone male (the very few women who have become *toreras* are fascinating not so much because they are bullfighters as because they are not male in this macho world). The human male must come within an inch (or even less) of death: he must see to it that the bull's horns sweep as close to his midriff as possible. *Aficionados* become furious if the horns do not come close, and it is a major public scandal, a kind of national disgrace, if, as in Mexico in the 1940s, it is found that a bull's horns have been shaved an inch or so short just before he enters the ring, so that when he moves his head to hook into the matador's belly, estimating his horns to be longer than they really now are, he is really at a relatively safe distance from it (a few centimeters is "relatively safe"). The matador must also kill the bull by going in over the bull's lowered head to place his sword between the scapulae or shoulderblades (if they are to be properly spread, the bull must have been maneuvered so that his front feet are close together). As the matador kills, a toss of the bull's horns could kill him, too.

The matador appears thus as a kind of fey male figure, doomed to meet death, but in this case to meet it so as to triumph in close quarters and with the maximum sangfroid: he must act with total "cool" all the time, supremely untroubled, unconcerned even, as though he had everything under control (as he had better have). For the bull is in fact the one that is the fey male, doomed to die. Torero and bull are curiously identified. For the encounter is not one between two enemies, but a kind of ballet around death in which one combatant dies for both. Recall what was said earlier: in human male ceremonial combat, the male must fight another male because he thereby faces up to masculinity itself and its inherent insecurities, so that male ceremonial combat often links combatants as "dear enemies," bonded together as surrogates for each other. Bull and torero have faced death together, and with equal courage. No matter what the consequences, the "brave bull" will never flee, but will always counterattack until he is too exhausted (maybe) for further effort. He is a surrogate for another human male and as much a hero as the matador.

The bullfight is unusual, however, in that it is vicarious combat that is more than half real, though carried on with the absolute maximum of ceremonial formality. Its linking of the ceremonial with the real produces what is abnormal in male ceremonial combat: real death. Bullfighting is not truly a "sport," not pure play. Unlike sports heroes, the torero remains always shrouded in the threat of death: a living but permanently tragic figure, death hanging over his triumphant head. This is what makes him a special kind of hero. Football or baseball or soccer heroes are not quite of this cut. Their *agōn* is all ceremonial.

In the past, human beings who were officially déclassé, such as criminals and war prisoners, have been made to engage in fatal combat on somewhat the same basis as infrahuman animals, as in the Roman gladiatorial games. They are surrogates for the noncombatant spectators, who can bet on or otherwise identify with one or another gladiator. The spectator's freedom from threat of death makes the combat that is fatal to the real contestants in effect a ritualized, nonlethal fight for him. Prizefighting seems to be a variant of vicarious male ceremonial combat: it is done basically for the spectators, and the heavy betting shows close identification of male noncombatants with the risk taking of the boxers. The term "prizefighting" itself clearly indicates that one is fighting for something more than just to win. It is not difficult to see the prize or purse as an acquirable possession that serves as a surrogate for territory.

The no-holds-barred, biting, kicking, eye-gouging fights that were brought to frontier America from the British Isles and became the antecedents of modern boxing and wrestling seem also to have served in part as vicarious modes of combat, for they attracted throngs of spectators, even though they at times arose as unscheduled, if formal, fights precipitated by disputes over such macho concerns as cockfights. Incredible as it may seem, gouged-out eyes of an opponent were at times exhibited by victors as trophies (Holliman, 1975:138-39). Men who engaged in such fights might commonly be regarded as somehow infrahuman, like criminal gladiators, but they were not always déclassé: it was not unknown for distinguished lawyer-politicians to have engaged in fights in which they went for one another's eyes and succeeded in biting one another's fingers to the bone. Still, these fights, horrible though they were, appear often enough to have been basically, though pathologically, ritualized: the objective was not to kill, as it can well be in fights between human beings, but to be known as the victor by performing certain vicious but also symbolic actions. Dueling has somewhat similar features, as we saw earlier.

Other vicarious contests besides Balinese cockfights bring out many of the deep dynamics of male ritual combat. This chapter can conclude by calling attention to the arcane but vigorous agonistic activity of "pigeon mumblers," who fight each other with flocks of birds. Pigeon mumbling (Kligerman, 1978:74-81) is less well known than cockfighting but perhaps almost equally ancient. It is a regular, if little publicized, activity over the roofs of Brooklyn, New York, and elsewhere.

Pigeon mumblers (the origin of the term is obscure) train their flocks of pigeons to circle above their homes after they have been released from their pens and shooed off the roof, and to continue circling until the owner signals them down. Until he gives his signal, pigeons in his flight know that they will not be permitted to return to their roost, where they always feed; but at his signal, they plunge in immediately; for they know that they will immediately be given food in abundance. Pigeons tend to follow one another's behavior, particularly when taking flight, circling in flocks, and descending. The objective of a mumbler is to have his own airborne flock circle into a flock of one of his competitors. If he can then flag his flock down at exactly the right moment, before his competitor can flag his own, his plunging birds will draw down with them onto his own roof the competitor's flock, or at least some of them. The confused visitors, seduced by their own mimetic drives, are then netted before they can get their wits together and fly off to their own roost. On a good day, a mumbler can bag over $100 worth of pigeons, and on a bad day lose as many.

The game is intense and hardly cordial. Captured pigeons are sometimes traded and sometimes condescendingly returned, but sometimes also ruthlessly slaughtered by their captors in the sight of their owners on neighboring roofs to dramatize total victory. But mumblers are typical male lone warriors, closely bonded and curiously friendly with their foes. At a Brooklyn pigeon exchange, where birds and equipment are bought and sold, "the atmosphere... is one of warmth and friendship, but up on the roofs... the game is called *la guerra*, the war." On the roof, explains Pat Sottile, owner of the Meeker Pigeon Exchange, "you are *natural* enemies [my italics].... In the street, you're friends, but up on the roof you don't talk to one another. It's dog-eat-dog on the roof" (Kligerman, 1978:77).

The use of birds in vicarious masculine—and often macho—competitions of various sorts deserves more careful study, along such lines as those traced by Clifford Geertz in his fascinating and profound work on the Balinese cockfight (1972:1–37). Birds rival horses, and in some ways surpass them, as symbols of power. Indeed, at times the horse and the bird are made into one, as in the figure of Pegasus. Birds' power of flight suggests the dominance that "superiority" or "overness" establishes—being "on top of" a situation, "overmastering," "overpowering," "overcoming," being an *Übermensch* or "overman," Superman (superstrong folkloric figures commonly have the power of flight), and so on without limit. Everywhere, "over" expresses dominance, excellence, "super-lativeness" or "over-bearingness." Birds use "overness" spectacularly for dominance, climbing above their foes or prey: cocks fly up to strike down with their spurs, falcons "stoop" in a breathtaking plunge onto their prey, male hummingbirds zoom-dive on other male hummingbirds, and the mumblers' pigeons power-dive in their own unbloody fashion. The airborne dove can represent not only the peace but also the irresistible power of the Holy Spirit. Moreover, because they are airborne, birds even better than horses represent the risk taking and vertigo that appeal to the male's titillating and adventurous insecurity. The air provides only precarious support, and the distance between the human agent and his surrogate combatants makes his control of them equally precarious.

Above all (and the pun is so fully intended as to be not merely a pun), the use of such high-flying birds as falcons and pigeons suits the curious abstraction and distancing that intraspecific male combat fosters and thrives on. As surrogates for the real combatants, human males, the birds give those real combatants an extraordinarily formal relationship with one another. And the remoteness of the combat in the air makes distancing even more real.

3

Separation and Self-Giving: Pietà and Quixote

And the servants came running to tell me the boy was in the tree. It was a cypress tree, that at the top grows frail and thin, and it was bending this way and that in the wind, and at the top of it the boy. I called out to him to come down, but he was drunk with the power to make us afraid. I was mad with fear, and cried and screamed. ... Then he stretched his arms above his head, and gripped the small branches with his knees, and bent over backwards and gave some kind of cry, so that if he had fallen he would have fallen to death. I could not watch it anymore, nor endure to be so shamed, and I threw my apron over my head and ran crying to the house. Then he was ashamed of his naughtiness.
—Tante Sophie, in Alan Paton, *Too Late the Phalarope*

Then they [the women] applied countless hands to the fir tree, and dragged it out of the earth. Sitting on high, from high he is hurled and falls to the ground with countless groans—Pentheus; for he was beginning to understand that he was close to his ruin.
—Second Messenger, in Euripides, *The Bacchae*
(translated by Geoffrey S. Kirk)

Externality of Masculinity

Masculinity for human males and, in ways explained earlier, even for infrahuman males engenders agonistic activity because it is something to be won, achieved, "always in a state of being earned" (Bardwick, 1971:204), not at all simply something one is born with. The genetic determinants of masculinity, notably for human beings, establish not so much a state of being as a program. A male finds his masculinity in some way outside of himself, especially in the higher animal species and most especially among human beings. Masculinity is difficult to interiorize, a kind of stranger to the human psyche. Since being human means living from interiority, masculinity is an especially acute problem for human beings.

A certain anatomical externality is obvious in the male sexual organs of humans and other higher animals, and it is also registered accurately and indeed exquisitely in certain ways of conceiving of these organs. Thus a male has two sexual organs, which in English, as in Latin, are called "testes" (Latin, *testes,* the plural of *testis,* witness) or "testicles" (*testiculi,* little witnesses—other languages deriving or borrowing from Latin use the same or cognate terms here). *Testis* is the word from which "contest" is derived, as we saw in Chapter 1. If the male is fully developed, the testes have moved outside of his body cavity, to be somewhat external to himself, though for no immediately obvious physiological reason, since they are not intromittant organs. The not-so-obvious but well-known physiological reason is, of course, reduction of temperature. How the need for reduced temperature of the organs producing the male gametes has evolved is not entirely clear. But whatever the evolutionary history, the lower temperature of the testes, once it becomes known to human beings, further advertises their differentiation from the rest of the organism and their relative externality. In line with what we have said about the etymology of "contest" (a confrontation of witnesses), the male finds himself anatomically entered in a contest, on trial, having to call witnesses (outside of himself to a degree, not himself) to give testimony as to what he actually is, not a woman, to "say" that he is a man.

This situation is one of the manifold deep paradoxes of human existence caught in the story of creation in Genesis, and perhaps in other ways in other creation stories. In Genesis 2:18-24, man is indeed created before woman, but he is essentially in more difficult straits, only half there. "It is not good for man to be alone." The male is presented as temporally prior to woman, but he comes into existence plagued with a need, a lack. From the beginning, he finds himself in a stress situation (like the male embryo and fetus). Woman is created to fill the lack, the male's deficiency. She came temporally second, but her situation was better: she did not have a comparable lack, for her needed companion was there for her when she arrived. To be feminine is, in a profound sense, to come into existence provided for—though not in every sense, of course. Male insecurity—the stress situation—and male dominance are advertised here again as functions of each other.

Self-Giving, Feminine and Masculine

The parlous situation of the male is probably better known to the unconscious than to the conscious mind, and is reflected and refracted in a thousand ways in folklore and all sorts of verbal art forms. A man must be willing to die for his country or for other causes. Of course, so must a woman, but somehow there is less point in a woman's being willing to do so. Others need her too much to spare her. Commonly, a heroine comes into her own in other ways.

Males frequently become ridiculous because of their drives to risk themselves. Don Quixote is a prototype of all masculinity—human masculinity and even infrahuman masculinity. There are no female Don Quixotes. A woman tilting with windmills or driven by impossible dreams is not a poignant figure. All real women have more sense. Not all real men do. Masculinity has something futile about it: as earlier noted, chivalric and other literature is full of men who are fey—fighters doomed to die—and who contrast with *das ewige Weib*, the eternal (or durable) woman. (Folklore sensed the comparative mortality rates for the two sexes long before the statisticians counted them out.)

The contrast between masculinity and femininity does not

mean that woman is simply nonman or man nonwoman. The contrast is not between contradictions, between a positive and a negative, but between two opposites, both positive. Male and female are not even fully complementary: they are an example of what in Chapter 1 I called asymmetric opposition. Just as she can be combative, so woman of course can be at least as heroic as man. Experience, with its reflection in lore and literature across the world, attests that woman is at least as capable of self-sacrifice as man is, if not more so. Her quintessential and typical (though not her only) self-sacrifice is truly heroic: creative self-giving at the death of a lover or son. Michelangelo's Pietà grips us by presenting a woman who in confronting death has become fully and overwhelmingly a symbol of life, in a way a man can never be. She has given up totally the possessiveness that is both necessary for womanliness and the abiding threat to full womanliness.

Possessiveness can be selfish and kill, and possessiveness relates particularly to woman, as in the widespread mythological symbol of the impersonal, possessive, unwittingly selfish Great Mother, whose children are for her not persons but possessions that she consumes or smothers (envelops to the point of death) (Neumann, 1954:39-101). But the psychologically sound woman knows how to relinquish, to let her natural protectiveness open into freedom for those she protects. Margaret Mahler (Mahler and Furer, 1963; Mahler, 1965 and 1971) has described in circumstantial clinical detail the processes that take place when the very young child begins to separate himself or herself from mother, the loving skill with which the psychologically sound mother permits and encourages her tiny child to achieve autonomy and individuation, physical and psychic. As the child plays peekaboo, scurries off in a sally of independence, glances back to mother for assurance, bravely allows mother to leave him behind in a strange room but then, just to be safe, quickly seats himself in the chair she has vacated, and otherwise zigzags toward self-confidence, the cooperative interaction of mother and child is truly a beautiful spectacle.

Separation and Self-Giving

In the Pietà the Virgin Mother has freed herself of all possessiveness, transmuted all eros (love involved in its own need) into agape (love as self-giving, involved with the other). She has done so by lovingly acquiescing to her now adult Son's doing what he was called to do, his Father's will. She leaves her Son completely free, though doing so returns him dead to her arms. And when she takes him dead into her arms, she does not clutch him, but leaves her arms open. The statue tugs at the hearts of women and men alike, but its subject matter is supremely feminine. And it is supreme human freedom: Mary has deliberately chosen to let her Son be about his Father's business. If she had the choice once more, knowing what it would cost, she would do it again. No regrets. Total courage. Her youthful choice is still part of her. Hence her youthful face, often commented on, despite her mature age. Her arms are open and relaxed. She is completely free, for she is fully aware of what she has chosen.

To be free, we must know our options and know our motives so far as possible: I want to do this, and for these reasons. Freedom is based on true and full knowledge. This Mary has. She is completely self-possessed, completely herself. Indeed, she had learned this self-giving all through her life, from the time when Jesus separated himself from her and Joseph to remain behind in the temple at the age of twelve ("I must be about my Father's business"—Luke 2:49) and even earlier in her Son's infancy when Simeon had told her that a sword would pierce her "so that the thoughts of many hearts may be laid bare" (Luke 2:35). "Mary treasured all these things and reflected on them in her heart" (Luke 2:19). Deliberately chosen self-giving had begun and ended her experience.

A father can suffer untold agony at the loss of a child, but there can be no male Pietà. Separation from father is achieved before conception. A father need not be alive when a child is born—or even when the child is conceived. Self-giving, and possible loss, comes to the male at a different angle, in questing, yearning for combat, courting stress situations for others' sakes, pursuing the impossible dream to his death. The typical threat of death from a father is not clutching or smothering or swallowing but brutal dominance. The father destroys by violent blocking or by delivering a direct blow. The masculine drive is to strike outward—the spear of Mars (♂)—to change things, to alter environment, and thus to counter the constant, restless male insecurity; the feminine urge is to incorporate, to harbor, to keep. (The analogy with sexual intercourse is evident and indeed commonplace.)

As the female counters her possessive drive by surrendering to others her dearest, the male counters his tendency to violent dominance by placing any violence in him directly at the service of others (the knight errant). The desire to work off violence by achieving for others against opposition can become pointless, amusing, and finally poignant when only an imagined other and a factitious opposition is there—Don Quixote, the feckless warrior, with no cause or opponent outside his own longing, his impossible dream. In another way also the male can counter his own proclivities to violence by containing or sublimating them even at the cost of death, which thereby puts his total self at others' service. ("Father, forgive them, for they know not what they do.")

The typical self-giving of men is the performance of valiant exploits (ultimately, from Proto-Indo-European *eghs*, out, *-plek*, plait) for others, women and other men. The typical self-giving of women is providing courage, conveying strength to others, men and women, but especially and paradigmatically to men performing exploits. Woman keeps other persons, both men and women, from being afraid. When a child is terrified and has a choice of running to father or to mother for strength, paradoxically mother is normally the chosen source for reassurance, though she is normally physically weaker. The expression "the weaker sex" is defensive male insecurity again when it hints—as it often does—that females are weaker than males not merely physically (as in fact they on the average are) but also in their entire being. Neither sex is psychologically or humanly "weaker." Each of these typical functions, performing valiant exploits or supplying courage and keeping others from being afraid, carries the individual outside of himself or herself, but in different ways. And the different ways are only typical of the two sexes, not sexually exclusive: women do perform exploits, and men serve as refuges and sources of courage—though in the deepest sense the drive to valorous exploits by women or men is rooted ultimately in relationships to a mother or a mother figure, however immediately it touches relationships to a father. *Cherchez la femme.* Or read D. H. Lawrence. A recent study (Isaacs, 1978:189-203) has pointed out that both fictional narrative and psychological and scientific writing attend to mothers far more than to fathers—two to three times as much. There is almost no literature by fathers about sons—in part, no doubt, because the deep narrative drives and structures underlying literature are radically retrospective (Ong, 1977a:230-71).

The differentiation of Don Quixote and the Pietà does not define all male-female relationships and it does not of course mean that a man cannot understand a woman's suffering or a woman a man's: the Pietà is the creation of a male artist, after all. And Don Quixote's impossible dream is incarnated in a female figure, Dulcinea. Understanding is interactive. One way to put it is to say with Jung that the male's psyche finds in itself the female anima (for creative work, the "muse"), the female's psyche finds in itself the male animus. Each sex understands itself and the other out of its own resources, but these resources themselves derive from the relationship of asymmetrical opposition to the other sex: a husband can understand a wife in ways she cannot understand herself (and she can understand that he does), and a fortiori a wife's understanding of a husband can reach deeper than his own self-understanding (and he can understand that it does—and she can understand that he can understand that it does, and so on, to depths we cannot consciously fathom).

Maximizing Male Risk

The structures being noted here are in some ways psychological or psychoanalytic commonplaces, but here they are intended to put into perspective the agonistic setting and behavior that have marked the earlier male-dominated world of academic and formal intellectual life. This setting and this behavior are seldom attended to. To prepare to understand them, we need to become aware of the extremes to which the male can find himself pushed in establishing his identity by setting up stress and performing under stress.

In an article earlier referred to, Clifford Geertz (1972) has shown some of these extremes as manifest in the Balinese institution of cockfighting, a totally and obsessively masculine, anxiety-charged, but on the whole cathartic activity. Other instances of performance under stress abound in anthropological literature, as in the Sun Dance of male Native Americans of the Great Plains, the Dakota and the Ponca, who whirled around poles to which they were attached by ropes skewered into their chest muscles, and in countless tests of endurance in male puberty rites around the world. For our present purposes, however, the extremes of the male identity crisis are perhaps nowhere more spectacularly evident than in the land diving of the Pentecost Islanders, as it has been explained in an article by Kal Muller in the December 1970 *National Geographic Magazine* (786-811) with a fascinating series of photographs by the author. Not only the activity itself, but even more the folkloric explanation of its origins, exquisitely reveals the male psyche—as does also the fact that Muller, in studying the activity, found himself obliged as a male, taunted by other males, to take the risk of a dive himself.

On the New Hebrides island of Pentecost, following a long-standing custom, in an annual celebration men from the village of Bunlap and nearby areas dive from tree-and-vine towers as high as eighty feet and more, headfirst, with lianas tied to their ankles, the woody vines just long enough to brake the men's fall as they hit the bare ground below. Women are barred from the construction site while the tower is being built and from the area in the forest where the building materials, tree trunks and branches and lianas, are stockpiled. (Woman is the threat because you have to prove you're not a woman; although you are not anatomically female, everyone, including you yourself, darkly suspects you are female anyhow since you were born and cared for by a woman: like females, males are a feminine product.) But though they are barred from construction activity—at least this tower is not a feminine product—the women assemble with the men about the completed tower and join in the dancing and singing of songs of praise as the diver mounts the tower, and they join in the celebration afterward. Just before the diver leans forward off the platform to plunge below, he makes a formal speech—often publicly airing his troubles (hostilities), typically including marital difficulties. Psychologically, the diving at least in part serves male adversative needs: it is a gesture to counter his psychological environment, the world as he has found it.

The land diving is in principle a ritual to ensure a good yam crop, but it is a ritual consisting of little more than male bravado—willingness to take an ultimate risk (as in a bullfight). The setting is impressively competitive. Individuals are given every inducement to dive from a maximum height, each diver building his own platform at whatever height he chooses on the tower. Nondivers are cowards. Muller proved to himself and to the spectators, male and female, that he was not a coward by making his own dive from a fifty-foot platform, after he had been told earlier, "Me no think white man he savvy jump, bambai you fright too much." Young Bunlap boys work up their skill and their courage gradually, some making twenty-foot dives by the age of five. The threat of death is real enough, though accidents, which occur with fair frequency, are generally minor (pulled muscles, sprains, contusions, skinned shoulders), since even if the lianas break, they generally do so at a point where they have already notably decelerated the fall. But death is in the air, literally and figuratively, and is meant to be. When one young man of sixteen dived from seventy feet, Muller reports, and both his lianas (one tied to each ankle) broke, he lay face down, feigning death, till his mother and sisters broke out sobbing, whereupon he leaped up, shouting and laughing. Of course. Having upset the women while not being upset himself, remaining "cool," he was now supersure that he was not female.

These performances bring to mind Erik Erikson's reports (1963:97-108) about young boys' propensity to use building blocks to construct towers to heights that invite collapse, as well as countless scenes from literature of males proving themselves by posing at great heights in trees, from the passage in Euripides' *Bacchae* in which Pentheus is hurled from a treetop to be torn to pieces by his mother to the passage from Alan Paton in which a boy risks his life in a treetop to have the satisfaction of terrifying the women—both quoted at the beginning of this chapter. In situations such as the one in Paton, the woman's reaction is complex. One reason for it is certainly that some women get a great deal of satisfaction, sometimes motherly, sometimes wry or even sardonic, out of strengthening the male ego. Innumerable Freudian phallic interpretations of males in tall trees also offer themselves. But no interpretation is more telling than the actual folkloric account that the Bunlap Islanders themselves provide to explain the origin of their land-diving practices.

Once, the Bunlap villagers explain, as Muller reports, a man named Tamalie quarreled with his wife, who ran away and climbed a banyan tree. Tamalie followed to recapture her, she jumped down to escape him, and he jumped after her. But she had tied lianas around her ankles to break her fall, while he, without lianas, simply plunged to his death. The other men took up the practice of land diving so that no woman would trick them again. The drive behind this fictitious explanation is clear: the male feeling of insecurity by comparison with the female, who had tricked and killed Tamalie by being secure when he was not. (Like Eve, Tamalie's wife had been provided for; like Adam, Tamalie had not.) Tamalie's wife had jumped not out of bravado, but for a very practical reason—to save herself. The Bunlap male imitates her action for no such practical reason at all but for reasons far more remote and tenuous (like the lianas themselves): in principle to ensure a good yam crop and also, in fact, to prove

Separation and Self-Giving

over and over again that in risk situations he can survive—and thus to convince himself and the world that he is not a woman and that he can live with his own male insecurity. Of course, what permanently dogs him is that the women do not really care that he can beat them in this particular way, are in fact pleased with the fact, since it makes him appear a bit childish and warms the cockles of their hearts. Women thus remain more secure or stronger after all. As the previously quoted Chinese saying goes, the woman always conquers because of her quietness (which again is not at all the same as simple passivity).

The symbolic components of the legendary explanation are further enhanced in the actual Bunlap practices. A tree (which grows of itself out of Mother Earth) will no longer do. There must be a tower, more incontestably masculine than a tree, not a work of Mother Nature but an artificially engineered structure, a work of the mind, made ready entirely by males, insulated from all feminine presence or influence. The men must compete now with men in full-blown ceremonial contest. Women can be present at the competition, for in a sense women are what it is all about: the male must prove his masculinity in the presence of women, though also, and indeed even more, in the presence of fellow males, to show by contest with them in their masculinity that he is freed from woman to the maximum.

Vocal and Physical Bravado

Agonistic drives find a major outlet in human verbal activity. It is noteworthy that the Bunlap villagers' test of physical prowess is accompanied not only by songs of praise from spectators but also by ostentatious speechmaking that airs a diver's hostilities as a prelude to his takeoff. Association of oral bravado with physical bravado is common in the animal world, as in the territory-defensive song of male birds (Wynne-Edwards, 1962), and it is a typical syndrome in both the literary and the lived worlds of human male combat. Ancient oral performances and ancient literature associate oral and physical bravado, from the Bible (e.g.,

Goliath's taunting of David—I Samuel 17:43-44) and the *Iliad* and the *Odyssey* through *Beowulf* and beyond, in the fliting of heroes, in which verbal insults are hurled by heroic fighters at one another often as a prelude to physical combat. In later literature, as writing and print are interiorized in the psyche, fliting becomes the subject of frequent parody, direct or indirect, as in various Rabelaisian figures, in John Lyly's *Euphues*, in Shakespeare's Falstaff, and more gently and poignantly in Don Quixote. Byron's *Don Juan* subjects it to ultimate romantic ridicule.

Today, when fliting or its equivalents reappear, they do so generally in a male oral ambiance. World Wars I and II generated in abundance bragging songs insulting the enemy, songs of course for oral use. In the United States today highly oral American black males still ceremonially taunt one another in the "dozens," topping an opponent's vituperation of one's mother by a worse vituperation of his mother—but without show of anger, for this is a ritual or game, and to break into anger is to leave the game arena. Roger Abrahams (1967:468-78; 1968b:62) and Manning (1973) have called attention to similar practices in the West Indies and to their African provenience, and Abrahams has also shown (1968a, 1972), as noted earlier, that in many oral cultures proverbs serve largely as equipment for verbal combat. The performances of "men of words" in black communities in the United States and the Caribbean are recognized by the communities as agonistic demonstrations of masculine strength (Abrahams, 1968b:62). Dillard (1972:250-51) has shown that throughout the Afro-American tradition the use of "fancy talk," or formally and often outlandishly ostentatious expression, is a masculine activity: the occasional woman who takes it up produces nothing so rhetorically showy as the male performance. Mostly, women are simply uninterested in engaging in that kind of bragging show. Muhammed Ali is. He continues a longstanding tradition, represented not only by blacks but by whites as well, especially those from highly oral cultures, such as Dizzy Dean.

The cheering at football games and other spectator sports in

Separation and Self-Giving

another way associates oral bravado with physical. The agonistic structures here have been modified—in some ways reinforced, in others attenuated—by the emergence of quasi-masculinized drum majorettes and, later, less masculinized female cheerleaders. Grotjahn (1957:240-45) has discussed the relation of the strutting majorette to what was and still mostly is essentially male combat display and has analyzed the quasi-masculine costume, complete with activated baton, which he sees as giving some kind of phallic significance to this taut feminine figure. The later female cheerleaders have discarded batons for pompons. Bunlap villagers have feminine cheerers but, so far as I know, not masculinized female strutters for mixed crowds.

The activity of the Bunlap women in praising their men, which can be matched in other highly oral cultures (Opland, 1975; Peristiany, 1966), suggests that praise can be understood as largely a feminine component of culture. Highly oral cultures rather uniformly make a great deal of male ceremonial combat, oral and physical, which determines personality structures of both men and women in such cultures far more than in cultures of high technology (Ong, 1967). And highly oral cultures use praise in formal discourse by males with a frequency and intensity that to technologized cultures appears affected and quite unreal. The male psyche is greatly exposed in many if not most oral cultures, which maximize stress situations for males. Bourdieu (1966:222-23) has shown that among the Kabyle in Algeria, certainly one of the most typically and profoundly oral cultures extant today, men must spend most of the time out of the house in the contentious public forum, under the gaze of others, to show that they are properly agonistic.

Roger Abrahams (1975:66-69) has identified comparable house-street polarities in United States black cultures: the street is an arena for masculine *agōn*. Spending too much time in the quiet security of the house renders suspect the manhood of a Kabyle male. Strangers might simply label this masculine display behavior useless loitering or "laziness," but Kabyle women understand it otherwise. They know that it is obligatory risk

Fighting for Life

taking, that it is flaunted masculinity, and that the "loitering" males do indeed stir up among themselves fights and feuds. Kabyle women consider this obligatory vagrancy a bothersome requirement for men: "O man, you poor wretch, all day in the fields like a donkey in the pasture." Boys will be boys. "Overt masculinity" marks the cult of "honor" elsewhere generally, and notably through the Mediterranean region, as in the "honor plays" of Lope de Vega (Larson, 1977:1-2).

Overmasculinized in a hyperagonistic culture, the male psyche appears to need complementary, nonagonistic, nurturing treatment, publicly administered, to keep itself functioning. Fulsome public praise, a kind of public mothering (even when proffered by other men) helps to fill this need for support in oral and residually oral cultures around the globe. The Kabyle men and other men in similar situations would have great difficulty in agreeing with this kind of analysis, I am sure, but difficulties in admitting dependence on nurturing are part of the abiding male problem in many cultures, and to some extent in all. Another instance of this problem can be seen in the young American male who exhibits the so-called junior executive syndrome, deeply troubled if he cannot feel himself completely in charge. Praise suits such males well: for them it is nurture disguised as tribute.

Bragging, from one point of view, appears as self-administered praise. But, since bragging so readily involves or modulates into fliting or vituperation of one's opponent, it reminds us that praise, even identified as public mothering, is not merely an irenic ploy. Praise can foster polemic, as cheerers at athletic events well know.

Bragging is thus complex, but it is rather thoroughly masculine. It is both self-administered public mothering and the oral equivalent of ritual physical combat between males, formalized, serious, and bantering at the same time. This fact was conspicuous in the 1973 tennis matches staged by a vociferously boasting Bobby Riggs against female opponents, who of course were not at all disposed to respond in kind. Riggs mixed "ungentlemanly" and "gentlemanly" behavior for confusion: after crowing outlandishly to the press about his superior prowess, he presented Margaret Court with a bouquet of roses before the match. She was completely unnerved—one perfectly normal female response.[1] Billie Jean King registered an equally normal, totally feminine reaction, stating, according to newspaper accounts, that she found herself responding alternately with anger and amusement—for Riggs's bragging, despite all its oral, literary, and other cultural antecedents, can strike the feminine psyche as nonsense, which it is, and nonsense can evoke either anger or amusement.

Women can be vain and verbally aggressive, as are Chaucer's Wife of Bath and Rojas's Celestina, but they are not typically loners singing their own praises in preparation for battle even when they are preparing for battle. There are no female Falstaffs. The vanity (and insecurity) of the Wife of Bath shows not in her battles with other women or the world in general but chiefly in her vainglorious reports of the way her husbands and others esteemed her. She is not engaged in or interested in ceremonial combat but in the deference she can command simply by being herself. She is an almost totally successful dominant person (suggesting Mae West, but lacking the latter's wry wit). Although Chaucer adopts a tongue-in-cheek attitude toward the Wife of Bath's success, the tale she tells is basically a putdown of males' routes to dominance: a woman will let a man have his own way in anything provided only that he lets her have her own way in everything.

The male stress-performances noted here, with some special reference to orality, pertain to the masculine asceticism marking stages in the evolution of consciousness in which the ego asserts its independence of the body—and hence of natural birth, hence of femininity—as described, for example, by Neumann (1954:310-11, and *passim*). Puberty rites for girls, less spectacular and often less demanding than those for boys, can in particular

---

[1] See *St. Louis Post-Dispatch*, May 14, 1973, pp. 1A and 7A, 1C and 5C. The accompanying photographs are fascinating in their psychological implications.

instances inflict fearful suffering, physical as well as psychological, and can call for great courage, but in them elements of contest are normally far less apparent or simply nonexistent: puberty rites for females are calculated to enable the girl fully to realize and make her own what she is, to "take her place" as a woman, whereas in male puberty rites the boy is made to undergo agonizing doubt as to whether or not there is a place for him at all. In the television series "Roots," Kunta Kinte was sent weaponless into the forest, with the command to capture a large wild bird and bring it back alive—otherwise never to come back to his village again.

This kind of exposure to maximum risk and stressful danger is typical of male puberty rites and other male initiation rites. The risk or stress situation can from time to time be fatal, as in hazing or initiation activities of fraternities and other male bonding groups. One of the most agonizingly stressful situations institutionalized by males for males in modern times was doubtless that imposed on generations of plebes at West Point, especially during "Beast Barracks"; the eating of all meals at rigid attention, eyes fixated, and other all but incredible hardships, artificial but inexorable and continuous (Ellis and Moore, 1974; Galloway and Johnson, 1973; U'Ren, 1974). This stress apparatus in great part collapsed with the admission of women to the academy in the 1970s, though some stress apparatus remains. The collapse of course brought agonized protest from males, who felt that reliability in combat demanded proven ability to function under the worst possible stress, preferably stress induced by other males.

Masculinity, Contest, Differentiation

Many folkloric and mythological logia are endorsed by present-day psychology. One is that "nature's primary impulse is to make a female" (Bardwick, 1971:87, quoting Money, 1965). Masculinity in this sense means becoming something different, separation from origins, a certain kind of getting away, abstraction, transcendence. Hence, as has been seen, the haunting male insecurity: born of a woman, how can I be sure that I am not what I came from, that I am not a woman, too? I have to do something difficult, something that only a man can do, to prove that I am not. Born to be different from my source of life, I must live with stress and must invent stress to assure myself that I can perform. Males, explains Judith Bardwick (1971:87, 95-98), are females to whom something has happened, to whom something has been added, making their physiological and psychological development more hazardous. Through the animal kingdom generally, males have to move farther from their starting points: males are usually more differentiated from the young than females are—in coloration, in such adornments as manes, beards, horns, tusks, in size, or in voice. Differences between related species of animals are often far more conspicuously marked in the males than in the females: in many species of birds in which males stand out spectacularly from one another females are almost indistinguishable.

Awareness, conscious or unconscious, that "nature's primary impulse is to make a female" admits of defensive formulations, such as that of Aristotle and others that females are imperfect or defective males. Contrariwise, a feeling that males are better off than females generates the common and normal wish of a girl at a certain stage of development to be a boy: I would like to have something more happen to me, too. This is the tomboy stage. With maturity, the girl becomes aware that she is much more than a defective male, that there are other ways to transcendence than this (for a woman) imitative way, ways of access to masculinity, as well as to femininity, forever unavailable to males. Among these ways, childbearing is paramount. A mature woman can *produce* a male as well as a female out of her own body, give birth to a male, mother one, nourish a male totally dependent on her—which is more than any male can do for either a male or a female. This state of affairs makes more understandable the often documented preference of a significant majority of women for bearing a male child: I am a woman myself, and it should thus be obvious that I can give birth to a female, but having a son will show that I have, besides my own femininity, this further potential, the masculine, within me. (This is not the same thing by any means as a desire to be hermaphroditic: it is the strictly feminine potential, not masculinity, that makes the mothering of both males and females possible.)

Masculinity is thus a testimony both to human insufficiency and to human potential, to a certain ability to move beyond insufficiency. This is not at all the same as to say that women do not sense human insufficiency and do not have human potential. Nor is it to say that the male ever totally moves away from his feminine origins even in his maximum realization of his masculinity. The human male remains permanently dependent psychologically on the female. As has been seen, he needs to have been enveloped from the beginning in a feminine environment, which is the only environment in which he can discover and begin to mature his masculinity. He needs not only this initial female ambiance to set him on the road to masculinity but also permanent feminine backing built into his psyche—the mother or the lover or the "muse"—in order to achieve any of his fuller possibilities. *Cherchez la femme*—the woman who may at the moment be lover or muse but who has her primordial origin as a mother figure.

Mother deprivation is often, and even normally, handicapping and at times paralyzing, and in special ways for males, producing characters such as Meursault in Camus's *L'Etranger*, who reacts to adversity not agonistically but with infantile passive aggression, calculated inactivity, consciously stubborn nonresponse—"No" or "Well, really I couldn't say" or "I had nothing to say" (Camus, 1956:6, 12, and *passim*). Meursault has not even regressed to the oedipal stage, for in many ways he has never arrived at it (Hofling, 1978). He hates his mother (and women generally) because he has never meant anything to her. She never effectively brought him into her world. He is still trying, by behaving like an infant, to evoke a response from her. She had never provided him the psychological strength that is available, for a male as for a female, only from the *mundus muliebris*. He is weak, and raging.

Separation and Self-Giving

This feminine psychological strength is related to the unconscious, which is feminine in character and thus somewhat "other" to the male, stranger to the male than to the female. Masculinity is differentiation here, too, differentiation from one's own unconscious, which is antecedent to one's consciousness. Consciousness arises out of the unconscious by differentiation and thus has a masculine quality (Neumann, 1954:121-22, 315-20), although its roots are feminine (Neumann, 1954:143-44). The male's "muse," the unconscious as source of creativity, is not himself or like himself, but other, out there, tantalizing, something of a threat (*la femme fatale*), yet alluring, as Kurtz's painting of the "dark lady" was to Marlow in Joseph Conrad's *Heart of Darkness* (Ong, 1977b:157-58). For threat, danger, can be alluring to the male: it provides the stress he seeks, the occasion to prove his masculinity again, his ability to cope with insecurity. The muse, being feminine, cannot have this relationship of tantalizing otherness to the feminine psyche. And there is no muse that is masculine. Feminine creativity would seem to be more unisex than masculine creativity is, to seek its inspiration not in the opposite sex but in woman's world (Gilbert, 1979:54-65). We recall that at the biological level the females of many animal species, such as aphids and even some reptiles, can perpetuate themselves for generation after generation with no males at all, whereas males have no such unisex potential.

In these ways and in many others, masculinity is thus differentiation. Unisex would be feminine. Interaction with a strongly masculine father in the confidence provided by a strong and caring mother fosters the full heterosexual development of a child of either sex, a being at peace with his or her own identity as something sexually differentiated (Stoller, 1968:146-47 and *passim;* see also Bardwick, 1971:40). In this sense sexual differentiation for both sexes is rooted in femininity and implemented by masculinity.

PART THREE

Past, Present, and Future

4

Academic and Intellectual Arenas

The Agonistic Heritage of Academia

The deep psychological and cultural changes that over the past few decades have come over the West and, to varying degrees, the entire globe register the basic sociobiological and noobiological patterns described in the foregoing chapters. Some of the most striking adjustments in agonistic behavior have appeared in the academic world. A few of these changes have been referred to in passing in earlier chapters, but we can look more directly here at the fuller academic pattern leading into the 1960s and 1970s. What we have thus far reviewed enables us to plot from one vantage point a good deal of what was going on.

Struggle in academia did not begin in the 1960s. In some ways, it disappeared. I recall clearly a remark made to me in 1967 by a middle-aged teacher, German by birth, in an all-boys high school in New York City. "Ach! These boys expect you in the classroom to be their friend. When I was a boy, everybody knew that the teacher was the enemy." The speaker's eyes twinkled, but he meant the statement seriously. The twinkle indicated that he knew, and knew that I knew, that the enmity he referred to, however intense, was on the whole basically a ritual or ceremonial one, accepted as more or less part of the game of boys' schooling. The boy whose teacher, "the enemy," would peremptorily order him out of the classroom as a confirmed nuisance for some misbehavior or academic stupidity might very well betake himself to the same teacher after class for help with his most serious personal problems.

This ritual enmity between teacher and pupils was of long standing in the all-male world of earlier academia. Christopher Jencks and David Riesman, in a report published the same year, 1967, noted that in eighteenth- and nineteenth-century American colleges "the students were continually struggling with the faculty, whom they almost regarded as the enemy," engaged in enforcing rules "often of the most trivial kind" (Jencks and Riesman, 1967:1). "Trivial" more than suggests ceremonial or ritual conflict. Had they worked back through history, Jencks and Riesman could have said much the same thing of Renaissance colleges and universities and of medieval universities (Ariès, 1962:241-68; Sylvester, 1970:16, 18, 112; Ong, 1971:129-38) and even of Saint Augustine's education as reported in his *Confessions* (I.ix-xi, xiv). And, working forward, they could have said much the same thing also of early-twentieth-century colleges and universities, though a lull set in at mid-century so that Richard Hofstadter and C. DeWitt Hardy (1952:17-18) could complacently write in 1952 that the earlier "episodes of almost hysterical rebellion, malicious pranks, and even personal violence against tutors and college presidents" were "unheard of in the modern college."

Although in my experience Hofstadter and Hardy's disavowal was certainly too sweeping even in 1952, by 1967 the old kind of ceremonial enmity between teacher and (male) student was largely outmoded or even outlawed. But the newly prevailing situation was more dangerous. Ritual contest had provided a way for the young to prove themselves. With such contest inoperative, out-and-out hostility could come into style. On the college and university campuses it already had. A new mythology of confrontation with no negotiation haunted academia, felt everywhere even though not universally effective. In the new mythology teachers were either students' friends or nothings.

Most histories of education attend only peripherally if at all to the ceremonially agonistic structures that dominated academia before the unrest of the 1960s. These structures were, however, pretty ubiquitous, as has been hinted in earlier chapters, even in higher education. They were often articulately programmed and they frequently determined not merely educational styles but even subject matter. I propose to excavate some of these structures here, not with the idea that they fully explain why the unrest of the sixties developed, for the agonistic structures were attenuated before the sixties, but because they may help us better to understand what the unrest was by giving it historical perspective.

By the agonistic structures in the academia of the past I do not mean anything so simple as grading systems, though these systems were related to the old agonistic structures and were, significantly, under attack in the 1960s. The *agōnia* referred to here was in the approach to the subject matter, and was operative in academia long before grades were even thought of. The old *agōnia* struck deeper than grades. Grades can be a combative gloss on a basically irenic situation, a kind of supplement affixed at the end of a term, an obligatory afterthought. The agonistic of the past resulted from a disposition to organize the subject matter itself as a field of combat, to purvey, not just to test, knowledge in a combative style.

Agonistic was more than a manner or a milieu. It had also to do with content, and that in absolutely crucial areas and in surprising ways. Certain kinds of subjects are favored by a disputatious academic milieu—ethics and political science, for example, or pre-Newtonian physics, rich in theories—and certain kinds are disfavored, as, for example, geography (Dainville, 1940) or laboratory subjects. The most striking example of the influence of disputatious style on subject matter is the case of formal logic, absolutely crucial to Western academic development. As noted in Chapter 1, this seemingly most neutral and objective of subjects, devoted to pure structure and terminating at one point in the computer, had its origins not in isolated scholarly musings but in the analysis of dispute. It was a product of the rhetorical world of the agora.

To sense the depth of the forces in play here, it is worth

recalling the fact noted in Chapter 1 that, in contrast to the West, early Chinese culture, which came to look with disfavor on disputatious intellectual situations generally, regarding them as incompatible with the decorum and harmony cultivated by the true sage, never evolved a formal logic, despite its other magnificent cultural achievements (Oliver, 1971:84-89; Levenson, 1964-1966:I, 9-14, II, 90-99; Richardson, 1960:240-42). Ancient Chinese culture sprang ultimately from oral roots, as all human cultures at some point have done, and shared the polemic structures that, as I explain, are inseparable from oral noetics, but, for reasons thus far fugitive, ancient Greece institutionalized its polemic where ancient China did not or where ancient China even deinstitutionalized it by denying it status.

In the West, the agonistic tradition of formal education was already deeply rooted in Greek antiquity, as suggested in Chapter 1. It persisted not merely through medieval dialectic and disputation and Renaissance scholarly polemic, but with remarkable vigor well into the eighteenth century, as shown, for example, in the formal, forensic, adversary-structured intellectualism of the Founders of the United States of America, and with still significant strength in certain sectors even into the mid-twentieth century. Only over the past twenty years have its last traces faded to the near vanishing point.

The Oral Roots of Agonistic Noetic

When the agonistic mode of education was functioning at its maximum—as, for example, in medieval and Renaissance universities—a student was not formally taught to be "objective" about knowledge. He may well have become objective in his approach to truth, insofar as such objectivity is possible, and in his regard for truth, as is more possible. But such objectivity was either a product of individual enterprise or academic spin-off, or perhaps a mixture of both. What was taught in the formal educational operation was to take a stand in favor of a thesis or to attack a thesis that someone else defended. Defense of theses and at-

Academic and Intellectual Arenas

tacks on theses marked procedures for the teaching not only of such subjects as philosophy (in the sense this term commonly has today), law, and theology, but also of physics ("natural philosophy"), sublunary and astral, and medicine. Young men at Harvard College in the seventeenth century defended theses about logic, rhetoric, and grammar (some of these theses are quoted in Morison, 1936:587-94). They learned subjects largely by fighting over them.

The roots of the agonistic procedures that prevailed so widely and so long in academia were doubtless manifold. Some were economic (contention is encouraged by economies of scarcity, widespread in earlier ages); others were sociological (the early stages of a culture can tend to heighten personal tensions, if only because their supply of information is relatively scant and hard to manage, so that abstract objectification eludes them). Among the deepest of the roots of the agonistic procedures, however, if not indeed the deepest roots of all, were those buried in procedures for managing knowledge: polemic is fostered by the oral noetic economy of early humanity. Oral modes of storing and retrieving knowledge have much in common in all cultures. They are formulaic in design and, particularly in public life, tend to be agonistic in operation.

Oral noetic processes are formulaic in design because we know only what we can recall. If I think of something once and never again, I do not say that I know it. To "know geometry" is to be able to bring it into consciousness. Knowing requires memory. But an oral culture cannot remember by formulating something first and then memorizing it afterward. Once the words are said, unless they are said in a way that is itself memorable, they are gone for good: there is nothing there to return to for memorizing. *Verba volant:* Homer's "winged words." That is to say, an oral culture does not *put* its knowledge *into* mnemonic patterns: it *thinks* its thoughts in mnemonic patterns. There is no other way for it to proceed effectively. An oral culture does not merely have a quaint liking for proverbs or "sayings" of all sorts: it is absolutely dependent on them. Clichés constitute its thought. Constant repetition of the known is the major noetic exercise. Narrative, poetic or prose, tells the old stories and tells them in formulaic style. The closer orators are to the purely oral tradition, the more their style, too, will be like the poets' and the prose narrators' styles, filled with commonplaces or formulas (Ong, 1967:57-58).

Largely because they deal in formulas, in what is already known, all oral cultures—which is to say, all early human cultures—foster agonistic performance, or virtuosity, in their management of their store of knowledge, and do so with a single-minded intensity sure to affect early formal schooling when it finally begins. If the narrative that a storyteller is going to present is familiar to the audience, if it is public property, as it typically is in oral cultures, the narrator's warrant for performance is likely to be superior skill. No competitor can tell it so well. What the narrator says is unimportant in the sense that others can say it. The way the narrator says it is what matters. An oral culture is performance-minded. Even in cultures long familiar with writing, if the oral life-style remains assertive enough, there are likely to be contests in oral virtuosity, as in the eisteddfod among Welsh poets today. Literate poets more typically give "readings," which are less overtly combative. Writing is a private activity, psychologically often aggressive enough but in itself not forensic, and its result is not an action but a product, a thing. A book of poems is so much a thing that it can be entered in a contest when its author is dead: such a contest is clearly not the same as one between living performers.

It is becoming a commonplace among anthropologists that highly oral cultures, across the globe, often cultivate combative life-styles, chiefly, and sometimes only, in verbal performances, though at times this life-style spills over from the verbal into the physical. In *Honour and Shame: The Values of Mediterranean Society* (1966), cited earlier, J. G. Peristiany has brought together studies that often brilliantly set forth the exquisitely agonistic structures in Mediterranean cultures, European, Middle Eastern, and North African, though with no evident awareness of the

Academic and Intellectual Arenas

intimate connection of agonistic with orality, which in these cultures is overwhelming. Raphael Patai has provided a more popularized and at points perhaps exceptionable account of an intensely combative oral life-style in *The Arab Mind* (1973).

Oral cultures thrive on the challenge and riposte. "Signifying" (also called "sounding," "joning," "screaming," "rhyming," and "the dozens"), the formalized exchange of remarks between opponents in various ways trying to put one another down, found throughout New World black cultures (Manning, 1973:61-63), is matched in other totally oral or residually oral cultures past and present across the globe—for example, in African drum talk (Bohannan, 1967b:57-58) or in the widespread fliting or ceremonial exchange of insults that marks oral or residually oral Western epic from at least the Homeric age through *Beowulf* and beyond into literary epics that take over as conscious conventions what had been integral and inevitable features of oral performance.

Residual Orality in Academia

The orality and concomitant agonistic mentality of early human culture persist in the Western literate, academic tradition in a multitude of ways, many of which I have treated in detail elsewhere (Ong, 1967:53-76; 1971:23-47, 284-304), so that it will suffice to enumerate them briefly here. The oral and agonistic roots of Western academicism are identifiable in antiquity in the dialectical procedures of the Socratic dialogues as reconstructed by Plato, a literate man who in the *Phaedrus* (274) and his Seventh Letter expressed serious reservations about writing, identifying it as a medium sure to reduce the living word and truth itself to lifelessness—Plato indicted writing for reasons essentially the same as those urged in indictments of the computer today. But the orality of both Greek and Latin cultures is more widely evident in their apotheosis of the *rhētor* or *orator*, the public speaker, who was considered in ancient academic tradition generally to be the ideal product of the overall academic educational effort—and with reason, since success in political leadership generally called for oratorical prowess, personal or vicarious.

The ancient Greeks and Romans knew and used alphabetic writing, but they felt it to be at the service of oral speech. So did the medieval universities, although these new institutions were far more script-oriented than antiquity had been: they depended on texts for their learning and they even lectured on texts, thus looking ahead to our present-day teaching style rather than back to that of classical antiquity. But for all their ascendant literacy, medieval universities remained basically oral and deeply agonistic in life-style and intellectual style. They did not use writing at all to test intellectual achievement: writing was employed to a considerable extent in the learning of Latin in elementary schools, but at the universities there were no assigned papers, no written examinations. All testing was conducted orally by disputation or by disputation-like viva voce examinations.

The contentiousness favored by the oral tradition was encouraged and abetted by the dialectical approach, typified in Abelard's *Sic et Non* and as inseparable from the universities as the universities were inseparable from scholasticism. Saint Thomas Aquinas cast what today would be a textbook or treatise, his *Summa theologiae,* in agonistic form, organized in "questions," each of which he handled by presenting first objections to the answer, then the answer with proof, then responses to objections. He fell into this agonistic organization because of the abiding strength of what I have styled the oral life-style: no other way in effect really occurred to him, as it did not commonly to his contemporaries. Even physics and medicine, as earlier noted, were taught much the same way.

The orality and the accompanying agonistic style inherited by academia from its remote past were simultaneously reinforced, weakened, and endlessly complicated by Renaissance humanism. The humanist revival of classical antiquity necessarily gave renewed life to the ancient rhetorical (oral) ideal: Renaissance humanism was much taken with Cicero's apotheosis of the orator as ideally the most learned and accomplished of all human beings. By comparison with medieval scholastics, Renaissance humanists were often activists and if anything more combative than their scholastic predecessors (Seigel, 1968:146-80). They favored involvement in existentially polemic decision making through rhetoric (persuasion to action) rather than pure scientific investigation, for which they often had very acerbic words.

At the same time, however, despite this reinforcement of the oral, Renaissance humanists intensified medieval preoccupation with texts and, with the help of print, in effect invented modern textual scholarship. Renaissance elementary schools and middle schools made much more of the teaching of writing than earlier schools had done—if always under the overriding supposition, not always entirely articulated, that the paradigm of all verbal expression was oratory. Shakespeare and his contemporaries were trained in writing—Latin, of course, with generally negligible attention to Greek (Bolgar, 1958:331, 333, 359)—but what they wrote consisted largely if not indeed entirely of bits and pieces of things designed to be incorporated into orations. Humanists patterned even letters quite commonly on combative oratorical models (Ong, 1967:216, 243-46). The universities remained even more oral, filled with disputation and declamation. What was taught, in physics for example, was a set of theses or positions felt as under permanent siege. Peter Ramus (1515-72) thought of his lectures on the various "arts" (logic, arithmetic, and so on) not as positive explanations of the arts themselves, which were supposed to be limpidly clear because of the "methodized" way they were presented, but as defenses against his adversaries, real or imagined (Ong, 1958b:193). As late as the mid-eighteenth century, and certainly in many places much later, when writing was made more and more a part of the students' work, even what was written often was written to be ultimately read aloud to others and thus injected into the contentious oral world (Sylvester, 1970:218).

This orality remained in more or less heavy residue throughout the nineteenth century, and in some places even until the 1960s. McGuffey's *Readers,* of which it has been estimated at least 120 million copies were printed between 1836 and 1920, were basically oratorical in conception and in the selections they included, orienting schoolchildren not to the fast silent reading normally aimed at today but to declamatory reading (Lynn, 1973:20) and to "sound-conscious" literature, as Daniel Boorstin has put it (1965:307), oratorically styled writing inviting memorization. McGuffey's *Readers* retained the noetic structures of the oral world in building their program on exposure to the lives of heroes (agonistic males—the female models in the selections were mostly little girls rather than adult women) (Lynn, 1973:5-27, esp. pp. 10, 12, 16, 20). The elocution contest, growing out of the elocution movement of the eighteenth century (Howell, 1971:143-256), which undertook to make oral recitation of a printed text sound like spontaneous oral performance (as theater had long been successfully doing), was a last attempt of the old orality to regain lost ground. Elocution contests appear to have vanished shortly before the 1960s in the United States, although I suspect they may linger, perhaps only vestigially, in the highly oral South and in various other places outside of the United States.

We are past elocutionism today, and far past the old, or primary, orality that elocutionism undertook to mimic. We have a new orality, not merely implemented but styled as well by electronic amplification, abetted by electronic visual images, as in television. We now speak to an audience of millions in a style of composition and delivery miles from Cicero's balanced and iterative periods, tending to irenicism where his tended to polemic. Television puts the speaker's face in your living room. Although some elements of contest survive in our secondary orality, it is basically an orality founded on literacy and its basic style is irenic as the basic style of primary orality was combative.

The absence of primary orality from academia in the United States is poignantly evident when persons from primary oral cultures of the Third World are transplanted as graduate students into our universities. In my experience, and that of many others with whom I have talked, such students are often paralyzed by the nondirective features of graduate education in the United States, features developed through massive use of print. These foreign students want, many have told me, to know what to memorize: Where is the list of questions for which the answers must be mastered (in primary oral, formulaic, rather than verbatim, chirographic patterns, of course) so that one can be assured of passing the oral comprehensive examination for the doctorate in English or history or chemistry? Who says the answers for us to hear? A brilliant and insightful Third World student put it clearly to me when we were discussing this difference: "Yes, that is the way education works in my country. You are not expected to read books the instructor never even talks about. *Whatever you have to know for the examination,* the teacher always *says out loud."* Here knowledge storage and retrieval, even in the classroom, still basically relate to the oral world. Much of this same orality of course governs the mind-set of a good many of our own American young people, particularly young men and women from the black ghetto, where early oral noetic modes and life-styles persist (Arthur L. Smith, 1972:x and *passim*). An intelligence "test" (written, that is) is as inapplicable as it is irrelevant in an oral culture, and at depths we seldom advert to.

The Latin Connection

Much of the thrust of the agonistic tradition in Western education sketched here was connected with the 1,500-year history of Learned Latin, which also was disestablished in the 1960s in such critical local settings as Oxford and Cambridge universities and globally in Roman Catholic liturgy of the Latin rite. We can sense the thrust, and its enfeeblement, by looking at the way in which Latin was functioning in a kind of peak situation, at the time of the Renaissance in Europe. I have treated this matter at length elsewhere, in "Latin Language Study as a Renaissance Puberty Rite" (Ong, 1971:113-41), on which I draw here. Since academic education—and we must of course remind ourselves that not all education is necessarily academic—was until long after the Renaissance, with negligible exceptions, only for boys, as it had commonly been from antiquity, the puberty rites to which this title refers and which concern us here are those for males. In such rites in many primitive cultures, boys are typically separated from their homes and from all contact with women to be inducted into the extrafamilial male life of the tribe. Puberty rites are *rites de passage,* transition rites. They are didactic, for in them the initiates are given understanding of more or less secret tribal lore. They involve calculated hardship: often the boys are snatched with violence or mock violence from the arms of their mothers and established in an all-male extrafamilial environment where they undergo various trials and often physical torture. They emerge with an *esprit de corps,* a feeling that they have gone through rough times together, which helps to establish the typically male "bonding pattern" discussed in Chapter 2.

By the Renaissance—and indeed for centuries before— Learned Latin was eminently qualified as an instrument for a puberty rite of this sort. First, Latin moved boys out of their families into the tribe. As it had gradually ceased to serve as a vernacular language between the fifth and seventh centuries and had become chirographically controlled, with its spoken use dependent on writing rather than vice versa, Latin had also become a sex-linked language, used only by males (again, with quite negligible exceptions). Learned Latin was no longer a "mother tongue" in the most real sense of this term: it was not used by mothers to raise their children, as vernacular Latin had been until the sixth century or so (see Chapter 1, n. 2). Learned Latin was exclusively a tribal language, learned in school or from tutors, and such Renaissance educators as Sir Thomas Eliot urged that boys as young as seven years of age be removed from women's company, including that of their own mothers, and put into an all-male environment to assimilate the language. Latin was the only entry into the tribal wisdom purveyed in academia: in the West in the sixteenth century, and even later, it was not possible, for example, to learn grammar or metaphysics or medicine or most other academic subjects unless one knew Latin, for there was no effective way to set forth academic subjects in the vernaculars, which had no adequate vocabulary or semiotic (interlocking language-and-thought processes) for such technical matters.

Second, the learning of Latin took place in the physical hardship setting typical for puberty rites. It normally entailed physical punishment, not as an incidental matter but as a regular procedure. In Renaissance art, a schoolmaster is recognized by his bundle of switches, and the literature attesting to their use is massive. The not infrequent protests against too much physical punishment voiced by some educational reformers are further testimony to its prevalence. Chastisement with the birch or various equivalents was only the ultimate among many physical hardships that the Latin schools imposed: early hours for assembling (six o'clock commonly, even on the dark winter mornings of northern Europe), strict rules of behavior (often including conversation in Latin, even in recreation hours), constant supervision by proctors, and all sorts of competitions that played on the boys' desire and need for agonistic activities but of course at the same time increased the stress.

Moreover, the very contents of the course for Latin learners were largely of a cut with the puberty-rite hardship setting and with the agonistic style of instruction. What the schoolboy read in Latin included epics and histories full of violence and tales of valor, together with orations pitting one speaker against another. The histories read were packed not only with war but also with such orations. In *The Boke Named The Governor* Thomas Eliot insisted, following Plato's *Republic,* that the boy must be given stories of military and other physical prowess to "inflame" his "courage." A widespread nineteenth- and twentieth-century doctrine, cited by Hofstadter and Hardy (1952:15-16), that the classics disciplined or toughened the mind, perpetuates the same agonistic framework. It merely shifts the *agōn* in Latin study into the interior: to acquire discipline and strength, the Latin student now does violence to himself instead of studying and imitating others in hardship situations.

Fighting for Life

The combined effect of physical threat from switching, agonistic methods of teaching and testing, and highly martial subject matter could often be an academic setting something like that of a present-day survival course, which romantic tradition now sets up in nature's woods rather than in the classroom. Although in *The Schoolmaster* (1570) Roger Ascham protested against the overapplication of physical punishment, citing the case of Eton students who so frequently ran away "for fear of beating" (Ascham, 1967:5-7), the overtones of the remarks by Sir John Mason and Walter Haddon, which Ascham reports, clearly suggest that the hardship situation in Renaissance schools produced the typical *esprit de corps* and male bonding pattern among "old boys" that has since been produced also by the British public schools and, *mutatis mutandis,* by the countless all-boy Latin schools in the United States through the early part of this century. The male bonding pattern, based on shared hardships in the school, is evident in *Tom Brown's Schooldays* (1857) and in innumerable similar stories for boys up to around World War II.

When alumni formed in this all-male tradition come together, as they still do, their stories inevitably turn on the rigors they endured and the teacher-enemies whom they outwitted but whom they often recall with evident affection. They are reminding themselves that they did successfully complete the puberty rites. They are grown, they once proved this fact by standing up to the ritual hardships imposed by adults, and they enjoy reliving the struggle with mutual support. They also still enjoy ceremonial oral combat among themselves redolent of their earlier marginal status: "razzing" one another and topping each other's horror stories.

The origins of the Latin term for school, *ludus,* are of interest here. The term means not merely a school or training place but also play or games. Earlier etymologists have suggested that the same term came to designate both play and school (which would seem to be work rather than play) simply because contrary ideas readily associate with one another. But it is more likely that the two meanings are associated for more circumstantial reasons, because of an original military use of the word to designate the training exercises for war, which were "play" or "games" by contrast with the stern reality of battle (Bonner, 1977:56-57). *Ludus*, play or a game, was used to mean a training exercise. In like vein, we speak in English today of war "games," simulated military action training for real war. Ancient Latin speakers felt school likewise to be play or a game training for life. Once they had thought of war training as "play" or a "game" (*ludus*), it was easy to think of academic training for life as *ludus*, too. For the agonistic mentality we have been examining made it normal to think of life itself as essentially warlike.

All of the agonistic play activity from the ancient, medieval, and modern world of the West rehearsed by Huizinga (1955:146-57) as making for the development of philosophy and of academic learning in general comes from the male agonistic milieu, although Huizinga himself does not advert to this sex-linked provenience of his material. The extra-academic play activity that he reviews (1955:158-72) as entering into art is less conspicuously agonistic. Differences here between intellectualizing, agonistic play and artistically creative play perhaps correspond in some way to the bicameral organization of knowledge and behavior in the two hemispheres of the brain, although the truth about bicamerality is still exceedingly ill defined. The agonistic would belong with the analytic, left, field-breaking side (masculine). The less agonistic or nonagonistic would of course be more holistic (feminine). (See Gardner, 1978.)

The male bonding pattern established in the West by Learned Latin had its parallels elsewhere. For when writing had been sufficiently interiorized most other larger cultures also developed learned academic languages, no longer anyone's mother tongues, learned exclusively by males more or less under duress, as, for example, Classical Chinese, Sanskrit, Classical Arabic, and Rabbinical Hebrew (Ong, 1977a:22-34). Far from considering the learning of such languages as attractive, women commonly shunned it as disabling. The exquisite Japanese writer Lady Murasaki Shikibu (b. 978?) reports in her diary that she learned Classical Chinese by sitting in on her brother's lessons in the language but hid her knowledge of it because she knew it would make her disliked, as, she notes, knowing it made even boys unpopular. She wrote *The Tale of Genji* in Japanese (Murasaki, 1935:vii).

From Agonistic to Coeducation: The In-Depth Revolution

Not all education is academic education. While it is true that early schools were, almost without exception, entirely for boys and that academic education for girls effectively began to take hold in a modest, limited way only in the late seventeenth century, this fact must be seen in perspective. First of all, most boys did not go to school either, in the West or elsewhere in the world. Second, girls of the more advantaged classes in the West often received intensive education, particularly in modern foreign languages and certain other liberal arts such as history, and in such performing arts as music, painting, and dancing, as well as education in the domestic economy of the time, which extended far beyond today's domestic economy. Even girls from less privileged classes often acquired formidable competence in the then domestic skills. These occupations included all sorts of health care, gardening and often marketing, the teaching of elementary reading and writing (schools usually admitted boys only after they had learned to form letters and read simple vernacular words), religious education, cooking and sanitation, textile manufacturing from the spinning of thread on through the making of garments, and many other skills, not to mention complex administrative work. A young girl of the more advantaged classes might at the time of her teenage marriage be expected to take over the round-the-clock management of a household of perhaps fifty to eighty persons (Hunt, 1970:70–74), among whom were dozens of often difficult resident servants. In a high-mortality culture with few if any hospitals, there was always the care of the dying and of the bodies of the dead. Women were busy. In a certain very real sense, academic education is a leisure activity, and most women did not have time for it. Besides, it was not all that attractive. It was not difficult for women to feel that they had more interesting and useful and rewarding things to occupy themselves with. Most men were not particularly enthusiastic about academic education themselves.

The academic world was thus a limited world, though a centrally important one, and it was strictly a male world, even though most males were not in fact a part of it. It was profoundly agonistic, and its agonistic structures registered masculine needs. If this fact is recognized, as it all too seldom is, academic education for girls and women, first in their own schools and then through coeducation, can be seen to have far deeper and more complex significance for psychic and social reorganization than that commonly assigned to it. Academic education for girls began first in the prepubertal lower grades, from which it gradually moved up to the higher levels, until in the mid-nineteenth-century United States we find colleges for women (often at first with highly specialized curricula) together with a very few precocious coeducational institutions. These developments were followed by limited admission of women to universities in the late nineteenth and early twentieth centuries and finally, mostly after World War I, by the large-scale presence of women students in a vastly increased number of women's colleges and on still more numerous coeducational campuses.

The entrance of women onto the academic scene everywhere marked the beginning of the end of the agonistic structures just described. None of the conspicuously agonistic structures had a place in early girls' schools. As females entered schools originally intended only for males, more or less *pari passu* these things happened: (1) Latin was dropped, first as a means of instruction and then as a required subject; (2) the agonistic, thesis method of teaching was replaced by less combative methods; (3) written examinations were substituted for public oral disputations and examinations; and (4), of course, physical punishment was minimized or suppressed.

Seldom, perhaps almost never, do histories of education discuss or even point out any particular connection between these developments. It is more or less assumed that their coincidence was accidental and superficial. In the light of what has just been detailed, it would appear that this is hardly so: the connections were as real as they were massive, deeply rooted, and hard to isolate in detail.

If and when the full history of these developments is written, it will doubtless be found that the exact sequence of the changes varied from one institution to another. And it will be difficult to establish that any one of these developments was the sole cause or effect of another or even which was cause and which effect or whether they actually stood in any direct cause/effect relationship. The point here, however, is not which was cause or effect, or both, but simply that the developments were not isolated but closely related phenomena, that is, paraphenomena, interlinked in various subtle ways, related to, among other things, ceremonially agonistic intellectual life-styles congenial to males as males. Although it may be difficult to assess all the factors in play, it appears no accident that the last bastions of Latinity in the British Isles, namely, the boys' public schools, have also been the last to maintain an exquisitely competitive life-style, to resist coeducation, to persist in regarding public speaking as a matter of major concern, and to retain physical punishment. George Orwell's solemn persuasion that it is impossible to teach Latin without physical punishment accords with the simple facts of history, if we are thinking, as Orwell apparently was, of the required teaching of Latin to a large school population. Such teaching, so far as I know, has never been carried on for any great length of time without physical punishment, which appears here as a part, and in the lower grades probably an integral part, of an agonistically structured academia.

A case I have been close to can be cited as an example of a microcosm manifesting the paraphenomena connected with the former use and the subsequent demobilization of Learned Latin. Although a good many medical books were still being published in Latin in the early nineteenth century and although dissertations in Hungary, and perhaps other places, were being published in Latin at least until World War II, it was probably in Roman Catholic seminaries or schools of divinity that the older oral-agonistic structures here noted were longest preserved in relatively intact form. When I was studying theology at the Saint Louis University School of Divinity in the mid-1940s, the basic or main-line courses, such as moral theology and dogmatic theology, which formed the core of the curriculum, were all given in Latin (once in a while the instructor would turn to English for a part of the lecture, but very rarely). Textbooks for these courses were in Latin. Only in ancillary courses, such as Hebrew, church history, special seminars, and the like, was English the language of instruction. In the basic courses instruction was by the thesis method: one was presented with a series of theses covering the entire subject matter, taught by oral lecture what they meant, encouraged to argue orally about them formally and informally in order to show up any weaknesses or ambiguities or misconceptions, and also in order to lay hold of them for oneself—to "interiorize" or appropriate their meaning—and made to prove them orally and to defend them orally against any possible objections. In these agonistic basic courses, but not in the irenically styled ancillary courses, "circles" or miniature disputations and large-scale public disputations (the latter by selected outstanding students) were regularly held. By and large, the theology course was thus proceeding as courses in all university subjects typically had earlier proceeded. In fact, the three-year philosophy course at Saint Louis University followed by Jesuit scholastics, preparatory to theology, had remained as Latinate as theology into the mid-1960s, too.

In this still live twentieth-century tradition, education was performance-oriented, and the major performances were oral contests. Once in a while a theological student of outstanding competence would perform the "grand act," the greatest performance of all, as did Father Joachim Villalonga, S.J., on April 29, 1903, when in impeccable logical form and equally impeccable Latin, he defended orally in open forum against all comers his 212 theses from theology and philosophy before an audience that included President Theodore Roosevelt. Roosevelt was visiting Saint Louis to inspect the site of the coming World's Fair, and, as a visiting dignitary with a university degree, he was politely asked if he had any objections to urge against any of the 212 theses (Ong, 1969). The question was put in Latin, of course, but immediately translated for President Roosevelt, who, the *St. Louis Post-Dispatch* reported, was intimidated for the first and only time in his life and failed to produce an objection. It is significant that on the occasion of such a disputation, at least in my day, the defender could use no notes or written or printed references except the two before him on the lectern: the Latin Bible and the small Latin Denzinger handbook of major selections from various church documents. We were still programmatically and conspicuously in the oral world.

There were of course no women in the Saint Louis University School of Divinity at this time or, so far as I know, in any other Roman Catholic schools of divinity or seminaries. The reasons that there were no women should be historically evident from the present work, and they are complex. For one thing, women had virtually never studied subjects in Latin in an academic institution, although a very few women occasionally learned Latin from tutors or otherwise, as had Margaret More (Saint Thomas More's daughter) and Queen Elizabeth I. (In the centuries of academic Latin, a fair number of women could read and write, but in the vernaculars—just as many tradesmen unacquainted with Latin could.) Of the tens of thousands of books written in Latin from the end of classical antiquity to the present (including some by men, now professors, who were in classes in theology with me), there are virtually none by women; it appears that the only Latin writings by any woman of which scholars are commonly aware are the Latin tragedies composed by the medieval abbess Hrosvitha.

Academic and Intellectual Arenas

Although by the 1940s the only academic field still Latin-bound was Roman Catholic theology (which was no longer entirely Latin-bound either, for there was very little theology available in Latin that was not also available somewhere in English), there was historically nothing properly theological about this Latin-binding. All academic subjects were Latin-bound even as late as Shakespeare's day—grammar, rhetoric, logic, physics, cosmology, ethics, metaphysics, law, medicine—and many of them much later, particularly in milieus using vernaculars that had relatively few speakers.

By the late 1960s, following the Second Vatican Council, Roman Catholic theology virtually everywhere in the West was loosening its connections with the Latin language. As it did so, certain spectacular correlative changes occurred, at times, it appears, rather automatically. Within two years, 1967 and 1968, the School of Divinity of Saint Louis University (1) ceased using Latin as a language of instruction, (2) dropped the thesis method as a method of instruction, (3) dropped circles and disputations together with oral course examinations as integral parts of its program, and (4) admitted women students. So far as I know, no one involved in these changes adverted to what appears to be the fact from the evidence adduced here: they were hardly four changes, but in effect one. They moved theological instruction out of the age-old rhetorical, oral-agonistic world of male ceremonial combat. The same thing had happened in the other higher education subjects of medicine and law in various stages from the eighteenth century on (or, spottily, from somewhat earlier). In the Saint Louis University School of Divinity microcosm it simply happened all at once.

Realignment of Agonistic Structures

The agonistic structures of academia have been only sketched here, though with sufficient references, I hope, for any who may wish to flesh them out further. But what relevance to the present academic situation is to be found in these structures, antique in origin, slow enough in collapsing to be sure, but conspicuously decadent already a century ago and clearly moribund or vestigial, though still clearly recognizable, by the end of World War II? In terms of direct "influence" or "action/interaction" theorems, probably little enough. In terms of deeper structures and their evolution, certainly a greal deal. The agonistic structures of academia suggest that in educational history beneath changes in teaching methods and curricula and classroom populations, and even beneath articulate theories of educators concerning the nature of education and of the mind, deeper forces move, registering a long cultural and psychic history that rests on an ancient genetic heritage. *Agōnia* lies at the heart of the evolution of consciousness, not merely in academia but throughout life. There is structure in academia deeper than in the Balinese cockfights reported on by Clifford Geertz (1972). *Ludus,* the Latin word for school, we have seen means also war games.

As must be apparent from the foregoing discussion, the agonistic elements in academia are entangled with the dialectic of masculine and feminine, the history of which makes the evolution of consciousness at least partly intelligible. To be more specific about this dialectic, one can say that a realignment of agonistic structures, to which the polemic climate of the 1960s is related, took place as the function of male ceremonial combat changed in the academic world, particularly in the realm of higher education.

The alliance between masculinity and an oral academic world is inevitable in early cultures for a grossly physical reason briefly adverted to in Chapter 2: the typical male voice can articulate intelligible words at a far greater volume than can the typical female voice. When, as in classical Greek and Roman antiquity, the overall aim of academic education was (and given the persistence of the oral heritage, probably had to be) the production of the *rhētor,* the *orator,* or public speaker, volume was crucial to academic success. The now well-known fact that female children normally develop such verbal skills as vocabulary and sentence structure at an earlier age than male children—and presumably did the same in classical antiquity—does nothing to counter the

Academic and Intellectual Arenas

disadvantage of lower articulatory volume. Until electronic amplification of the human voice, few if any women's voices could project articulate, intelligible speech to audiences of hundreds and indeed thousands of persons to whom male orators from classical antiquity through the early twentieth century often had to bellow their orations. A woman's scream can carry a great distance, but intelligibly articulated speech is another problem. Women frequently narrate folktales with great skill and effect for smaller groups in oral cultures. But for large crowds, conspicuous public display of what many philosophers considered the human race's most distinctively human activity, speech, was almost exclusively the business of postpubertal males (before puberty males' voices, too, did not have the needed timbre). Before electronic amplification, the very size of an audience could build up the agonistic temper of discourse. It is hard to project irenic gentleness in roaring vocalization, which lends itself readily to combative situations.

The physical requisites for effective oral delivery were imperious: they encouraged, if they did not entirely determine, many of the typical features of the pre-electronic oral style of speech and of thought, particularly the elaborate and formal development of various kinds of repetitiveness: antithesis, parallelisms, enumerations, and the whole battery of formulary expressions that the old-style orators and their audiences knew and reveled in. Many of these repetitive features of style and thought were the result in great part, of course, of the mnemonic patterns demanded originally by an oral noetic economy. But they persisted after writing and often governed academic styles, too, oral and written, as anyone who has read Renaissance classroom lectures or learned controversy knows. So long as acoustic problems were constant and inevitable even with the strongest male vocal cords, the repetitive patterns had the advantage of providing the overload of information that could help to solve the problem. If the audience missed the "not only" item, they might catch the "but also" and thus follow the sense. If they heard only part of the familiar formula, their memory filled in the rest. Such heavily loaded, formally redundant, ostentatiously ceremonial oratory, so far as I have been able to find, was never taken up by women. There has been no female William Jennings Bryan or Everett Dirksen. In cultures where "fancy talk," one of the regular show performances of oral cultures, is practiced, such public ostentatious flaunting of oral powers, though occasionally practiced by women in minor forms, is predominantly and often exclusively male. So also "joning" or the "dozens" or fliting generally is practiced all but exclusively by males: women who resort to it are more or less "public" women, who live in and off the extrafamilial male world and whom other women hardly esteem (Abrahams, 1972:15-29; Manning, 1973:165).

Heavily loaded oratory persisted into the beginnings of the present century, but has completely disappeared from all but the most antique speakers of our electronic age. On radio and television we address thousands and even millions in a style like that of a tête-à-tête. On television contending presidential candidates do not stomp about a platform flailing their arms or even stand out in the open, like earlier orators metonymically claiming possession of a field, but install themselves behind protective lecterns for genteel exchanges of words projecting images of their self-contained selves instead of pacing up and down a rostrum flailing verbally at one another. They have texts in front of them—a state of affairs unknown to orators from antiquity through the Renaissance and beyond.

Writing governs our oral delivery as never before, and since, as has been seen, writing is interiorizing and nonforensic, the agonistic edge of oratory is dulled. The bellowing male voice is out, and the style that went with it is now only quaint and amusing. Many of the first television generation, who populated the colleges and universities in the 1960s, have no idea of what most oratory was like for thousands of years up to their own grandfathers' or fathers' days, or of the older styles of classroom teaching paralleling such oratory.

A second connection between masculinity and oral polemic is psychological or psychophysiological and has been adverted to

Academic and Intellectual Arenas

frequently in several ways throughout this book: the connection via ceremonial combat. Oral combat is necessarily ceremonial rather than physically disabling: it cannot kill, even though those who indulge in it may have murderous desires. So long as persons continue talking to one another, they show that they are less than totally hostile. Talk can preface complete hostility. But it is itself essentially social, communicative, and to that extent unitive. When complete hostility takes over, talk ceases and opponents take to court or to blows or "cut" one another metaphorically by not communicating at all. We speak of glances or looks as killing, but not of words. Bourdieu (1966:200-201) has made clear that among the oral-culture Kabyle in Algeria an insult or challenge from an equal constitutes a compliment and sets up a ceremonial combat, although an insult or challenge from an inferior may demand that an assassin be hired to do away with the insulter, who receives no verbal response at all, but is dealt with as a thing, disposed of by someone employed to kill him.

Earlier chapters have suggested other forces in play in and around the oral academic world of male ceremonial combat. The basic ontogenetic insecurity of males, beginning in the womb amid the mother's threatening female hormones, is matched by their phylogenetic insecurity. Males are expendable for the good of the species. Intraspecific male-with-male combat, however furious, is normally ceremonial rather than lethal and often effects territorial distancing. This distancing reduces intense individual interaction, thereby among human beings giving more play to the "objective" elements in conscious attention. The corresponding relatively nonceremonial character of combat in females tends to be either perfunctory or furiously real. Masculinity often leans toward braggadocio. Males feel a defensive need to advertise the female as the "weaker sex," which basically means weaker in ceremonial combat and all that it entails, for in other arenas the female is probably the stronger. (Of course, what ceremonial combat entails is a great deal indeed, as has been seen.)

Early oral combativeness and the early ascendancy of rhetoric, which established the ancient academic and intellectual milieu of the West, I would suggest, were ways of dealing with this same insecurity. So, too, in the perspectives suggested here, were the activities giving rise to and governing the old academic world itself. I do not mean to intimate that dispute determined everything in the academic world or that everything in the disputatious climate of early academia can be reduced to male insecurity and to ceremonial combat, only that much in the cult of dispute and in academia can be related, directly or indirectly, and often intimately, to male insecurity and ceremonial combat. It may even be that virtually everything in the academia of the past can be related to male insecurity and ceremonial combat, but "related to" does not mean "caused by" or "the same as" or "reducible to." It may mean "affected by." The thrust of these reflections is intended to be not reductionist but relationist.

Much more could be said about the agonistic structure in academia than has been said here, and still more about the other factors in academic life interacting from antiquity to the present with agonistic factors. These limited reflections are presented chiefly to call attention to the existence and importance of the agonistic structures and to suggest that educational history cannot be written simply as the history of consciousness without attention to the history of the unconscious as well. Puberty rites and ceremonial combat and the masculine/feminine dialectic warrant attention as they are represented on the academic scene because they are phenomena in which the conscious and the unconscious meet. When they change in academia, it is not academia alone that is changing, but consciousness as well.

The New Setting

It appears evident that ceremonial combat no longer operates and no longer can operate in the academic and intellectual world of the West as it did in the past. The intellectual world is still competitive, surely, but in ways more muted and less scholastically programmed than during the ascendancy of the centuries-

Academic and Intellectual Arenas

old, and indeed aboriginal, rhetorical-dialectical tradition. Even the defense of the doctoral dissertation, the last grand remnant of the old agonistic way of teaching, appears today clearly doomed in the few universities in the United States where it still survives. The combat that marked the 1960s was no longer of the old self-consciously ceremonial kind. Something had happened to the previously ascendant masculinity of academia—and of course at the same time to femininity as well. Connections between the campus crisis and the women's liberation movement were more direct, and at the same time more profound and veiled, than many have made them out to be.

For some generations, the gradual attenuation of academic ceremonial contest had shown that masculinity was in some sense on the run in academia. At the subconscious level, this retreat was what the shifts in faculty/student relations and also the quite irresistible drive in the 1960s toward intervisitation and coeducational residence halls and equal budgets for women's athletics were ultimately about. These were final steps in the phasing out of the academic male-puberty-rite world, concluding what coeducation had begun. Now the bisexual milieu of the home would purportedly continue into adulthood uninterrupted.

But coeducation had not been the beginning of the liquidation of the old ceremonial academic *agōnia*. It had been rather the beginning of the end. Earlier beginnings can be discerned in the Romantic movement and before that in the Renaissance: both of these movements marked a refocusing of academic attention away from agonistically tooled abstractions, which represent the masculinizing movement from the subconscious to the fully conscious, and a closer attention to the human lifeworld in its concreteness. The Renaissance and the Romantic age each in its own way marked a movement away from the agonistic, which, paradoxically, has historically generated objective thinking, and a movement toward increased attention to self-fulfillment, typically a feminine objective, even in the male psyche, contrasting with the typical masculine objective of proving oneself capable of survival in a permanently hostile environment on which one is dependent—which in one of its phases means finding a permanent foe and making him keep his distance. (See Hennig and Jardim, 1977:14, 31; Duncan, Featherman, and Spence, 1979.) The self-fulfillment emphasis that has marked curricular reforms since the 1960s has a long history, in the subconscious as well as in consciously advanced educational theory.

The paraphenomena of the developments here treated are countless, and individual readers can doubtless think of many that have never occurred to me. Since these reflections are intended to be suggestive rather than conclusive, a few paraphenomena might be suggested here.[1] First, the conflict of the 1960s tended to be between students and administration rather than between students and teachers: in effect, the principal arena for academic ceremonial combat had been vacated. Faculty members were beset by a seemingly unprecedented wish to be liked by students rather than by administrators. (It is true that student/administration conflict had not been unknown earlier, but earlier the administration was not too distant from the faculty—college presidents often also taught and faculty shouldered many disciplinary tasks, so that the focus of contest had been student versus teacher.)

Second, attacks on faculty members in the 1960s tended to be made because of their personal beliefs, not because of their behavior as teachers or disciplinarians: again, combat had moved from the ceremonial arena and had become an ad hominem attack, in which the attackers pursued their opponents anywhere and everywhere. (In male-with-male ceremonial combat, one male never pursues another beyond a given territorial limit; for infrahuman conspecific males, flight is normally an inhibiting mechanism for the victor—in human ludic terms, the football player who steps outside the gridiron cannot be tackled.)

Third, there was a feeling that if one argued with a teacher about the teacher's own subject, one risked losing. Of course, but

---

[1] For help in working out these paraphenomena, I am deeply indebted to Carl Bereiter of the Ontario Institute for Studies in Education, who generously gave his time for many discussions at the Center for Advanced Study in the Behavioral Sciences a few years ago.

here the rationale of earlier academic struggle is lost sight of: one argued, with some risk, against a more skilled opponent in order to acquire that person's skills and knowledge, and that person attacked one, ritually, in order to teach.

Fourth, the academic world itself was often attacked not on academic grounds, but on grounds of social injustice as such: the academic arena was bypassed again.

Fifth, whereas agonistic educational methods had prepared for the subsequent extra-academic give-and-take of politics and diplomacy—here the classic example was the exquisitely agonistic British Latin public school—the new agonistic proposed in the 1960s (by some, not by all) was revolutionary guerilla combat, a different sort of thing, perhaps highly intellectualized, but designedly lethal, not argumentative and ceremonial.

Sixth, the advancing of "nonnegotiable" demands was, superficially at least, an attack on formal negotiation, with its rules of give-and-take—though, in fact, the urging of such demands became itself quite ceremonial, for reasons suggested earlier: as long as two parties keep talking, even to say they will not negotiate, their total verbal hostility is only a fiction, for verbal hostility cannot be total hostility, but always has a ceremonial frame. In an article to be discussed at length in Chapter 6, Richard B. Gregg (1971) has shown the constructive thrust of even purportedly nonnegotiable demands.

Most of these paraphenomena are often loosely subsumed in statements about anti-intellectual or antirational elements in the conflicts of the 1960s. Without denying this quality of the conflicts, the present reflections suggest that something historically and psychologically deeper was at stake. Ceremonial contest was being rejected or bypassed or otherwise done away with. The antirationalism occurred within this larger framework of rejection of ceremonialism, for it was through ceremonial contest that rationalism itself had historically come into the ascendancy.

Finally, among the paraphenomena of the 1960s one finds not only a female identity crisis but, I strongly suspect, an even more intense male identity crisis, to some degree reflected today in the widespread male addiction to sports on television—which brings male ceremonial contest into the home (with the commentator's oral accompaniment, simultaneously combative and objective) in a safe and nurturing feminine ambiance. While the teams slug it out, the spectator sips beer. Some of the implications of today's spectator sports I shall touch on in the next chapter.

But the recent changes have certainly increased insecurities. Erich Neumann (1954:410) has observed that the absence of such institutions as puberty rites in present-day technological culture "is one reason for the incidence of neuroses in youth." Perhaps so, but in academia, we certainly cannot go back to the old puberty rites. Should we have new puberty rites? It appears quite impossible consciously to design puberty rites: most of the effective patterning in them has always been from the subconscious and doubtless has to be. Are there new ones already on hand? For men and women both? Whether there are or not, the academic present and the academic future are things of the past perhaps more profoundly than we have commonly known.

5

Some Present Issues

The shift in agonistic structures within academia has not been a consciously managed change in strategies or tactics. For the most part, it took place without anyone's understanding what was going on and even without conscious awareness that anything special was going on at all. The shift represents a deep, largely unconscious adjustment in psychic patterning, a new stage in the evolution of consciousness—for we must remember that by the evolution of consciousness we do not mean something consciously programmed or directed but rather unconsciously powered shifts that result in a new orientation of consciousness to the world around it and to itself. Changes in academia that reflect and/or help to cause a new stage or stages in the evolution of consciousness are likely to be accompanied by other shifts, complexly related paraphenomena, elsewhere in the human lifeworld. In an age undergoing the rapid evolution of consciousness that we find in the present, what are some of the arenas of human activity other than the academic where agonistic forces are eminently at work and possibly undergoing adjustment?

I have selected four, somewhat arbitrarily, for examination and reflection: (1) spectator sports, (2) politics, (3) business, and (4) Christian life and worship. These four are by no means the only arenas that could be looked into, and I can treat none of them exhaustively—nor, I suppose, can anyone else. But these four appear to be representative of a diversity of human activities and in their diversity likely to yield information showing the complexity of many currently urgent questions. Is the element of contest in human life growing or diminishing? With what effects? As women move more and more into areas of activity previously more or less reserved to men and marked by a distinctively male ceremonially combative style, what is the effect on this style and/or women's and men's behavior? Of course I do not propose to provide final answers to such large questions but only to note and reflect on some well-known or readily verifiable developments, suggesting in the light of the foregoing chapters certain perspectives that need to be considered when such questions are studied, as they are destined to be studied more and more.

Since highly stressful agonistic behavior typically and significantly sets off males from females, examining shifts in agonistic structures and behavior inevitably entails studying the feminine-masculine dialectic, which patterns so much in the history of consciousness. It must be noted, however, that intensity of an individual's agonistic behavior in a given human activity does not necessarily correlate with success of the individual in that activity and in fact may often correlate negatively with success. Some recent sociological studies have suggested that, at least among scientists and business people (the studies are thus far incomplete for athletes), competitiveness and (personal) success do not correlate either for men or for women. (Corporate success might be another story.) In fact, they often correlate negatively for both: the most successful persons, women and men, were those high in "work mastery" (which means that the most successful were the ones who could do their jobs best—hardly a surprising finding) but *low* in competitiveness (Spence, in Duncan, Featherman, and Spence, 1979:34-36; cf. Duncan and Duncan, 1978). One might conjecture that successful persons are so attentive to doing their jobs well that they have no time or concern to measure themselves against others, or perhaps even to watch how others are doing. Or perhaps for those at the top, dominance is largely a *fait accompli*. In the cases reported, only for those whose success was slight did competitiveness correlate with success: if you were not very good, competitiveness helped you to achieve your modest success; if you were good, it hindered you. The negative correlation between competitiveness and success in the most successful individuals does not of course mean that the whole process engaged in by scientists and business persons would work without competitiveness. That is another question, I suspect impossible to lay hold of statistically but, it is hoped, somewhat illuminated by the present study.

The negative correlation between high success and competitiveness means that the total relationship between agonistic behavior and the evolution of knowledge and of consciousness needs further investigation. In the past, the intellectual world advanced through markedly agonistic behavior. Was any other route to advancement possible? If so, why was it not taken? Did agonistic behavior pay off because no one was really very good at what he was doing? The positive correlation between competitiveness and success found among poor performers only would seem to suggest this possibility. Does agonistic behavior pay off when human effort is at a disadvantage, not likely to succeed? In many ways early human beings functioned normally in hardship situations that modern people rarely know—most human beings born never lived to adulthood. These are questions that the present work does not undertake to answer. It is essential, however, that they be raised.

The same studies that show that competitiveness relates negatively to high success also show that it relates positively to sexual differences. They find that "the most significant differences between the sexes are in competitiveness" (p. 32), males being uniformly and strikingly more competitive than females in every factor tested, as might be more than suspected from the sociobiological and noobiological information in the present work.

The four arenas looked at here and reflected upon are for the most part public either in the sense that they involve a public

Fighting for Life

audience, often a mass-media audience (spectator sports), or in the sense that they affect the interrelated lives of large numbers (politics, business, Christian life and worship).

Spectator Sports

Rapid transportation and modern mass media have made it possible today to mobilize agonistic drives, normally nonmartially, in huge agonistic spectacles reminiscent of the ancient Roman public games but immeasurably surpassing those games in the extent and intensity of the partisanship that they arouse, for they engage national and global audiences of millions and even hundreds of millions. (For brief histories of various sports, see *Encyclopaedia Britannica* articles; also Holliman, 1975.) All societies manifest interest in athletic events. The ancient Greeks lionized Olympic winners, as Socrates mentions at the end of the *Apology,* and the ancient Romans passionately followed the savage and murderous combat in the Colosseum. But this interest was restricted to city dwellers largely and other specific groups and was not continuous through every day of the year, as spectator's or listener's involvement in athletics can be today, when involvement is unlimited. No contest in the pre-electronic world could command the simultaneous attention of so many persons across the globe as the Muhammed Ali–George Foreman 1974 boxing match in Kinshasa or the Olympic games of the past few decades. The float of written, printed, and electronic discourse concerned with sports events which is taken for granted in high-technology cultures today and is becoming more and more common in the countries still moving into high technology has no counterpart in the pre-electronic age. Millions of males across the world know virtually no subject of sustained conversation other than spectator sports.

Women can of course engage in the same conversation, but few care to do so and virtually none so totally immerse themselves in the conversation as males regularly do. In earlier ages sustained conversation among males about agonistic events often

Some Present Issues

turned largely on wars, as in the case of Uncle Toby in Laurence Sterne's *Tristram Shandy*. Modern spectator sports provide consciousness, mostly that of males, with an agonistic surface that contrasts with the agonistic texture of earlier cultures. The huge salaries that professional athletes command today—among the largest of all salaries ever paid human beings—or in communist countries the equivalent privileges accorded athletic stars show the tremendous investment of consciousness and of the unconscious in mass sports in the present age.

In the context of the foregoing chapters, one of the more fascinating features of mass spectator sports is their relation to academia. Mobilization of agonistic drives around teams made up of students is largely but not uniquely an American phenomenon. While some of the reasons for the mass attention to college and university football, basketball, and other sports in the United States are fairly obvious—such as the unprecedented numbers and proportion of United States youth in colleges and universities—not all of the reasons are clear, and neither are the effects on the psyche in the United States and elsewhere. The phenomenon is relatively new. Certainly the spectacle of two institutions of higher learning battling it out on the football field before fifty thousand or more spectators would have nonplussed Erasmus. A sixteenth-century scholar transplanted into the present world might well notice a significant displacement of agonistic drives: the growth of mass interscholastic sports has occurred within the past seventy years, at the very time when agonistic structures in classroom instruction have declined, as explained in Chapter 4. Programmed contest has moved in academia from the classroom and the disputation hall to the athletic field.

Despite the relocation, however, certain continuities can be seen. One is in the association of the agonistic with the oral. Not only in radio and television sports reporting but even more in sports journalism, the oral cast of the discourse is marked: the sports page is regularly the closest thing in a newspaper to oral chatter and to male agonistic banter. Its style and vocabulary are historically allied to that of war reporting, and both styles developed with the telegraph and later electronic devices, which made possible near-instantaneous accounts of contest, polemic, or gaming, as has just been noted above. The banter and fliting that have marked male ceremonial contest from Homeric times to those of Muhammed Ali continue all through the sports world to advertise the alliance of the oral with the agonistic. For many males on a baseball team, "talking it up" is almost as much a part of the action as is the playing itself.

Furthermore, as oral polemic was likened to war, so are sports events in the mass media. The vocabulary in the sports-page headlines is unabashedly martial, even distastefully so. For sports victories are often heralded in terms suggesting gross violence such as would be out of place in war reporting, which is concerned with lethal, not ritual, disaster. Sports teams "slaughter" and "annihilate" and "bash" and "clobber" one another with well-advertised violence seldom so highlighted in war headlines. The conspicuous violence in sports headlines compensates for the lack of lethal intent on the part of participants (at least most of them) and for the disengagement from which the spectator as a spectator suffers. The more violent the imagery that bombards you, the more it appears that you really are in the contest—and indeed even in real war. The effect of mass spectator sports as surrogates for martial activity is probably salutary on the whole, but it needs serious assessment.

Mass spectator sports at first involved almost entirely males set against males. Females at first took part as members of mixed-sex hortatory support groups ("fans" and cheerers) reminiscent of the groups urging on the Pentecost Island land divers. Gradually women become more and more central in the support groups themselves not merely as members of a cheering crowd but as cheerleaders (see Chapter 3). More recently women in large numbers have taken up sports as direct participants. The changed pattern here is evidence of the new stage reached at present in the dialectic of the sexes that marks psychic and cultural history over the ages. The full effects of the changed pattern of course cannot be known in much depth until the passage of time allows fuller

Some Present Issues

perspectives. There is evidence that increased pressure on women to engage in sports—as well as in other conspicuously agonistic activities such as law and politics—steps up their insecurity, making it something like that in men, though not the same either (Bardwick, 1971:177-87). But if the psychic significance of such shifts remains on the whole uncertain, some reactions of spectators to women's engagement in spectator sports are already clear.

Women show superb skill in team sports and a great many persons, women and men, have put every effort into developing spectator interest, but for the most part team sports engaged in by women have had at best only limited public appeal. It has proved possible to create a sizable, largely family-backed following for basketball teams of high school girls in sections of the United States, but team sports for female adults, despite superb playing and vigorous promotion, have no following among either women or men even remotely comparable to that of male team sports and seem to give no promise of developing such a following. (On women's professional basketball, for example, see *Newsweek*, February 19, 1979, p. 55.)

This is not to say that women's team sports are not successful, for they are. It is only to say that women's teams, it seems, do not convey to mass spectators the sense of desperate urgency created by the male's peculiar type of insecurity—the appeal of lone warriors sternly united in tight bonding patterns for survival. The action photos, for example, in the 1979 "Year in Sports" issue of *Sports Illustrated* (February 15) show what is at stake: the photos concentrate mostly on moments of utter desperation, often defined by violence. Few women are interested in creating or cherishing such moments, nor are persons of either sex otherwise supportive of women much interested in supporting them in such moments. The war vocabulary normal in reporting team sports, which accords well enough with one's image of dad, no matter how peaceable he may be, somehow does not suit mom. The roots of this situation spread through the sociobiological past so widely and deeply that those aware of the past can hardly look for

155

any great change, even if they should want it. More than any other human contest, the violent contest of athletes directly continues the ritual combat of conspecific males that regularly marks the upper reaches of the entire animal kingdom.

In many single-combat sports (figure skating, gymnastics, golf, tennis—which can modulate into double combat but no further) and to some extent in track, the body of the performer is dramatized somewhat as in the dance. Such sports attract more women participants, who can mobilize large crowds. But otherwise, athletes drawing large live audiences in the tens of thousands and media audiences of tens or even hundreds of millions and often preempting hours of prime time on television screens are almost exclusively males: in high-violence single combat (boxing), in high-violence teamwork (United States football, rugby), in adroit teamwork (world football or soccer, basketball, hockey—though the latter might also fit under high-violence teamwork in fact if not in principle), and in combined single combat and adroit teamwork (baseball, a game conspicuously designed for the needs of the male psyche: the single-combat figures of pitcher and batter against the background of the entire team, a typical bonding group responsive to the situations that the pitcher-batter, lone-warrior duel creates).

The appeal of mass spectator sports, even those thus conspicuously male-styled, can reach to women as well as to men, for there are women sports buffs, and intensive cultural conditioning, such as is being undertaken now in some places, will doubtless produce more. But team sports exert their deepest psychological appeal on males still. Those who go to a stadium to watch football are attending a social as well as a sports event, and for a wide variety of reasons: as a result the stadium crowd is very mixed. Those who watch football on television are captivated by the sport itself, and they appear to be overwhelmingly male, not only in fact but also, more important, in symbolic interpretation. The male television sports addict has become a near-mythological character in hundreds of cartoons, as noted in the immediately preceding chapter, slumped alone with his can of beer before the

Some Present Issues

screen under the glare of his justifiably outraged sports widow, who, according to one story, found that the only way to attract her husband during the World Series or a Superbowl game was to dress in Astroturf. This story is even more apt than it first appears: early chapters here have presented massive evidence that males engaged in ceremonial combat are often more directly concerned about territory or "turf" than about females of the species. The appeal of football has roots in the distant sociobiological past: the two sides are gaming for territory like two male robins or two Uganda kob bucks. The wife proposing to dress herself like a bit of territory shows greater wisdom than perhaps she consciously knows, although it is not at all impossible that she senses the deep relevance of her proposal.

The selectivism or abstractionism fostered by male ceremonial combat has been discussed earlier. Even at the biological level, contest isolates, selects, abstracts certain issues and certain gene pools. At the intellectual level it quite formally sets abstractionism in motion: formal logic grew out of oratorical combat, and the high level of abstraction developed in the West from classical antiquity through the eighteenth century was sustained by the deliberate and systematized agonistic structures characterizing academia.

Modern spectator sports manifest in a peculiarly direct way the intimate relationship between combat and abstractionism in the propagation of statistics. Statistics hold together much of today's spectator sports world. "This is the first time in the history of professional football that three linemen with Polish names have broken their right collarbones simultaneously on the twenty-five-yard line"—this sort of thing can be found without end in sports reference works, along with endless lists of statistics concerning world and other records.

The importance of statistics in sports perhaps has an indirect effect in reducing women's place in the sports world: women's records in almost any kind of sport do not even approximate those of men in abstract figures because of the greater bodily strength of the male. The bottom line is what counts. But more significant, it is the men viewers and writers who characteristically brandish the statistics: this is their sort of world.

Abstractions show also, even more spectacularly in the strict sense of this word, in the instant replays made possible by television. Here the viewer can reanalyze the pattern, catch more accurately the abstract design of a movement or movements. A well-known story registers at least unconscious awareness that the instant replay appeals primarily to the men who make up most of the sports television audience. The little old lady, who figures in so many stories projecting male insecurity onto woman, is portrayed as being totally unresponsive to any structural appeal. She is not a field breaker, not an analyzer, but a holistic observer of people as human beings. "No wonder," the story has her say, "that those poor boys are so tired after all those instant replays."

Nevertheless, to a degree the accumulation of abstract figures generated out of the male-polarized agonistic situation tends to depolemicize the situation itself. For abstractionism is "objective," impersonal. In a way, ceremonial contest tends to destroy itself, to move operations to another plane. (Biologically, it moves often from territorial and other conquest to mating activities.) Historically, the agonistic, masculinizing era has given way to one of greater femininity. In a sense, the male television sports watcher with his *Guinness Book of World Records* is a product of a highly feminized culture: no earlier oral-agonistic age could have produced this abstract half-disinvolvement with the *agōnia* in the arena. You need a writing-and-print world to bring about this effect and a computer world to mature it.

Politics

Politics is everywhere so basically and pervasively agonistic that it is futile even to think of identifying all of the shifts in its agonistic patterns. But a more or less worldwide basic shift can be identified that is intimately related to the themes with which the present work has been dealing. This is the shift that takes place when the less technologized cultures of the world move closer and closer to a high-technology culture. In the perspective of the present work, this movement shows as one from the pristine oral and subsequently residually oral world, which polarized political issues largely in terms of "good guys" and "bad guys," to a chirographic-typographic-electronic economy of thought attending more to vast accumulations of factual knowledge in analytic, "objective" fashion. The older politics was marked by full-blown, impassioned oratory and was conspicuously agonistic. The new politics is in principle polarized in terms of more objectively enunciable issues, formulated in a world of low agonistic tolerance, although in fact it may be highly agonistic beneath the enunciable, "objective" surface, where inarticulate, unconsciously operative forces are always in play. The older world would be represented in Cicero's orations or in more recent times by the oratory of a William Jennings Bryan, the new world by television debates between presidential candidates in the United States, discussed in Chapter 4.

The depolemicizing and objectifying of politics showed dramatically in Fidel Castro's famous speech of July 26, 1970, a speech that marked a turning point in Castro's career and probably in Cuba's history. The *New York Review of Books* for September 24 of that year recognized the importance of the speech and printed it in full in English translation. The principal subject of Castro's speech was the failure of the *zafra* or sugar crop. For this failure, Castro in his speech took full personal responsibility, though he did not deny other additional causes. His dramatic *mea culpa* aligned the speech with the old oral agonistic world of good guys and bad guys, giving the audience the unusual experience of having the principal "good guy" accuse himself of being in some way bad—and thus, in the last analysis, showing himself as good, for the Revolution demands self-criticism. Self-criticism subjects the personal to the "objective" scrutiny fostered by writing, which facilitates treatment of the self as an object. Castro, however, here fed his objective self-criticism rhetorically back into an oral, agonistic, personalist context. The speech thus mingles the old world and the new, but moves resolutely into the new. In noting these complexities I do not accuse Castro of dissembling or other dishonesty, for his self-accusation and the rest of his performance here seems eminently honest, however dramatic.

This was the epoch when Castro's audiences had been used to hearing from him two-hour to four-hour speeches, the length of which alone testifies to the primary oral ambience in which his thought and that of his auditors was moving, as also does the fact that he normally never delivered his speeches from a text, as he might have done in a dominantly chirographic culture. Lee Lockwood, who provided the Introduction to the speech in the *New York Review of Books* and who has had long direct experience of Castro's Cuba and frequent personal contacts with Castro himself, makes it clear how deep in the tradition of primary orality Castro's speechmaking was situated. "Fidel's orations," he writes (p. 20), "have really no analogue in Anglo-Saxon culture" (meaning present-day Anglo-Saxon culture, for they have plenty of analogues in ancient Anglo-Saxon oral culture). They were "meant to be listened to rather than read." His audiences formed not only a part of the scene but also "an element of the speech itself." Lockwood notes that most natives of the United States would find it virtually impossible to have "a sense of the excitement, the level of noise, the physical, almost sensual experience of being in a packed audience of that magnitude" or of "the interrelationship of speaker and listener"—all characteristics that, however strange to a visitor from the high-technology culture to the north, have never been other than normal features of oral performance in primary (preliterate) oral cultures and residually oral cultures across the world. John Donne's sermons for residually oral Elizabethans went for hours.

Castro begins (p. 21) by telling his audience, "I don't usually come to events such as this loaded down with papers." As an exemplary primary oral-culture performer, he had always made his speeches performances arising out of the living contact between himself and the particular audience he was addressing on a given occasion. But this time he says, "I had no alternative but to bring some papers with me [applause], since there are a lot of data and figures." Harking back to the oral world, he talks much of heroes (the people are the heroes), of the enemy, and of shame and honor and glory, the old oral ultimates (pp. 23-25). But the figures turn up massively. Castro calls them "objective difficulties" (p. 27): "objective" refers to the extrahuman, inarticulate world of facts, "difficulties" to the warm, human lifeworld, a world of struggle, an agonistic world. Castro has a foot in both worlds, but he wants to free himself and Cuba from too great subjugation to the verbomotor, human lifeworld. Like Plato, as Havelock (1963) has explained the Greek philosopher, he wants the people he is concerned with to distinguish the known from the knower more effectively than a primary oral culture or even a residually oral culture can.

Significantly, he refers specifically to, and rejects, the oral or residually oral tendency to trace all problems to "bad guys." "Some people believe... that it is just a matter of replacing certain individuals" (p. 30). It has sometimes "been necessary to remove some ministers.... But... there might be some confusion when the masses think that the problem can be solved simply by replacing individuals." What is needed is analysis, including hard statistical analysis and policy based on this objective analysis: only thus can the generous effort he hopes for from everyone be productive.

This is truly an "extraordinary speech," as Lockwood labels it (p. 18). It climaxes the general movement in Castro's thought and expression from his early "dramatic and heightened rhetoric" to "a much more pragmatic and businesslike tone," like that of "the annual report of a corporation executive." In brief, Castro was shifting his style from orality to literacy. The July 26, 1970, speech at its core is a corporation executive's report and it shows that Cuba was by that time on its way out of primary oral culture. But only on its way, for, as Lockwood notes (p. 20), the old resonant redundancy is still present in this speech and the corporation executive's statistics are conveyed through explosive speaker-audience interaction, which served to accommodate the new "cool" rhetoric to the still assertive "hot" personalized life-style that the new rhetoric was undertaking to alter.

This mix of the new visualist noetic with the old oral tradition can be discerned all over the so-called Third World today and elsewhere in societies engaged in technological development. Passing over the abundant instances in the Moslem world and in Christian cultures of subsaharan Africa, we can note a spectacular instance in the largest nation of the world. At about the same time as Castro's speech, Mao Tse-tung was undertaking to move the highly oral masses of the People's Republic of China toward literate technological culture through his own kind of juncture of old and new. He was providing them with collections of his "sayings" that would encourage them to make the move out of orality.

"Sayings" lie at the heart of primary orality: only in "sayings" or proverbs or other formulas can an oral culture store its verbalized knowledge for retrieval. In purely oral cultures, however, "sayings" are common property, the voice of the ages, of the entire past, not of any particular person, and much less of a particular living person. On the edge between orality and literacy, collections of sayings might be made by an individually identified wise man such as Confucius or Qoheleth or Jesus, Son of Eleazar, Son of Sirach, or circulated under the name of a wise king such as Solomon, and the sayings of an individual wise teacher might be gathered from his community of followers and recorded by a Matthew, Mark, Luke, or John. But all of these sayings, even though their utterers are literate, as Jesus of Nazareth was, come out of a functionally oral culture. They were not generated in a committee setting. Only in the twentieth century is the confrontation between primary orality and the chirographic-typographic-electronic culture of high technology so stark that one encounters the "sayings" of a chairman. Mao was a chairman in a culture unaccustomed to chairpersons, and his performance is consequently somewhat quaint, however affective. Fully acculturated chairmen are not particularly interested in sayings as such but rather in "facts" and the complex details that they know they must work with.

Some Present Issues

The special problems confronting Chinese culture in moving into high technology without the alphabet are massive, so that their existence needs to be mentioned. But they are altogether too massive to be discussed here. These problems can be solved when the present program of the People's Republic to teach all of its citizens Mandarin achieves success. Once all can speak the same language—for many so-called Chinese "dialects" are in oral utterance mutually unintelligible languages—the Roman alphabet can and will be introduced, it appears quite certain.

Business

The agonistic cast of business or commerce is in many ways obvious. The aggressiveness of business executives and of business operations in capitalistic economies is conspicuous and has long been a commonplace in literature and drama, whatever the relationship of competitiveness to personal success (see the beginning of this chapter). Business regularly uses contests of various sorts to encourage productivity—service contests, sales contests, and many others. The laissez faire principle would put agonistic activity at the heart of commercial operations and make it essential to their functioning and their well-being.

Nevertheless, the setting of person against person and the resulting polarization of personal loyalties is much less obvious in business, at least in the West, than it is in politics. Business enforces a certain dispassionate objectivity. The person who typically votes Democratic out of personal loyalty to Jimmy Carter does not typically buy a Chevrolet out of loyalty to the president of General Motors or to his local dealer—at least not ordinarily. Commerce is no respecter of persons. The bottom line is what counts. Businessmen are essentially bookkeepers, writing folk, dealing in the last analysis with commodities, things: they are not jousters, oral debaters—at least not in principle. Writing developed largely to serve economic purposes: nearly all of the earliest writing we have (that in Mesopotamian cuneiform script) takes the form of records of ownership, transfers of ownership, and related matters. As schools in the West from the Renaissance on adjusted more and more to teaching pupils who would go into commerce rather than into politics or the professions (Eby and Arrowood, 1934:520-26, 606-9; J. W. Ashley Smith, 1954:158-63 and *passim*), they moved slowly but surely away from the old classical rhetoric and dialectic to a curriculum of "reading, writing, and 'rithmetic" and more practical knowledge. The classical schools representing the traditional agonistic education of the West had not been interested in such matters, for they were training more for diplomatic and other verbal jousting in a world of interpersonal human exchange. Computation had no place in main-line academic education, at least in principle. Practical arithmetic was for tradesmen and housewives.

An agonistic charge, however, can be found not far below the surface of much commercial advertising. Use of a given product assures the user's social ascendancy over nonusers. Advertisements for liquors (notably vodka and Scotch whiskey, drinks for risk takers) and for speed vehicles (motorcycles and sports cars), as well as for perfumes, feature death threats (nightfall, the "dark lady," high-risk situations of various sorts). In this sense, commerce attends, unconsciously, to threat and to death. But business people do not as individuals engage one another in open debate, as politicians and academicians do. They never did, for the most part, engage in person-to-person rhetoric. And recently, the visual persuasion developed by advertising that presents pictures of commercial products and of ways to use them or photographs of smiling, satisfied users has moved rhetoric in commerce to a great degree out of the verbal field, where the pitchman urges his product with seductive words. Visual rhetoric reduces the agonistic charge common in oral argumentative rhetoric. It is hard to develop a dispute merely by flashing pictures. While the business world does of course use oral communication and argumentative written and printed communication, it does not usually live in the world of oral confrontation normal in politics and academia.

The remarkable growth of commerce in the Renaissance and post-Renaissance world, in so far as its direct effects are concerned, marked a major decline of the old agonistic world, the pristine oral world that survived in European feudalism, where literacy was inconsequential but fierce personal loyalties and fighting prowess, physical as well as verbal, were of prime consequence. In the feudal world, fighting was governed by elaborate ceremony, whether the fighting was physical or verbal. The feudal world could not contain the burgeoning commercial world or even live comfortably with it. All over Europe commercial centers had to obtain exemptions from feudal law in order to operate. The Hanseatic League (league of merchants' guilds—*Hansa* is a Middle Low German word meaning guild) ruled its own towns as extrafeudal, commercial territories. The City proper of London received special exemptions from feudal law: to this day, the king or queen of England, representative of the old feudal order, has to ask permission of the lord mayor to enter the central part of London which is the City. The Church, keyed in reflectively to feudal law but not to commerce, could relate only with difficulty to commercial practice: the ethological problems in adjusting to usury and other commercial realities constitute *loci classici* of economic and theological history (Dempsey, 1943). In France, the Low Countries, Germany, and England, when Protestantism came, it had a strong drive to literacy and a strong appeal in commercial milieus, which fostered democratic trends alien to feudalism.

Even when managed largely by males, modern commercial society has not had the strong macho cast often met with in aristocratic, feudal cultures, with their masculinizing ethos, not infrequently defensive. Competitors, when referred to publicly, have normally been anonymous: "Ours is the best of all brands." The more openly agonistic style adopted by the Avis car-rental company in recent years first referred to an identifiable competitor only by inference, not by name: "We're number two [Hertz is number one], so we try harder." The pitch here was to an almost entirely male clientele, frequently salesmen whose activities were plotted in "territories," the old, even prehuman, stake in ritual competition between conspecific males. The tone of these advertisements was gaming, that of male ritual contest and the bragging that accompanies it. But this ritualized gaming approach has yielded to factual analyses. More recently, explicit mention of competitors has come into fashion in the United States, and for a great variety of products. The more recent style tends to objective, fact-based statement: specific qualities are compared in the brand advertised and competing brands. It is not the competition as such that counts, but the facts.

The commercial and business world is in fact more related to the home than is the world of the agora or the world of sports. Manufacturing was at first, and in many places often still is, a home activity, unlike politics. The family cast and exclusivism in trade unions today is a heritage from the time when guilds of tradesmen often operated out of and as extended families, with apprentices living in the master's house and marrying his daughters. Much of commerce is in direct contact with woman's world, even in societies where sexual distance and tensions are maximized, for in such societies even more than elsewhere, women often engage in manufacturing and marketing and also have complete charge of the domestic economy, which even in high-technology cultures still provides a major market, if not ultimately the major market, for commercial products. Its large-scale orientation to household needs helps to give the business and commercial world its characteristically nonagonistic tone. Moreover, despite war and armament profiteering, commerce needs peace in order to function effectively. Wars may be waged because of tensions created by commerce, but business even in wartime has to be conducted under an umbrella of peace. You cannot negotiate prices with the enemy while firing on him. Even when its managerial population is all but entirely male, as it was until very recent years, the business world, it appears, in significant ways works more for the feminization than the masculinization of culture (Ong, 1967:192-262; Douglas, 1977, *passim*).

Marxist doctrine produces its own special alignments of the industrial world with agonistic structures. By directly politicizing industrial production, dialectic materialism reinterprets such

Some Present Issues

production as fundamentally agonistic. Moreover, its insistence on ownership and control of material resources as the paradigmatic issue underlying all human struggle suggests some deep, unconscious reference to the pristine territorial contests focusing male ritual combat and a preference for the feudalism related in so many ways to such combat. The possible results of these agonistic alignments are too complex and specialized to be treated here.

Christian Life and Worship

Christianity cannot be understood in any depth without some explicit reference to the history of consciousness. Basically, the Christian Church is not a body of doctrine or an "institution" but a community with a shared memory. "Do this in memory of me" were Jesus' words at the institution of the Eucharist, words repeated certainly billions upon billions of times since and still repeated whenever the Eucharist is celebrated. The Church came into being through the witnessing—the sharing of the memories—of those who had known Jesus of Nazareth, and the Church was continued and is continued today by those who have subsequently witnessed to the witness passed on to them by generations tracing back to the first witnesses to Jesus' words and deeds. The most honored persons in the liturgy of the Church are the martyrs (from the Greek *martys, martyros,* witness), men and women who witnessed to the maximum, who continued to speak the Gospel, the Good News of Jesus Christ, even when doing so brought death. The shared memory that marks Christian faith had as its antecedent the Jews' memory of God's dealing with his chosen people. The essential rootedness in memory that marks the Hebreo-Christian tradition makes it unlike other religious traditions. But Christian faith is even more concretely rooted in memory than the Hebrew faith, for it sees all of God's dealings with all human beings as centered in the Incarnation. The Word was made flesh, God took to himself a human nature, became incarnate, "enfleshed," in the man Jesus of Nazareth, through whom all redemption is given. All Providence is centered at this point in historical time. All of God's dealings with human beings are through the historical person Jesus Christ in historical time, the ground of real memory. There is no direct, ahistorical access to God "from eternity." "Only through time time is conquered," writes T. S. Eliot. Memory dwells in real time.

Memory lives. It lives in real time. It constantly reinterprets itself, relates itself to the present. Otherwise it is no more. The kerygma, or continued proclamation of what Jesus said and did, based on memory coming from the direct witnesses to his life through their successors, is a continued historical event in the preaching and liturgy of the church. As consciousness evolves, the kerygma continues to work itself out, making itself felt somewhat as a human person does, as a presence always set in a living, developing relationship to the human psyche that reflects the current state of the psyche to which it relates. As stages of consciousness succeed one another, the kerygma reflects the changes. In a highly mythological era, it speaks to the mythologically tuned mind. In our historicist age, it attends to its own historicity, and even "demythologizes." But throughout, memory must keep itself straight: must remember and keep alive what it is remembering.

Its rootedness in memory and thereby in the history of consciousness has made Christianity a gold mine for depth psychologists. Because its involvement with psychohistory is so deep and urgent, some relations of Christianity to questions concerning contest, sexuality, and consciousness that have been earlier discussed here are worth reviewing, if only cursorily. Seeing these questions in relation to Christian belief today opens fresh insights into the present and future of consciousness. I shall direct reflections here chiefly to the Roman Catholic ethos, not only because the Roman Catholic tradition is more familiar to me in depth than other Christian traditions but also because links between the biological and the psychological (including the noetic) worlds are more evident in Catholicism (and in Orthodoxy) than in Protestantism. The sacramentalism that marks Roman Catholic (and

Orthodox) faith interprets the relationships between the material world and the spiritual world in a more dynamic way than classical Protestantism does. In Catholic belief, the material signs of the sacraments—the water of baptism, bread and wine, oils, the externalized consent of the spouses in matrimony, the laying on of hands—are not mere external accoutrements but are rather a part of the dynamism whereby God gives his graces to his human creatures. These graces relate to the "soul," psychic life, directly, not to the body as such. But in the sacraments they involve the body. Roman Catholic doctrine is inexorably psychosomatic and in this sense essentially hospitable to noobiological insights, despite recurrent Manichean or Cartesian drives that occasionally inhibit recognition of this fact.

The development of the Roman Catholic ethos, as of consciousness generally over the past three millennia (at least) has been that of a strongly masculinizing era, marked by the agonistic patterns treated here. The Bible itself took shape in this era. From its earliest books through to Revelation, the Bible, though its deeper message is peace, presents human life on earth, not exclusively but repeatedly, as spiritual struggle or warfare carried on paradigmatically by male against male. The concept of Satan takes form in this agonistic milieu—the name Satan means adversary. God is above the struggle—there is no self-sufficient power of evil independent of him with whom or with which he struggles—but in our struggle God involves himself, helping on the side of good. Preaching Jesus' gospel of faith, hope, and divine love, the Church has from the beginning been very much at home in the agonistic male world, and nowhere more than when engaged in intellectual activity.

As shown in Chapter 4, Catholic theology in the West has been the last academic enterprise to abandon the agonistic proceedings and thought forms rooted in the ancient masculinized, residually oral academic world. The Roman Catholic Church clung longest of any group in the West to Learned Latin, the extrafamilial, sex-linked, distinctively male language that carried with it the old agonistic mind-set and thought forms. Indeed, the Roman

Catholic Church clung so long to Learned Latin that the impression has prevailed for several recent generations that Latin had always been a peculiarly ecclesiastical language, whereas in fact it had been simply the language of virtually all learning and scientific or scholarly expression in the West until by the seventeenth century vernaculars had developed to the point where it was possible at long last to use at least some of them to carry on and express scientific and scholarly thinking. As Latin ceased to be the medium of instruction, the agonistic economy of academia collapsed. In the Roman Catholic Church the discontinuation of Latin and the collapse of agonistic theology are not yet two decades old.

Down through Pius IX's *Syllabus* of modern errors (1867) a conspicuously agonistic stance has commonly marked conciliar and papal doctrinal pronouncements. Indeed, it has been a commonplace of theology that the Church needs heretics (adversaries) to sharpen its understanding of the truth it possesses. This is another version of the assumption in academia that all intellectual action is of its nature agonistic. We can suspect—as, with Huizinga, I more than suspect—that this is indeed so. But the agonistic can be a central or a peripheral concern: of late, it has moved from the center to the periphery. The tone of the decrees of the Second Vatican Council (1962-65), while often forthright and firm, lacks the agonistic edge typical of many earlier church pronouncements.

Elsewhere Roman Catholic life has followed suit. A statistically analytic recent study (Dengler, 1971) has compared the sixteenth-century *Catechism of the Council of Trent* and *A New Catechism: Catholic Faith for Adults* (1972), the widely used post-Vatican II "Dutch Catechism," and found the former distinctively polemic in presentation of Catholic doctrine in high contrast to the less agonistic approach of the latter. The old *Breviarium romanum* had included in the round of its weekly readings all of the 150 psalms: the new *Liturgy of the Hours* (1971-), which replaces the Breviary, omits three execrative psalms calling down God's wrath on the psalmist's enemies,

Psalm 58 ("Smash their teeth in their mouths"), Psalm 83 ("Let them be confounded and perish"), and Psalm 108 ("May his days be few... his children... fatherless"). (The Church's liturgy has never considered as adaptable for public liturgical reading absolutely every text in the Bible, but it had hitherto included in such reading all of the 150 psalms.) In similar nonagonistic style, instead of writing off the human city as inimical to the heavenly kingdom, the *Liturgy of the Hours* now prays, "May we work together to build up the earthly city, with our eyes fixed on the city that lasts forever" (fifth Sunday of Lent, morning praise; this passage is typical of many others). The duality is still there, but the intensely agonistic stage of consciousness has been superseded by another stage, and existence is no longer defined so utterly by polemic.

Given the reduced adversativeness in the Roman Catholic Church's stance since Vatican II, one might think that the Church could simply slough off various more or less agonistically toned masculine accoutrements, including such things as the practice of ordaining only males to holy orders. This is no place to discuss the question of ordaining women as clergy, but it is certainly the place to note some of the complex and rich ways in which the incarnation and redemption at the center of Christian teaching are tied intimately to sexuality, that is, to a differentiated maleness and femaleness, as they relate to contest and associated phenomena.

The Church's teaching is structured permanently in the deep feminine-masculine polarities that shift dialectically through time to produce, for example, today the needed and welcome ascendancy of the feminine in consciousness signaled most conspicuously by women's liberation movements and also perhaps even more by worldwide ecological concern, which regards the whole universe as a house, a home. Since sex is a biological phenomenon, the masculine-feminine dialectic is basically biological, however complexly related to much, or indeed virtually everything else, in human life. Catholic doctrine has a biological base in the sense that the female-male relationship forms the human ground in which redemption, freedom, and love take root. A residual Manichaeism—from which Christians have still not entirely liberated themselves—would downgrade the material universe and make a biological foundation for anything human distasteful. But the foundation is there nevertheless, and should not be dismaying to those who truly believe that the Word became flesh.

The Church is sexually defined. To the psyche, the Church is always feminine, Holy Mother Church. Psychoanalytically as well as theologically there is no way to have a "Father Church." The femininity of the Church is connected with the nature of the Incarnation itself and of redemption. The Incarnation has a fundamentally feminine human base, particularly as related to the church's teaching regarding the virgin birth. In the economy of the Incarnation, the great advantage of the birth of Jesus without the ordinary process of sexual intercourse and thus without a human father is that, through the totally effective free assent of a woman, it assured the absolute freedom of humankind in humankind's own redemption.

Freedom is essential in the Christian's relation to God, and it manifests itself in response to God's grace, his call. One of the features of the Hebreo-Christian faith, as distinguished, it appears, from all other religions (except, to a degree, Islam, which is related historically to Judaism and Christianity), is that, whereas other religions are commonly concerned with the human quest for God, the Hebreo-Christian faith is not: it appears as a free response to God's free quest for humans. Biblical characters are not typically God seekers, but responders to a solicitous God. "We, for our part, love because he first loved us" (I John 4:19). From Genesis through Revelation, the Bible is almost entirely about God's quest for humans and humans' uneven response. God cares, and he comes. In Genesis he volunteers to speak to Adam and Eve before the fall, and after the fall he is back again with "Where are you?" (Gen. 3:9). He calls Abraham, the prophets, others. The word of the Lord came to Jeremiah: "Before I formed you in the womb I knew you.... What do you see,

Jeremiah?" (Jer. 1:5, 11). "God put Abraham to the test. He called to him, 'Abraham.' And he said, 'Behold, here I am'" (Gen. 22:1). "I have called you by name; you are mine" (Isa. 43:1, cf. 45:4). As the deeply learned literary critic Erich Auerbach has made clear (1957:5-9), no god of ancient Greece or Rome ever behaves that way, calling out to a human being to elicit that kind of response. The God of the Bible summons. He summons finally by sending his Son, his Word, who is himself God with the Father and the Holy Spirit. Sending the Son was God's idea, not man's. The initiative is God's. The Greek term for the Church, *ecclesia,* means those who are "called out"— *ex-,* out; *kalein,* to call. The Church is free response to God's initiative.

The Incarnation through virginal conception and birth fits the pattern of free response par excellence. The angel Gabriel came to Mary (Luke 1:26-38) with the word that Mary had found favor with God: "Blessed are you among women." Mary was fearful and puzzled: "She was deeply troubled by his words and wondered what his greeting meant." She is told, "You shall conceive and bear a son and give him the name Jesus." God's will is preemptive, for his messenger straightforwardly states, "You shall conceive . . ." But God's will does not force Mary's will. The statement "You shall conceive" suggests the omniscient God's foreknowledge, but clearly not coercion, for the climax to which the passage builds is Mary's own act of consent, interiorizing God's will as manifest to her, freely making his will hers: "I am the servant of the Lord. Let it be done to me as you say."

Whatever theories are advanced to explain the interrelationship of God's foreknowledge and human freedom in Christian teaching—and the theories are legion—the passage clearly presents Mary's response as freely given to God's freely designed plan. There is a vast theological and devotional literature on this free choice of hers, her free surrender, which sometimes develops into speculation on what might have happened had she said no. Mary, as Saint Leo the Great observes in a homily excerpted in the Roman Breviary (Leo I, 1948:393-94), "conceived Jesus in her mind before she conceived him in her body.'' The Incarnation resulted from her acceptance, which had to be an act of faith, free assent to God's once concealed Word, now revealed. That free assent of faith brought the Word (the Second Person of the Godhead, as later theology would work it out) into her conscious mind through intellectual conception—we speak of "conceiving" a thought—whereupon the physical conception in her womb immediately took place.

The Incarnation was thus immediately consequent on Mary's saying yes. Conception by sexual intercourse cannot be so direct a result of a free act. Although sexual intercourse may be freely intended and, with it, conception freely wished for, hoped for, prayed for, these acts of the will in connection with sexual intercourse do not directly result in pregnancy. The symbolic effect of the virgin birth is massive: a human being gave free consent to, accepted the redemption of, mankind and thereby made it a reality. Because of Mary, mankind's redemption is not only God's work, it is humankind's own—or, more specifically, woman's own.

For there is no way for a male to do what Mary did. The freedom of the Incarnation insofar as it depends on human choice has to depend on a woman's choice. Males are disqualified from making this central decision for all humankind, and on biological grounds. As the Incarnation is presented in Luke and throughout Christian teaching generally, this is not simply a theological requisite but also inevitably a biological one. The biological base has been discussed often in earlier chapters: there is no way for a male to produce a child without a female, though many female organisms, as has been seen, produce offspring without a male.

The dynamisms here help to show some of the ways in which sexuality is a factor in the Hebrew and Christian concept of God. God is not an organism, as human beings are organisms, female and male. He is likened to the masculine not because he has a masculine physical constitution but because he is a source of existence that is other, different, separated (*kadosh*, the Hebrew word translated *sanctus*, *hagios*, "holy," means at root "separated'') from all his creation, even from human beings, though they are "made in his image and likeness." Masculinity stands in the human psyche for a kind of otherness, difference. Among the higher forms of life, above the egg-laying species, the male's physical relationship to his offspring is distinctively distanced. The male reproductive cell becomes effectively reproductive when it is totally detached from the male's body and joins the cell that, in the higher forms of life, remains attached to the female. Fathers are essentially distant from offspring physically. They can even be dead and buried when the child is being formed and is born.

Human fathers can be and normally are deeply affectionate and devoted to their children, but the male kind of affection is always a function of this real physical male relationship, as has been seen. A sparring match setting up a ritual distance between father and son and even, within limits, between father and daughter can express deep affection. Neither sons nor daughters spar with mother as they can with father. To mother they have been physically and physiologically attached.

Human beings, female or male, never have a comparable problem of separating themselves from father: there was no male umbilical cord. Nor do human beings, female or male, have a problem of separating themselves from God. We are distanced from God as from a father. We have never been physically and physiologically attached to God, yet Hebreo-Christian teaching insists that he loves us—hence he calls us, his children set off from him, and draws us near to him with love. In this sense, related to the biological sense though not entirely the same, God is male. He is not nature. Nature is feminine, Mother Nature. Out of her we grow. We do not grow out of God, or out of any consort of his. Mother Nature is not his consort. He has no consort and no seed (and thus is not male in the strict biological sense). We are God's creatures, his creation. Since we have not grown out of him, rupture from him is not required for our individuation.

It should be noted that in Christian Trinitarian theology, the relation of Son to Father is somewhat different: Son and Father are totally distinct without ever being at all separated. Where one is, the other always is totally. And so with the Holy Spirit, who is distinct from Father and Son yet never separated from either as they never are from him. This is one thing meant by the absolute unity of the three persons in one God. The Son's unique union with the Father establishes distinctness without a process of separation such as motherliness would require. The pattern of distinctness-establishing-unity in the bonding pattern of human and infrahuman males is remotely analogous here.

The Bible at times compares God to a mother: "Can a mother forget her infant, be without tenderness for the child of her womb? Even should she forget, I will never forget you" (Isa. 49:15). "As a mother comforts her son, so will I comfort you" (Isa. 66:13). Jesus says to Jerusalem, "How often have I yearned to gather your children, as a mother bird gathers her young under her wings" (Matt. 23:37; cf. Luke 13:34). These passages show God's love tender as a mother's love and indeed show intimacy. But never is there any suggestion of creatures' being formed from God as from a mother. In Isaiah 49:15 God's love is not simply commensurate with that of a mother for "the child of her womb" but rather transcends such love: "Even should she forget, I will never forget you."

Always distinctive of God is that, with all his tenderness and concern and closeness suggested by such passages as these, he is always also other, different, separated, as a father physically is, and not by becoming so but simply by being so. Though he reaches out to creatures, they cannot of themselves reach him. Human beings cannot be made *of* him but only "made in his image and likeness." This is why he "calls" men and women and why the Church is *ecclesia,* meaning "those called," those invited to come near.

God is so different, so separated, that, although human beings, his creatures, are like him, made in his "image and likeness" (Gen. 1:26), he is not like them. "My thoughts are not your thoughts, nor are your ways my ways" (Isa. 55:8). St. Thomas Aquinas develops this subject at length in his theory of relations, explaining that while "creatures are really related to God him-

Some Present Issues

self, in God there is no real relation to creatures" (*Summa theologiae*, 1941:836-42—pt. I, ques. 13, art. 7, response). That is, while each creature comes into existence necessarily bearing in itself a relation to God, the creature's existence establishes nothing new in God, whose "love is everlasting" and was there in its fullness from eternity, before the creature's existence.

If God is masculine, appreciation of God as other, different, comes not from the masculine but from the feminine side of human nature, in both females and males, because among other things, of the feminine sensitivity to otherness, a sensitivity due to the fact that otherness arises biologically by contrast with the female: femininity is the abidingness in nature from which masculinity, too, takes its organic beginnings. "Nature's first impulse is to make a female" (Bardwick, 1971:87, quoting Money, 1965). This is to say that for human beings, males as well as females, the way truly to conceive of God as he is presented in Hebrew and Christian tradition is to conceive of him by means of feminine insight, not masculine. In relation to God, through Roman Catholic tradition (the Protestant tradition is less outspoken here), we are all, men and women alike, basically feminine. Macho insights reveal nothing of God.

Hence Mary's centrality as the paramount member of the Church, and indeed as the figure of the entire Church (Rev. 12:1, where the "woman clothed with the sun" is commonly interpreted as both Mary and the church, fused). Mary's acceptance of the Word of God by an act of faith in her mind that resulted in her conceiving him within her body and giving birth to him was the paradigmatic act on which is modeled that of all Christians who receive God's word. To receive God's word is to conceive his Word as conceived in Mary, who thus, in Gerard Manley Hopkins's phrase, "makes... new Nazareths in us." All Christians, men as well as women, can accept this free gift of God only by molding their acceptance on the initial acceptance, which had to be that of a woman. This fact establishes the overwhelming femininity of the Church and all her members vis-à-vis God. The essential human response to God is womanly. The redeemer, Jesus Christ, is a man, but all men as all women are born of woman, and Jesus received his masculinity, his male-sexed body, from a woman as a result of her own free choice. His entry into the human lifeworld was through a woman, and his entry into the individual consciousness follows suit.

This overwhelming femininity of the Roman Catholic Church from the human side suggests that a male clergy is basically not a characterizing feature of the Church so much as a countervailing feature. Despite the masculine clergy, in macho cultures (of which there are many), where the male labors under more than the usual male insecurity, open association of males with Church services is relatively rare, so great is the threat of being swamped there in the feminine. In such cultures even an all-male clergy is likely to be regarded by other males as somewhat feminine because of the close alliance with the feminine Church. Insight into this situation does not resolve the question of the ordination of women but it shows some elements involved.

The otherness and separateness of God, which defines in one way the Church's and the individual person's relation to him in sexual terms, has as a counterpart the sexually defined role of Jesus in the redemption of the human race. This role can be examined in countless ways. Here it will be looked at in terms of the agonistic structures and behavior with which the present study is concerned.

In one of its principal aspects Jesus' work is diaeretic, differentiating, field breaking, as the masculine *agōn* and style are. "I come into this world to divide it" (John 9:39). "My mission is to spread, not peace, but division. I have come to set a man at odds with his father, a daughter with her mother, a daughter-in-law with her mother-in-law: in short, to make a man's enemies those of his own household" (Matt. 10:34-36). "I have come to cast fire upon the earth" (Luke 12:49). "He who is not with me is against me" (Matt. 12:30). All this despite Jesus' central and overarching mission of peace.

The *agōn*, the struggle, is a liberating one. Those who engage in it, Jesus says, will find "I am the way and the truth and the life" (John 14:6). "The truth will set you free" (John 8:32).

Some Present Issues

But at the same time the struggle that Jesus engages in is also a curiously nonviolent one from his side: it is his enemies who use violence on him. He goes out to meet it, undergoes it, in his "passion," which means his "enduring." But he never passively surrenders, even to hatred or resentment. "Father, forgive them, they do not know what they are doing" (Luke 23:34). His last act at his death is a free act of self-giving: "Father, into your hands I commend my spirit" (Luke 23:46). Some philosophers have made the point that such an act, the free acceptance of the death that simply comes to one (not suicide), is the freest of all possible human acts. For such death comes without my bidding, and in that sense is not my own. Yet it is totally personal, my own death. If one can make his or her own this overwhelming intrusion into one's deepest interior, freely taking it to oneself, then one is truly free—for freedom means being master of one's actions from within one's own consciousness. Jesus so appropriated his own death: "Father, into your hands I commend my spirit." Such acceptance of death is not passive: though it may not involve external activity, and indeed may be a decision to desist from external activity, true human acceptance always is a positive, active decision, often demanding tremendous energy.

This free quietness, related to Jesus' nonviolence, differentiates his struggle from the purely male, aggressive, violent *agōn* through which so much has been effected in biological evolution but which in a human being bespeaks some sort of insecurity and weakness. The masculine in Jesus' redemptive action is complemented by this feminine strength-in-quietness—which is not passivity at all but a free and active choice. Such free choice, free response, is what makes woman in her "quietness" appealing to man—not passivity, which is infrahuman—and what makes woman "always conquer," according to the Chinese proverb. For this quietness bespeaks power.

Its free quietness makes Jesus' redemptive action in significant ways unlike that of the archetypal slayer of dragons. On the one hand, Jesus is like the mythological dragon slayer, the masculine

Fighting for Life

ego (Neumann, 1954:262-65, 433), in that he wins from captivity his bride, the Church. But he is quite unlike the dragon slayer in that he conquers by his free obedience to his Father in freely submitting to death. He is unmistakably male but not so insecure as most males. Epic heroes tend to be dragonslayers archetypically and Jesus is not an epic hero, as Kierkegaard has made clear (1968), for Jesus' meaning is not that of a "heavy" paradigmatic figure representing a given culture. Jesus is a personal friend, related to each individual human being, male or female, personally in real history.

Yet, if he is not entirely like the dragon slayer, Jesus' work is still that of the male fighter. He had to go it alone. Though he has male followers and also a large number of close and more reliable women followers, when the time comes for the agony in the Garden of Olives and for the trial, torture, and death that follow, he has to fight the fight by himself, the male loner, destined for high-risk combat. To the Roman cohort and temple guards who arrested him in Gethsemane, Jesus says, referring to the disciples with him, "Let these men go" (John 18:8).

For the followers of Jesus, female and male, faith is also a high-risk undertaking, involving struggle. "Work out your salvation in fear and trembling" (Phil. 2:12). "While all the runners in the stadium take part in the race, the award goes to one man. In that case, run so as to win!" (1 Cor. 9:24). And although Christian faith is never a private faith but always faith shared as a member of the Church, each individual Christian, male or female, is held individually accountable for his or her own efforts. Christian peace is not nirvana or totally *islam* (resignation), though it includes elements of the latter.

In the Roman Catholic ethos (as in the Orthodox), the persons who are most honored publicly and liturgically for their profession of the Christian faith are the martyrs, the supreme witnesses, men and women who contest death in quietness, who go freely to their deaths because they will not desist from proclaiming the Gospel, the Good News, from telling what Jesus did and said, what he means to them. The struggle that is martyrdom was not

Some Present Issues

characteristic of the ancient pagan religions; indeed, for them it was normally pointless. *Cuius regio eius religio,* went the old Latin saying: you follow the religion of the country you are in. Christian martyrs had been preceded by Jewish martyrs, who, like Eleazar or the heroic mother with her seven sons (2 Macc. 6:18–7:42), decided to die rather than act against Yahweh's law. They witnessed to Yahweh's presence to his people through Hebrew history. Christian martyrdom is witness to Jesus' presence among human beings and to his actions in real human history.

Like Jesus, the martyr, male or female, is a nonviolent agonistic figure, struggling to stand upright in obedient love against attack. Though martyrdom is agonistic, a struggle, a contest, it is totally nonaggressive. Suicide cannot be martyrdom, for martyrdom comes not from one's own action but from the action of another or others. There is no way to arrange it for oneself, to make oneself a Christian martyr. Like Jesus, the martyr does not actively cause or even seek death ("Father, if it is your will, take this cup from me"—Luke 22:42), but freely accepts death if it comes, and thereby becomes the ultimate witness.

Witnessing to Christ is a grace, a gift of God, and witnessing crowned by martyrdom, total witnessing, total self-giving, is the maximum gift, a maximum free offer met with a maximum free acceptance. In the Catholic liturgical calendar, martyrs, nonviolent agonistic figures, outrank all other saints except the Apostles and Evangelists (who for that matter are themselves all remembered in liturgical tradition as martyrs except for John), John the Baptist (who was also a martyr), Joseph, and Jesus' mother, Mary, who herself is reckoned not only as a martyr but indeed in the Litany of the Blessed Virgin as "Queen of Martyrs," since her appropriation and interiorization of her Son's death, at which she was present (John 19:25), constituted martyrdom for her—again by way of feminine prerogative, since her maternal identification with Jesus in this supreme act of his, his free offering of his death, was closer than any identification possible for a mere male.

Not all martyrs, perhaps, have been sure, theoretically or practically, of the issues involved in martyrdom, much less able to state them explicitly. Some, out of generosity or sheer fatigue, may have acted rashly and precipitated death. Not all Christian martyrs have been learned and articulate, but some have been. Saint Thomas More, humanist scholar, lawyer, statesman, and martyr, was able to treat of his own agonistic but nonaggressive stance before his martyrdom with beautiful clarity (Chambers, 1958:291-350). As More knew and stated, like other human beings, the prospective martyr may not risk his or her life needlessly. If doing his or her duty brings death, that is another matter. In More's case it did. But he had felt obliged to make every effort he could to avoid death short of denying his faith. His efforts failed. It was take the oath of supremacy or die. The issue was joined. He would not swear the oath. The gift of martyrdom thus came out of loving obedience, when there was no other way to be lovingly obedient. Martyrdom is the sublimation of all aggression but a contest for all that. And it is one to which all Christians, male and female, in principle may be called.

The agonistic forces in the Christian, and particularly the Roman Catholic, ethos have only been touched on here. But perhaps enough has been noted to suggest how deeply and complexly Christian teaching involves and is involved in the agonistic structures running from the biological world through the social and noetic worlds. The old polemic theological style, as Chapter 4 has shown, had roots that run through the evolution of consciousness on down to biological evolution. But the agonistic in the Christian ethos is more than theological style. It involves the highest reaches of doctrine.

Shifts in agonistic structures due to the dialectic of the sexes, which enters so deeply into the history of consciousness, show in many places in the development of Christian teaching. One of the places is in the central action of the Christian liturgy, the Eucharist. In an earlier highly masculine state of consciousness, when agonistic behavior determined social institutions more conspicuously than it does generally today, the sacrificial element in the Eucharist was stressed in Catholic theology: sacrifice of a living victim typically entails violence. In the present, more feminine stage of consciousness, theological interpretation tends to center on the nurturing element rather more than on the sacrificial: the Eucharist is seen chiefly as a sacred banquet, a meal. Both elements are integral to the Catholic view: the sacred banquet is the partaking of the victim of the sacrifice. But attention fluctuates from one age to another.

Agonistic structures enter paradoxically even into the Christian desire for peace. Christianity calls for peace, the peace of Christ, in terms of struggle, asceticism, training for a contest, for only through struggle, carried on out of love, can peace be secured. How much agonistic in life-style does the Gospel presuppose or need? And what is the relationship of this agonistic to the respective roles of the sexes in the Church? How much masculinization can the Gospel tolerate? How much feminization? These are urgent questions that affect the respective roles of men and women in the Church. Answers to them can hardly be shaped in advance. They have to be lived out in history.

6

Contest and Interiorization

The Variable Settings of Contest

This account of the prehuman and human history of contest does not provide a complete explanation of human nature or of sexuality or of the evolution of consciousness, or even of consciousness itself. By tracing the history of contest through some of biological and noetic history, it has merely brought attention to bear on otherwise neglected features of human existence. The density of existence cannot in whole or in part be forced into any simple, linear, total explanation. The present account has been "phenomenological" in a sense close to that explained by Lyman (1978:90-95). It has undertaken to order historical data and experience in a form of related "interests" generated by the present state of consciousness and thereby to provide partial, but real, understanding that can be further developed as later "interests" may demand.

Obviously, this account does not make it possible to predict the next thousand or ten thousand or fifty thousand years of conscious history. But it does, I hope, give some idea of certain structures that are part of our past and present and which in one way or another will affect our future.

Male insecurity and the agonistic drives characterizing male insecurity will, it seems, remain in one form or another as long as men and women are born of women. Whether this insecurity and these drives will in the future remain so determinative of social

Contest and Interiorization

structures as they have been in the past is unsure. It may seem that they will not remain so ostentatiously determinative on some fronts—in political organizations, for example, where the old-style fliting oratory has atrophied—but if they operate more subterraneously they will not thereby necessarily be less powerful or effective. Whether in the future they will be so productive of change and discovery as they have been in the past remains to be seen. They will certainly not affect society in exactly the same way as in the past, although they may always affect society as much as they have in earlier ages. Meanwhile, we shall manage agonistic structures and all that is related to them, including sexuality, not by abolishing or blurring or denying the structures or sexual differences but by better understanding the structures and the differences. It is impossible to work effectively against discrimination and other abuses of sexual differences when these differences are swept under the rug.

With the advent of human consciousness, the operation of contest even at the biological level changes, and not only among human beings. Even among infrahuman species human consciousness has for millennia interfered with the effect of contest in determining heredity. With our increased knowledge of genetics, it will certainly interfere more and more. The males that father progeny in domesticated species or laboratory animals are selected by the conscious deliberation and decision of human beings, women and men, not by the evolutionary processes that have produced and are in turn affected by combative prowess. Human beings have artificially evolved organisms—helplessly ornamental dogs or helplessly overweight bovines, for example—that natural evolution could never have produced. In the case of the "brave bulls" for the Spanish *corrida de toros* or of gamecocks or of Siamese fighting fish (*Betta splendens*), artificial selection precisely for agonistic mettle has outstripped nature and produced gene pools with an agonistic charge perhaps too high for survival in the wild. But in most cases, artificially selective breeding has downgraded agonistic masculinity by seeing to it that males qualify as breeders on quite other grounds—

obesity, abnormal wooliness, tractability in harness, sheer running speed, cuddlesomeness (as in the case of lapdogs), or simply bizarre appearance.

Yet the effect of conscious human planning on the total biomass of the globe is thus far picayune. We selectively breed only an insignificantly tiny fraction of the total number of species of animals, and in many species that human beings selectively breed, only a few relatively tiny populations are affected: there are innumerably more fruit flies (*Drosophila*) outside laboratories than inside.

Among human beings, contest, however biologically grounded, virtually always involves human consciousness, the reflective, calculating element in psychic life that is uniquely humankind's. Human beings do not merely plunge into contests: they also plan them. Unlike a contest between stags, a football game is preplayed, thought through, in the minds of coaches and contestants in countless hypothetic forms before it is actually begun. The reflective processes here, however, do not override the biological but rather interact with them. For, as has been seen, reflective processes themselves have been shaped by the agonistic structures in academia, which have biological as well as intellectual roots. Logic governs a football contest, but logic itself, even as a formal discipline, grew out of rhetorical contest.

The reflectiveness that marks human consciousness is itself becoming more intense. Since at least the time of Hegel, Western philosophy has been aware of the drive of human consciousness to greater and greater interiority. Consciousness obviously focuses on and affects the exterior world. The ecological crisis has brought home how much consciousness has done to the world around it, intentionally and unintentionally. But even while it continues to affect the outer world, consciousness drives more and more inward through the course of history, in an always accelerating pattern. This growth in inwardness shows on many fronts, from the plastic arts to city planning. Developments on two fronts appear particularly relevant to agonistic behavior, the narrative and the scholarly-scientific fronts, which can be examined briefly here.

Contest and Interiorization

In narrative we organize reality as it presents itself to us flowing through time. In scholarly and scientific accounts we organize it in terms of causal relationships.

From Violence to Inwardness in Narrative

A valuable and now standard work by Erich Kahler, *The Inward Turn of Narrative* (1973), drawing on Hegelian insights, has documented in great detail how fictional narrative over the ages has moved the focus of its concern from exterior happenings more and more to occurrences closer to or inside the mind, eventually producing such works as James Joyce's *Ulysses* and *Finnegans Wake,* which are so inwardly directed that they can be read as stories about the workings of the mind itself (Ong, 1977a:238, 247-49). Narrative, with related dramatic enactment, provides a particular instance of the greater and greater interiorization of consciousness through history noted by Hegel. It has long been a commonplace of classical scholarship that, historically, Greek drama moves from concern with external proprieties and improprieties to a study of the agonies of the interior conscience. The Bible similarly moves from a relatively exteriorized world of external ritual observance in its earliest books to a stress in the New Testament, roughly a thousand years later, on interior activity: "It is not what goes into a man's mouth that makes him impure; it is what comes out of his mouth," says Jesus (Matt. 15:17). Ortega y Gasset (1956:99-120, esp. 104) and others have made a similar point about the progressive interiorization of painting and other art forms in the West.

The "inward turn of narrative" correlates with a reduction in certain agonistic structures related to modes of verbalization. For it correlates with a reduced orality and a more dominant literacy. Oral traditions across the world and all early, residually oral literatures narrate stories of heroic model figures esteemed largely for their conspicuous external agonistic performance. As noted earlier (Chapter 4), "heavy," highly polarized type figures, identifiable by external behavior, psychologically uncomplicated, are needed for oral noetic processes. These "heavy" heroic figures can be either men or women, but partly because of the need to counterbalance the overwhelming femininity of earlier stages of human existence and partly because of the need for high and even violent contrast in oral management of knowledge, major narratives of early cultures feature heroes, males involved in often spectacular external violence, far more commonly and more conspicuously than heroines. In the struggle to break away from the early stages of consciousness dominated by the "totality orientation" of the Great Mother, vigorously combative heroes are helpful to females and males both, for the entire culture needs a strong injection of masculinity (Neumann, 1954:39-169). The frequent result is machismo, which in most if not all cultures marks the "heroic" stage of consciousness, that is, the oral stage.

This oral stage of consciousness is concerned largely with exterior struggle. The *Iliad* is full of gore, quite competitive on this score with the most violent television productions today. Today we might concern ourselves with an imputed inner agony of soul that Achilles or Hector or Odysseus might suffer. Such agony is of no concern to Homer or his congeners. Indeed, as Havelock has shown (1963), there was no effective way for the Greek mind at the Homeric stage to deal explicitly with deep interior consciousness.

Male ritual combat, which governs so much of early narrative, is conspicuously external, however deeply interior its sources. Over the centuries, from classical to modern times, in narrative the incidence of this externally violent male combat diminishes, but gradually and slowly. Tales in which external agonistic activity yields to intense personalized interaction between individuals, usually a man and a woman, put in their appearance quite late. One of the earliest major narratives featuring such interaction comes from the Far East: the precocious *Tale of Genji* by Lady Murasaki Shikibu (978?-1026?), whose millennium has just passed. It is no coincidence that the author was a woman.

Contest and Interiorization

Shortly after, comparably interiorized narratives develop in the West as a "movement," on a large scale, with the courtly love tradition of the twelfth and subsequent centuries. Again, woman's influence is strong and essential: though the troubadours and their successors were males, they wrote largely for female audiences and commonly under the sponsorship of women, from Eleanor of Aquitaine and Marie of Champagne to Mary Sidney, countess of Pembroke. Nevertheless, in these stories interiorized personal interaction of lover and beloved is still intermingled with jousting and other boisterous and violent male external combat. Only some seven centuries later, when consciousness has appropriated the silent world of print sufficiently to produce the novel, could lengthy serious narrative be purely interiorized and domestic in locale and/or tone, totally freed of male ceremonial agonistic even when concerned with the lives of males. A Jane Austen novel or a Thomas Hardy novel is in the strict sense unthinkable as oral narrative or even as written narrative before print.

Lady Murasaki's males were fascinating refractions of an essentially and intensely feminine sensibility, exquisite projections. Novelists in the nineteenth-century West can portray male personality structures from the inside more directly, and that is exactly what they do, concerning themselves with intracacies of characterization, of both males and females, as for example in Dostoevski, unrealized earlier even in drama. Novels develop in full form only with the Romantic movement as a product of the interiorization encouraged and implemented by print (Ong, 1971:276-83; Ong, 1977a:286-92). They are little interested in masculine agonistic externalization, and, like romances earlier, are indeed written largely for female readers, even when their authors are men. Novels are also the first major verbal art forms to be produced by women in considerable numbers. Apparently the greater tolerance for the feminine in public life encouraged women's extradomestic activity, including writing for publication, and simultaneously encouraged public interest in the in-close, nonformalized, domestic woman's world, thereby fostering treatment of the entire human lifeworld, male as well as female, in a less ritualized, less agonistic, more directly interiorized fashion.

The continuing popularity of the in-close world of the novel and its derivatives is permanent evidence of the presence of a high overtly feminine charge in the modern psyche. Even the supergothic violence of Anthony Burgess's *A Clockwork Orange* is focused ultimately on the human interior: quintessential violence is calculatedly used to change the characters' state of consciousness. Indeed, the gothic style generally, while it treats of violence, does so to create atmosphere and mood, not to celebrate contest as such: most violence in gothic narrative is not agonistic. And gothic narrative has long been a specialty of women writers, from Ann Radcliffe and Mary Shelley down to Joyce Carol Oates.

Narrative centered on raw male combat, such as the Western or the typical television whodunit, is today usually regressive, for it can no longer be made to carry the serious psychic load of combat stories in oral cultures. The seeming exceptions in such novels as *Native Son* are dealt with at the end of this chapter. Violence as such today is trivial as a narrative ploy—which is one reason its use in the mass media comes under such constant attack. As one element in a deeply resonant psychological setting—such as that of Faulkner's *Absalom! Absalom!*—violence can be effective, but in the Lone Ranger's or Kojak's world it is meretricious. The more psychologically violent world of *Oedipus Rex* (a chirographic construct, composed in writing) has outlasted the more exteriorly violent oral world of the *Iliad*.

Contest and the Inward Turn of Scholarship

Scholarly, closely reasoned thinking, including nonfictional or historical narrative, has taken its own kinds of "inward turn," resulting a century and a half ago in Hegel's inward view of history as *Geistesgeschichte* (history of ideas) and in countless other related modes of thought, including psychoanalysis and the deep and careful introspection used in phenomenology and in personalist philosophy. But here again change has been slow. Like all other human activity, scholarly and scientific work shapes itself in great part by responding to unconscious needs. Even after writing had been interiorized in Western classical antiquity deeply enough to make possible history in something like the modern sense, as in Thucydides, historiographers continued, through no possible conspiracy but simply in the natural course of events, to serve the old need, always more unconscious than conscious, to heighten masculinity in its characteristically agonistic ambience. As a result, scholars today, such as Kenneth Neill Cameron in his *Humanity and Society* (1973), find ample cause to complain that, throughout the past, history has been written almost entirely as the record of the doings of prominent males.

In historiography's earlier stages the males whose records are being kept are typically and overtly engaged in spectacular contest. Early annals in Mesopotamia and Egypt were written largely to glorify military conquest or the triumph of ostentatious architectural work. Even when such historians as Herodotus and Thucydides produce something resembling cultural history or descriptive sociology, the whole is set in a general context of wars—wars with the Persians for Herodotus, the Peloponnesian War for Thucydides—and of such other agonistic activities as debates in public assemblies and diplomatic jousting (Barnes, 1937:3-40). The texts of the most analytic histories in antiquity often consist in great part of orations put into the mouths of historical characters. In the absence of a developed science of sociology or economics or cultural anthropology, the oration often was the best means to present issues in a sharpened, relatively abstract form. But the orations were normally polemic. In fact, their polemic pitch helped to sharpen their abstractions. The results in historiography are about the same as in epics: plenty of combative heroes and/or villains, few heroines, a dominance of external action over psychic subtleties. The Bible introduces a notable inwardness, but, as just noted, it is far more inward in later books than in earlier.

Several developments help to account for the shift in historiography from its early preoccupation with heroic masculine *agōn* to more interiorized, less overtly combative foci of attention. First, in historiography as in fictional narrative, highly polarized "heavy," heroic, combative type figures, which had been useful and necessary to manage the organization of knowledge in an oral culture, became less necessary and even interfered with the more complex categories encouraged by writing. Second, the success of technology in gaining control of the external world, the "environment," gave more confidence to masculinity, which, as has been seen, is driven even from before birth to fight environment in order to survive. With masculinity thus more secure and struggle less urgent, there was no need to be so programmatically macho in construing history, and thus life itself, as a series of male ceremonial combats. Finally, the technologies of writing and, more especially, print had implemented the accumulation of knowledge, making possible the development of new fields of study that eventually took shape as sociology, anthropology, economics, modern psychology, artistic, literary, religious, and intellectual history, and the like. These new fields of study provided a rich variety of consciously controlled categories for use in dealing with human action and thereby made obsolete heroic polarization of issues in grossly agonistic terms. Public disaster that used to be assessed as the result of personal disloyalty or the evil nature of one of the king's advisers was now understandable as the product of involved, but not entirely indescribable, sociological, psychological, economic, and other human factors. Fidel Castro's seemingly successful negotiation of the passage from oral agonistic to visualist objective analysis has been discussed in Chapter 5.

Older accounts of what was "going on" in existence tended to be simpler and more gripping and, by the same token, more agonistic than accounts in recent histories. Greeks versus barbarians, Romans versus Carthaginians or Gauls, settlers versus Indians—such dyads have wider appeal and are more manageable by the oral or residually oral mind than are analyses terminating in the complexities of psychohistory, individual or collective, and descending finally into analysis of "deep structures" and of stages of consciousness. Children today in their early, oral stages of development prefer agonistic to analytic presentations of history.

The inward turn in historiography is symptomatic of an inward turn marking the general development of explanatory thinking over the past few centuries. The Romantic movement, with its attention to the mysterious, the obscure, the hidden, the inside rather than the outside, manifests an inward turn. So does psychoanalysis, in which the inner "dark side" of existence breaks through into consciousness even more dramatically than in other romantic manifestations: consciousness directs its closest attention to the unconscious. Phenomenology, existentialism in its diverse forms, personalist philosophy, dialogic philosophy, and related currents of thought have undertaken to articulate descriptions of the psyche at interior depths previously inarticulable, though familiar to the unconscious. Even the physical sciences have brought the observer (who, in the last analysis, must be an interior consciousness) into consideration. In a remarkable work E. M. Barth (1974; see also Barth and Krabbe, in press) has shown that even formal logic is part of a personal, dialogic world from which it can never be completely detached. She has thus directly related the "distances" of formal logic itself to interior, personal awareness.

The present book is obviously a product of the same interiorizing movement that marks so many areas of thought today. It has considered contest, which originates biologically as quite externalized, directly observable behavior, not merely as a phenomenon in the arena of purely external activity but as something impinging on the interior development of human consciousness itself.

Contest, Consciousness, and the Self

Although contest has its roots in the infrahuman lifeworld, in our distant biological heritage, it is in significant ways more important for human beings than for other living creatures. For contest is related to "othering": even among infrahuman species it maximizes difference between individuals of the same species in the very process of maximizing their likeness and interaction. Because they are allied in being conspecifics, individuals of a species distance themselves from each other. In the interiority that characterizes the human person, this paradoxically intimate distancing is maximized. The human person is radically both more closed and more open than any other being, so that relationships between individuals become crucial in human existence at depths utterly unrealizable among infrahuman species.

The closure of human consciousness is most apparent in its reflectiveness, its being turned back on itself. This reflectiveness makes possible the saying of "I." For the "I" identifies itself by its self-awareness and by this alone. The "I" has no name. Others know me as Walter, but of myself and to myself I am no more Walter than I am Tom or Dick or Harry, however much I may have accustomed myself to referring to myself or being referred to as Walter. To myself, I am simply "I." This "I" I alone can find. A child grows into full self-consciousness slowly and usually or normally refers to himself or herself first by his or her own "given" name, which keeps the self at a distance from itself, and soon after by "me" (which is truly an objective case, treating the agent as passive recipient rather than originator of action). The child only gradually comes into the full possession of self signaled by the ability freely to say "I." Names—Cathy, Caroline, Cindy, Michael, Paul, Patrick—do not come from inside, from self-possession: they are stuck on, like labels on containers. They are assigned code marks such as can be fed into a computer. Names are "given," applied from outside, usually by others, and often refer the one bearing them to others (family and/or given names refer to father and/or mother, favorite aunt or uncle, family line, and so on). Because names are applied, thinglike, children are able to manage names before they can negotiate more reflectively with their own interiors, before their full individual human potential has been actualized, before they can reflectively find the "I" who he or she is.

Contest and Interiorization

In contrast to names, which are given from outside, what I refer to when I finally am able to say "I" comes to me from within. "I" is the most inward center of my consciousness, which only I can find. Mother or father cannot lead me to it or even point directly to it. When they point, it is at best to "me" (whom they call "you").

All others besides myself, even father and mother, can contact this "I" only indirectly, for they are in maximum contact with the "I" when they are in my presence and we are communicating—but then, to all but me, the "I" that I know as "I" is precisely not "I" but is inevitably "you." For full intimacy, "I" and "you" must be used, and names are put aside: "I love you," not "John loves Jane." In all conversation, names when they occur are always off to the side, adventitious, incidental, parenthetical, a fact indicated in writing by "setting off" (distancing) in commas: "I do not love thee, Dr. Fell." When names are introduced into a conversation, they inevitably to some degree distance the parties. Distancing may be human and desirable. But it does not work for lovers' intimacy: "I, John, love you, Jane" does not normally mean so much as "I love you." Law resorts to this sort of interjection of a name after "I" precisely to achieve the formal distance that law requires. "I, John Doe, do hereby . . . ."

The "I" is no incidental phenomenon in my consciousness. It is absolutely central. When I say "I," the "I" is in me and I am in the "I." "I" in a sense is all that I am, all of me. It is this "I" that I knew as myself from the first dawning of my consciousness as a very young child. It is present in all of my waking hours, and even in my dreams. No matter what else I attend to, what else I think of, it is always there alongside of or enveloping my thoughts. It flushes my being the moment I attend to it. I am unthinkable without this "I," though it is veiled from others. Its interiority is total, for female and male alike: neither is more closed or more open as an "I" than the other. Paul's famous denial of all distinctions in Galatians 3:28 (cf. Rom. 10:12; Col. 3:11), "There does not exist among you Jew or Greek, slave or freeman, male or female," is at root a recognition of the paramountcy of this "I" as the ground of what is most profoundly human and the ground of each human being's relation to God.

Each "I" is unique and knows that it is unique. I do not fear that one of the other four billion human beings in the world today might also be me. This "I" is not the sort of thing that admits of duplication. I know that simply in experiencing the "I."

Since others all say "I," I know that there must be something in them like what is in me, but since every "I" is totally different from every other, the likenesses are in a certain sense specious. In the deepest sense, we are all more alike in our bodies than in the "I" that each one of us says. Our bodies resemble those of our parents. The "I" that I say is not more like my mother's or father's "I" than it is like anyone else's. It is different totally from all. What is the body of one person can become the body of another, as a mother's milk does. But the "I" that the child at her breast will one day be able to say is as inaccessible to the mother as the "I" of a total stranger.

The "I" cannot be defined, broken down into constituent parts. For it is utterly simply as I know it, my model for all simplicity. When I conceive of a unit, a one, an individual separate from all else and one in itself, my model is this "I" in my own consciousness. Being individual, indivisible, is being in one way or another like this "I."

The "I" exists in a state of terrifying isolation. No matter how close another is to me, he or she can never break through into this center of my being, into what really matters. A husband and wife who have lived together in great love for fifty years so that they can read each other's thoughts are still separated here: the one does not know the direct experience of "I" which is the other. They may almost forget this fact, for the chasm that this situation opens and keeps open can be crossed and is crossed by love. But the chasm remains. We are divided from one another. The veil that separates each of us as a person from the other is never lifted in this life, though it may be pierced by love.

Contest and Interiorization

We cannot find this veiled person in infrahuman animals. They are not veiled, for they cannot turn in on themselves. They never say "I" or do anything to indicate their experience of an "I," although if we feel affection for favorite animal pets, we may like to pretend that they do. Significantly, very small children, whose sense of self, of "I," is less fully developed than the adult's, commonly experience a more overwhelming identification with animal pets. Animals live in a world that José Ortega y Gasset (1956:164-66) nicely identifies as a world of *alteración*, "otheration" or "othering," a world in which they are forever lost to themselves, fixated on the object world outside of themselves (which of course includes their own bodies as objects). The outward gaze has back of it no inward gaze. Rainer Maria Rilke writes of the horrible emptiness that the human gazer seeking response finds staring out from an animal's eye. Perhaps, some may argue, an infrahuman animal has a self-consciousness like that of a human being, only it does not show. But the reason you know that the animal does not have self-consciousness is precisely because it does not show. Reflective consciousness, deeply interior though it is, is essentially and irrepressibly self-manifesting. A reflectively self-conscious ape would share his self-consciousness with you, as even a tiny child does.

Paradoxically, because they are not reflexively aware of themselves, infrahuman animals cannot get as close to one another as human beings can. The dialectic of interior and exterior with which contest is engaged takes over here in its distinctively human form. Infrahuman animals cannot enter into one another's interiors, however indirectly, for they possess nothing veiled enough to be fully interior in the human sense. When chimpanzees are taught sign "language" to "speak" to one another, the real interlocutor for each chimpanzee is the human experimenter, who is deeper into each chimpanzee than the chimpanzee is and who alone sets up the arrangements. Only persons, deeply interiorized, secluded from one another, are truly able to share themselves reflectively—"I" with "you." Only beings isolated as human beings have anything to say. Only they can communicate. For communication is not mere passing of "information" as a commodity back and forth between "terminals." It is a movement from secret interior to secret interior. When I say something to you, I invite you to enter into my interior consciousness, and when you listen, you invite me to enter into yours. I listen as I speak to make sure I am speaking truly, and you form the words you hear as though you were speaking them to make sure they touch what is real. Mechanical transmission systems do not work this way.

Since we are isolated, in the sense just described, we cannot directly enter into one another's personal awareness. I cannot share your direct knowledge of yourself, nor can you share my direct knowledge of myself. The gap between our two inner selves cannot be closed. But we can bridge the gap, as we have seen, by love. All human communication, even the most vapid, involves some kind of love, communion, union, some regard for the other person as a person. This love may be so mingled with other attitudes, disdain, fear, brutality, that it becomes itself cruel. But it is there. Even shouted hostilities show some kind of union or affection between the clamorous enemies. Indeed, shouted hostilities are perhaps most common where there is most clearly an admixture of affection in the hostile relationship, as among members of a family group. When total hostility sets in, as has been seen, verbal communication ceases and the person is "cut," no longer addressed at all, treated as a thing.

It is precisely this isolated, closed human person, thrown back on himself or herself, who is also paradoxically the most open of beings. For persons have intelligence, are capable of intellectualized knowledge, and through such knowledge are open to the entire universe, to everything. Through their intelligence, women and men can take into themselves, in one way or another, all there is—which is not of course to say that they all do so or that even one of them ever does so, but only to say that the possibilities of knowledge open them to all the universe and all the universe to them. A human being is open closure—and thus is more than a "system," for no system can have such openness and such closure (Ong, 1977a:332-41).

Adversativeness in the Service of the Person

The ability to say "I," with the sense of self and of other and of community which the saying of "I" involves, marks off human from infrahuman animals. When in the series of anthropoids and prehominids some beings appeared who were capable of the reflective self-possession expressed in the saying of "I," at whatever point they did so, the leap into human existence had clearly taken place. Although we shall doubtless never be able to ascertain for ourselves exactly when this frontier into full reflectiveness was first crossed, whenever it was, beings whom we recognize as persons were present on the globe, each in reflective possession of himself or herself, savoring himself or herself as unique, totally other than all else, and yet prepared so far as possible to sweep all else into the circle of her or his unique consciousness—deep interiors of consciousness, through intelligence open to all. (You have to have an interior to be open.)

Open closure or open interiority has thus marked human beings from the beginning. But generations of reflection have made interiority more and more articulate about itself. The concept of person was gradually given articulate formation, beginning to shape up first in the early Christian centuries, when Christians experienced the need to define for themselves better what they meant in holding that the Three, Father, Son, and Holy Spirit, were one God. In the New Testament, these were clearly three different "I's" or "thou's," even though it was later worked out that, unlike human beings, each was fully aware of the interior of the other, fully present inside the other, as the Council of Florence (1438-45) would ultimately define (Denziger, 1947:704). The concept of person, missing from previous ancient Western philosophy in any fully articulated form and yielding ultimately the modern senses of this term, was worked up from the fourth century on to make more explicit the trading about the Three.

But here the concept of person was a rather specialized concern, centering on theological issues even though it involved the human in these issues, for in Christian teaching Jesus Christ is one person, though both human and divine. Very recent times have activated concern with the human person as person to a degree of explicitation unknown before, and that at many levels of awareness. At the highest level of speculative thinking such philosophers as Martin Buber and Gabriel Marcel and many phenomenologists have worked out self-consciously personalist philosophies. Such theologians as Hans Urs von Balthasar have pointed out that in the past, when nature overshadowed humanity, human beings had approached God through nature, whereas today, when technology has reduced nature's dominance and put human beings more over nature, philosophy has become anthropologized and tends to approach God through the human lifeworld and the human person. Existentialism is a by-product of the technological scenario.

At the social and operational levels, whole constellations of thought forms and expressions have emerged to turn around the concept of the person: personal relations, personal fulfillment, personal interaction, and other kinds of interpersonalism. These new thought forms have appeared together with widespread somewhat mythological concern about the "depersonalization" imputed to industrial and technological society. Obviously some sort of complementarity or compensation is at work here. For only high-technology cultures have given rise to personalist philosophies. To treat the person as person explicitly and in depth, thought must have been technologized by writing and print. And although one can indeed identify certain specific kinds of depersonalization that technology and industry can impose, it is of course quite impossible to show (Ong, 1978) that modern technological society is any more depersonalizing as a whole than earlier societies, which in myriads of ways were brutalizing, often built on slavery, by modern standards incredibly cruel and unfeeling in physical punishments—and yet, like all cultures, capable of humanizing, too. All known cultures have in one way or another depersonalized as well as personalized, so that no human culture has been worth preserving the way it was—though all have been worth improving. Earlier cultures, less able to analyze themselves than is a high-technology culture infused by thought processes made possible by the technologies of writing and print (and now electronics), were less explicit about both depersonalization and the personal problems of the human person.

The present focus of attention on the human person as such signals a deep reorganization of consciousness. This reorganization—which of course is not the only reorganization of consciousness discernible today but is a central reorganization—has implications for the role of contest in the future psychic development of human beings. For contest, as we have seen it here, has a particular bearing on both exteriority and interiority.

Ceremonial or ritual contest is certainly external, an exteriorized fracas—nothing is more exterior, more "out there," than the shattering head butting of two bighorn rams. But contest is also isolating and interiorizing. Warring peoples, engaged in basically nonritual combat, will normally directly enlist others on their side—the more allies the better. Those in ritual contest or games do not. A prizefighter cannot call his supporters into the ring to help him to subdue his opponent. The stag or ram engaged in ceremonial contest with another of its own kind is in it alone. Often enough, the rest of the herd simply stand by quietly awaiting the outcome. The *agōn* is normally a lonely struggle, from that of hercules beetles (Edward O. Wilson, 1975:321-24) to that of boxers in a ring. The contestants are thrown back on their own interior resources.

At the biological level, the isolated agonistic system is, however, closed only in order to open, for upon the outcome of the contest between loners in its maximized male-against-male form will depend the genetic constitution of future members of the species, the distribution of genotypes, who will mate with whom.

At the noetic level, a similar situation obtains. As explained in Chapter 4, in the classic disputation the defender was thrown back on his own resources. Everything had to come from within: exterior resources, such as notes, were not permitted. And as the objector attacked the defender, the rest of the audience sat back to hear how the disputants would comport themselves.

But this struggle based on interior resources had external effects. Intellectual combat made public many intellectual issues otherwise hidden or obscure, and clarified them. It made accessible publicly apprehensible truth. The potential of intellectual contest to disclose truth lay at the root of Socratic dialogue and lies at the root of the adversary procedure that still prevails in law to this day. The result of individual contest is thus felt outside of the individual contestants in others, in knowledge uttered (that is, etymologically, "outered"), knowledge shared.

With the inward turn of consciousness manifested in narrative, in scholarly work, and in the explicit attention to the person—the human interior—as person, the place of contest in the human lifeworld would be expected to shift. This is particularly true because of the relationship that contest can have in establishing individual identity, whether the all-out contest in male ritual combat that has been a principal focus of this book or other, less intense forms of contest that define one individual's relationship to others in terms of dominance or in related terms. The need of individuals to organize or define themselves by contest appears greater in the upper reaches of the animal kingdom. In a flock of chickens, hens will interact agonistically with one another to organize themselves in a pecking order in which each hen fits herself into a particular place in a dominance-submission hierarchy. But the hen on a modern egg farm has no peers to set herself against: each individual layer is isolated in a separate small pen so that pecking-order battles never occur—each hen, the sole inhabitant of her little kingdom, is by definition a nonpareil individual, an "alpha" hen (the dominant individual in a group). A hen in such a noncompetitive situation nevertheless appears to be well adjusted, a happy hen. She does not have to set herself against other fowls to achieve a sense of identity. Higher animals, such as chimpanzees, do. They must interact in patterns that include agonistic, though not necessarily hostile, activities (Van Lawick-Goodall and Hamburg, 1974:36-48). But most of all human beings must so interact.

When the human ego is threatened with dissolution, often there is nothing like a good nonlethal fight, a contest, to get it back together again, even if the contest is lost. This is particularly so when the psyche is threatened by dissolution merely from neglect, from being not noticed by others. Some of the forces at work here can be seen in the protest rhetoric of the 1960s.

By comparison with earlier ritualized combat, this protest rhetoric was likely to present itself as nonceremonial, confrontational, nonnegotiating, "for real," all-out, honoring no rules, a manifestation of existential desperation, prepared to be lethal. And there was an element of the nonceremonial, of anomie, in protest rhetoric, as has been suggested in Chapter 4. But very soon, if not from the start, protest rhetoric developed into a ritual performance. Surprisingly to some, it was the mass media, led by television, that implemented or even induced ritualization. Counting on media exposure, playing for such exposure, the protesters soon modulated their purportedly lethal rhetoric into a game, which generated its own rules.

The purpose of protest rhetoric, moreover, was intensely interiorized, calculated in depth—whatever its announced aims—not only to affect externals but even more to affect the interior consciousness of those engaging in the rhetoric. That is to say, with protest rhetoric particularly of the 1960s, the inward turn of consciousness manifests itself with particular poignancy. What does this mean?

A study by Richard B. Gregg, "The Ego-Function of the Rhetoric of Protest" (1971), has shown how groups that can feel themselves neglected, unattended to by others, generate an agonistic situation in order to call not merely the attention of others to their existence, but even more to call their own attention to their own existence. The groups studied were three from the 1960s in the United States: blacks, university and college student activists generally, and women's liberation activists. Examination of their agonistic protest statements shows that such statements were in fact largely "self-addressed" discourse, concerned with a definition of self, implemented by the setting of the self against others as enemies.

As explained in Chapter 4, the old ritualized adversativeness in society, particularly ritualized adversativeness in academic settings, had been eroded, and confrontation tended to become more destructive. But in the past certain relationships had included no provision at all even for ritualized adversativeness, as in black-white relationships, where blacks had been prevented even from poking fun publicly at whites (which could have been a form of ritualized adversativeness). The result was that blacks had a long history of feeling unnoticed. Like the "invisible man" of Ralph Ellison's novel, they felt passed over by the majority of their fellow citizens, who were white. Eventually, by a kind of refraction, blacks could feel themselves unimportant even to other blacks. Stokely Carmichael told the students at Morgan State College in 1967, "We have to learn to love and respect ourselves. That's where it should begin. That's where it must begin. Because if we don't love us, ain't nobody going to love us" (Gregg, 1971:76). Black is beautiful. Blacks had been trying to gain respectability and status or selfhood by imitating whites. What was needed now was adversativeness, Carmichael went on to point out. Whites had to be stood up to, boldly, not kowtowed to. In his "Message to the Grass Roots" (quoted in Gregg, 1971:81), Malcolm X protests:

> As long as the white man sent you to Korea, you bled. He sent you to Germany, you bled. He sent you to the South Pacific to fight the Japanese, you bled. You bleed for white people, but when it comes to seeing your own churches being bombed and little black girls murdered, you haven't got any blood. You bleed when the white man says bleed; you bite when the white man says bite; and you bark when the white man says bark.

The literature of women's liberation and of the student activists shows the same concern with building self-esteem and setting up oneself, or one's group, clearly in some kind of adversary relationship with another person or group. An adversary, if he or she is effective, is sure at least to be noticed.

Gregg concludes that rhetoric itself needs to be redefined. It has traditionally been discussed and justified in terms of moral ideals and "rational" discussion. Understanding a rhetorical transaction as one in which "a speaker undertakes to produce a message for the purpose of affecting the perceptions, beliefs, attitudes, and behaviors of a listener or group of listeners" (Gregg, 1971:72), Gregg contests the common view that rhetoric is to be understood solely in a setting of "moral ideals which presuppose the principles of 'rational discussion'" (p. 89). "Communicative intent" or "reasoning together" or even "feeling together" do not exhaust the "primary goals of men's and women's serious discourse" and do not yield a plausible explanation of protest rhetoric, which is a real phenomenon to be accounted for, too. Rhetoric is turned inward as well as outward. Thus rhetorical contest itself has lately been conspicuously redirected inward to the human person, as so much else in life today is.

Gregg has pointed out what we all should have known: every address to another is also an address to oneself. The ego-building functions of rhetoric are as real as its exteriorizing, rational functions—and, it might be added, not necessarily in collision with the rational functions. For rationality has no existence of its own: it is always tied to elements it has not processed. Rhetoric has both rational and infrarational, more primitive roots—as in fact all discourse and all thought do. It serves the purpose of giving a person self-possession by setting him or her firmly against an "other." As with the Kabyle, the challenge or response to challenge is by no means totally hostile: it is a complement, affirming the value of the other as well as one's own value. No one challenges a nonentity.

In identifying a function of rhetorical contest central to contemporary consciousness, Gregg supports the contention of the present work—a work that I am sure is profoundly rhetorical, and which has come into being because, in many deep ways for the most part even now still unconscious, it helps to establish and affirm the identity of the author as well as, I trust, to serve the cause of truth, without which nothing is really established or affirmed. The present work contends that contest has been and seemingly will remain a constituent of human existence, if in constantly adjusting forms, from the biological base of this existence to its noetic peaks. Contest comes to human kind out of the race's distant evolutionary past and enters even into the intimacies and ecstasies of self-consciousness.

In *Burnt Norton* T. S. Eliot has deftly caught the distance and the intimacies in a few beautifully nostalgic Darwinian lines about his own past and everybody's past:

> The trilling wire in the blood
> Sings below inveterate scars
> And reconciles forgotten wars.
> The dance along the artery
> The circulation of the lymph
> Are figured in the drift of stars
> Ascend to summer in the tree
> We move about the moving tree
> In light upon the figured leaf
> And hear upon the sodden floor
> Below, the boarhound and the boar
> Pursue their pattern as before
> But reconciled among the stars.

As the ancients well knew and as the European Renaissance liked to remind itself, the human being is a microcosm, the "little world," representing the macrocosm or "great world," the universe. We know now that the human being is the peak of the organic evolution in which cosmic evolution culminates—and indeed even more than the peak, for the human person, woman or man, in his or her ineffable sense of self, his or her interiority, the "I" that each utters and that is more than a name, is a leap beyond organic evolution, a leap into the full reflective consciousness that has no ascertainable organic source, although it has an organic base on which it depends and from which it operates, a leap that is alluded to in the Hebreo-Christian tradition by the teaching that, transcending the rest of the universe, we are made not only of matter but also in the image and likeness of God. In the human lifeworld, contest catches up some of the lowest dynamics and some of the highest. It is a genetically advantageous factor in organic evolution, indeed in the large an absolutely indispensable factor, one that is the product of natural selection, and thus part of humankind's genetic heritage, linking us to lower forms of life and them to us. But it is also at the same time an element in humankind's intellectual development, our development of abstract thought, of noetic distance, and, even beyond that, in the development of the identity of individual human persons, male and female, in finding one's own person, in saying "I."

Connections with the biological do not subvert human freedom any more than they subvert human thought. Human beings make free decisions, but to understand these decisions and indeed even to make them more humanly and effectively we must understand the base on which they are made. Our free choice can work only with the given: we cannot create the world in which we exercise free choice. We cannot freely choose to have a history other than that which we actually come from. The present study has attempted to detail some of the history that establishes the ground on which we stand, with particular attention to the relationship between developments in human consciousness and the biological world.

Contest is not only a part of humankind's past but also a part of the future evolution of consciousness itself. How it will serve the future remains to be seen. I have treated it here largely in terms of male ceremonial contest, not only because this is, biologically, sociologically, and noetically, the paradigmatic form of contest, but also because the evidence regarding contest coming to us from the past 5,000 years comes from an intensely masculinizing period in psychic history. The new roles of women in academic and public life and elsewhere will certainly complicate matters greatly. The complications will be all the greater because it appears quite impossible to do away with the relatively greater biological and psychological insecurity of males on which their peculiar predisposition to spectacular forms of contest is in so great part founded. Nor do I see any reason why it would be even desirable to do away with this peculiar male insecurity or to undertake to convey it to females—though we, men and women, are, it seems, willy-nilly conveying to females something related to it, and in the process learning that insecurity is by no means fun, though it may be tremendously productive.

Whatever their continuing differences in relation to contest, males and females will be interacting—are already interacting—with a feminine world and feminine forces differently than they did in the past, though in ways never discontinuous with the past. In *The Feminization of American Culture* (1977) Ann Douglas has provided some deep insights into the paradoxes already manifest in the nineteenth century as woman's power in society shifted and increased with the growth of industrialization, commercialization, and mass culture, and has suggested some of the ambiguities that lie ahead in female-male relationships. Beatrice Bruteau, in "Neo-Feminism and the Next Revolution of Consciousness" (1977), conjectures, as many others have conjectured, that the future holds promise of a new synthesis of masculine and feminine, different from earlier syntheses and more comprehensive, and different for men and women. No doubt it does, and inevitably: every age has been marked by a new synthesis of masculine and feminine. The entire history of consciousness can be plotted in relation to the always ongoing male-female dialectic. Any new synthesis will certainly be different, for the synthesis has been different in every age. Whether the new synthesis will be more different from its past than earlier new syntheses have been from their pasts remains to be seen. This book has not undertaken to assemble or reflect on all of the data relevant to the evolution of consciousness or to relations between the sexes but only on some data that relate to contest

Contest and Interiorization

(which, it will be well to recall, is not exactly the same as aggression or conflict or war).

If in the evolution of consciousness we include the growth of consciousness out of the unconscious, it is evidently impossible completely, or even significantly, to plan what the next stage of consciousness will be. Consciously developed plans may affect the next stage of consciousness but they themselves will not define it. What will define the new stages will be their relationship not simply to our conscious planning but, more basically, their relationship to the unconscious organization underlying our conscious planning. We had better do our conscious planning humbly, paying attention not only to what we think we can make ourselves to be but to what we really are. Out of what we are, and our relationship to what we are, comes the future. Discovering what we are and acknowledging what we are has never been easy for human beings. It is always an ongoing project. This book is intended as a contribution to our unfinished business.

References

Abrahams, Roger D. 1967. "The Shaping of Folklore Traditions in the British West Indies." *Journal of Inter-American Studies* 9:456-80.

———. 1968a. "Introductory Remarks to a Rhetorical Theory of Folklore." *Journal of American Folklore* 81:143-58.

———. 1968b. "Public Drama and Common Values in Two Caribbean Islands." *Trans-action* (Washington University, St. Louis), pp. 62-71.

———. 1972. "The Training of the Man of Words in Talking Sweet." *Language in Society* 1:15-29.

———. 1975. "Negotiating Respect: Patterns of Presentation among Black Women." *Journal of American Folklore* 88:58-80.

Alcock, John. 1975. *Animal Behavior: An Evolutionary Approach*. Sunderland, Mass.: Sinauer Associates.

Ardrey, Robert. 1967. *The Territorial Imperative: A Personal Inquiry into the Animal Origins of Property and Nations*. New York: Athenaeum. Though Ardrey is not a professional biologist, this book is highly informative on many points and no more romanticized than some ecological and behavioral studies by some professionals.

Ariès, Philippe. 1962. *Centuries of Childhood: A Social History of Family Life*. Translated from the French by Robert Baldick. New York: Alfred A. Knopf.

Ascham, Roger. 1967. *The Schoolmaster* (1570). Ed. Lawrence W. Ryan. Ithaca, N.Y.: Cornell University Press.

Auerbach, Erich. 1957. *Mimesis: The Representation of Reality in Western Literature*. Translated from the German by Willard Trask. Garden City, N.Y.: Doubleday Anchor Books. First published in Berne, Switzerland, 1946, by A. Francke.

Baldick, Robert. 1965. *The Duel: A History of Duelling*. London: Chapman & Hall. The Irish *code duello* appears on pp. 34-36.

Balthasar, Hans Urs von. 1972. *Die Wahrheit ist symphonisch*. Einsiedeln: Johannes Verlag.

References

Bardwick, Judith M. 1971. *Psychology of Women: A Study of Bio-Cultural Conflicts*. New York: Harper & Row. To avoid multiplication of references to the many and scattered works that Bardwick cites and pulls together, in the present work reference is often made simply to Bardwick, 1971, through which the various works directly relevant to the matter in hand can be traced.

Barnes, Harry Elmer. 1937. *A History of Historical Writing*. Norman: University of Oklahoma Press.

Barnett, Samuel Anthony. 1963. *The Rat: A Study in Behavior*. Chicago: Aldine.

Barth, E. M. 1974. *The Logic of the Articles in Traditional Philosophy: A Contribution to the Study of Conceptual Structures*. Translated from the Dutch by E. M. Barth and T. C. Potts. Synthèse Historical Library, vol. 10. Dordrecht and Boston: D. Reidel.

Barth, E. M., and E. C. W. Krabbe. "Formal$_3$ Dialectics: Language-Invariant Systems for the Resolution of Avowed Opinion." *Studia Semiotyczne* (Warsaw). In press.

Biebuyck, Daniel, and Kahombo C. Mateene, eds. and trans. 1971. *The Mwindo Epic from the Banyanga* [as performed by Candi Rureke]. Berkeley: University of California Press.

Bochenski, I. M. 1961. *A History of Formal Logic*. Trans. and ed. Ivo Thomas. Notre Dame, Ind.: University of Notre Dame Press.

Bohannan, Paul. 1967a. *Law and Warfare*. Garden City, N.Y.: Natural History Press for the American Museum of Natural History.

———. 1967b. "Drumming the Scandal among the Tiv." In *Law and Warfare*, ed. Paul Bohannan, pp. 262-65. Garden City, N.Y.: Natural History Press for the American Museum of Natural History.

Bolgar, R. R. 1958. *The Classical Heritage and Its Beneficiaries*. Cambridge, Eng.: Cambridge University Press.

Bonner, Stanley F. 1977. *Education in Ancient Rome: From the Elder Cato to the Younger Pliny*. Berkeley: University of California Press.

Boorstin, Daniel J. 1965. *The Americans: The National Experience*. New York: Random House.

Bourdieu, Pierre. 1966. "The Sentiment of Honour in Kabyle Society." In *Honour and Shame: The Values of Mediterranean Society*, ed. J. G. Peristiany, pp. 171-90. Chicago: University of Chicago Press.

Bruteau, Beatrice. 1977. "Neo-Feminism and the Next Revolution of Consciousness." *Cross Currents* 27:170-82.

Caillois, Roger. 1961. *Man, Play, and Games*. Translated from the French by Meyer Barash. New York: Free Press of Glencoe.

Cameron, Kenneth Neill. 1973. *Humanity and Society*. Bloomington: Indiana University Press.

References

Camus, Albert. 1956. *The Stranger (L'Etranger)*. Translated from the French by Stuart Gilbert. New York: Vintage Books.

Carthy, J. D., and F. J. Ebeling. 1964. *The Natural History of Aggression*. Proceedings of a Symposium held at the British Museum (Natural History), London, October 21-22, 1963. London and New York: Academic Press.

Castro, Fidel. 1970. "This Shame Will Be Welcome... : A Speech by Fidel Castro" [delivered July 26, 1970], translated from the Spanish with Introduction by Lee Lockwood. *New York Review of Books*, September 24, pp. 18-32.

Chambers, R[aymond] W. 1958. *Thomas More*. Ann Arbor: University of Michigan Press. First published London: Jonathan Cape, 1935.

Chapman, Valentine J. 1974. "Algae." *New Encyclopaedia Britannica: Macropedia* I:490, 496.

Chess Life and Review. 1977. New Windsor, N.Y.: United States Chess Federation 36, no. 12.

Cole, Charles J. 1978. "The Value of Virgin Birth." *Natural History* 87, no. 1:56-63.

Curtius, Ernst Robert. 1953. *European Literature and the Latin Middle Ages*. Translated from the German by Willard R. Trask. Bollingen Series, vol. 36. New York: Pantheon.

Dainville, François de. 1940. *La géographie des humanistes*. Paris; rpt. Geneva: Slatkine Reprints, 1969.

Dempsey, Bernard W. 1943. *Interest and Usury*. Washington, D.C.: American Council on Public Affairs.

Denenberg, Victor H. 1969. "Animal Studies of Early Experience: Some Principles Which Have Implications for Human Development." In *Minnesota Symposia on Child Psychology*, vol. 3, ed. John P. Hill, pp. 31-42. Minneapolis: University of Minnesota Press.

Dengler, Ralph, S.J. 1971. "Hot and Cool Catechesis: A Content Analysis of Technological Determinism in Selected Sixteenth-Century and Twentieth-Century Texts Based on the General Inquirer System." Ph.D. dissertation, New York University. Ann Arbor, Mich.: Xerox University Microfilms. Tests four hypotheses extracted from the writings of Marshall McLuhan, Harold Innes, and Walter Ong.

Denziger, Henricus, Clemens Bannwart, Ioannes B. Umbero, and Carolus Rahner, eds. 1947. *Enchiridion symbolorum definitionum et declarationum de rebus fidei et morum*. 31st ed. Freiburg-im-Breisgau: Herder.

Dillard, J. R. 1972. *Black English: Its History and Use in the United States*. New York: Random House.

Dollard, John, et al. 1939. *Frustration and Aggression*. New Haven: Yale University Press for the Institute of Human Relations; London: Humphrey Milford, Oxford University Press.

References

Douglas, Ann. 1977. *The Feminization of American Culture*. New York: Alfred A. Knopf.
Duncan, Beverly, and Otis Dudley Duncan. 1978. *Sex Typing and Social Roles*. With the collaboration of James A. McRae, Jr. New York: Academic Press.
Duncan, Otis Dudley, David L. Featherman, and Janet T. Spence. 1979. "Sex Typing and Achievement in American Women." Stated Meeting Report, *Bulletin of the American Academy of Arts and Sciences* 32, no. 5:19-36.
Durand, Gilbert. 1960. *Les structures anthropologiques de l'imaginaire*. Paris: Press Universitaires de France.
Eby, Frederick, and Charles Flinn Arrowood. 1934. *The Development of Modern Education*. New York: Prentice-Hall.
Eibl-Eibesfeldt, Irenäus. 1970. *Ethology: The Biology of Behavior*. Translated from the German by Erich Klinghammer. New York: Holt, Rinehart & Winston.
Ellis, Joseph, and Robert Moore. 1974. *School for Soldiers: West Point and the Profession of Arms*. New York: Oxford University Press.
Erikson, Erik. 1963. *Childhood and Society*. 2d ed., rev. New York: W. W. Norton.
Euripides. 1970. *The Bacchae*. Translated from the Greek by Geoffrey S. Kirk. Englewood Cliffs, N.J.: Prentice-Hall.
Ewer, R. F. 1968. *Ethology of Mammals*. New York: Plenum Press; London: Logos Press.
Ewing, Arthur W. 1977. "Communication in Dyptera." In *How Animals Communicate*, ed. Thomas A. Sebeok, pp. 403-17. Bloomington: Indiana University Press.
Farrell, Thomas J. 1979. "The Female and Male Modes of Rhetoric." *College English* 40:909-21.
Faulkner, William. 1954. *The Portable Faulkner*. Ed. Malcolm Cowley. New York: Viking Press. Contains *The Bear*, pp. 227-363; *Spotted Horses*, pp. 367-439; and Faulkner's own Appendix, pp. 737-56.
Freilich, Morris. 1977. "Lévi-Strauss' Myth of Method." In *Patterns in Oral Literature*, ed. Heda Jason and Dimitri Segal, pp. 223-49. The Hague: Mouton.
Friday, Nancy. 1978. *My Mother / My Self*. New York: Dell.
Galloway, K. Bruce, and Robert Bowie Johnson, Jr. 1973. *West Point: America's Power Fraternity*. New York: Simon & Schuster. A somewhat alarmist, journalistic work, but filled with useful information about Beast Barracks procedures and other stress-inducing situations.
Gardner, Howard. 1978. "What We Know (and Don't Know) about the Two Halves of the Brain." *Harvard Magazine* 80, no. 4 (March-April):24-27. A knowledgeable and helpful assessment, distinguishing what is scientifically known from what is merely asserted in more popularized accounts.

References

Geertz, Clifford. 1972. "Deep Play: Notes on the Balinese Cockfight." *Daedalus: Journal of the American Academy of Arts and Sciences*, Winter. Issued as vol. 101, no. 1, of *Proceedings of the American Academy of Arts and Sciences*, pp. 1-37.

Gilbert, Sandra M. 1979. "Literary Paternity." *Cornell Review*, no. 6 (Summer 1979):54-65.

Gilley, H. M., and C. S. Summers. 1970. "Sex Differences in the Use of Hostile Verbs." *Journal of Psychology* 76:33-37.

Goody, Jack [John Rankine], ed. 1968. *Literacy in Traditional Societies*. Cambridge, Eng.: Cambridge University Press.

———. 1977. *The Domestication of the Savage Mind*. Cambridge, Eng.: Cambridge University Press.

Gouldner, Alvin W. 1965. *Enter Plato: Classical Greece and the Origins of Social Theory*. New York and London: Basic Books.

Gregg, Richard B. 1971. "The Ego-Function of the Rhetoric Protest." *Philosophy and Rhetoric* 4:71-91.

Grotjahn, Martin. 1957. *Beyond Laughter*. New York: Blekiston Divison, McGraw-Hill.

Harlow, Harry F., and Margaret Kuenne Harlow. 1962. "Social Deprivation in Monkeys." *Scientific American* 207, no. 5 (November 1962):136-46.

Havelock, Eric A. 1963. *Preface to Plato*. Cambridge, Mass.: Belknap Press of Harvard University Press.

———. 1978. "The Alphabetization of Homer." In *Communication Arts in the Ancient World*, ed. Eric A. Havelock and Jackson P. Herschell, pp. 3-21. New York: Hastings House.

Heagle, John L. 1973. "Conflict Resolution and the Future of Man: The Perspective of Teilhard de Chardin." *American Benedictine Review* 24:46-58.

Hediger, H[eine]. 1955. *Studies in the Psychology and Behavior of Captive Animals in Zoos and Circuses*. Translated from the German by Geoffrey Sircom. London: Butterworths Scientific Publications.

Heinrich, Bernd, and George A. Bartholomew. 1979. "The Ecology of the African Dung Beetle." *Scientific American* 241, no. 5 (November):146-56.

Hennig, Margaret, and Anne Jardim. 1977. *The Managerial Woman*. New York: Anchor Press.

Hibbert, Christopher. 1963. *The Roots of Evil: A Social History of Crime and Punishment*. London: Weidenfeld & Nicolson.

Hofling, Charles K. 1978. "Notes on Camus's *L'Étranger*." In *The Human Mind Revisited: Essays in Honor of Karl A. Menninger*, ed. Sidney Smith, pp. 159-203. New York: International Universities Press.

Hofstadter, Richard, and C. DeWitt Hardy. 1952. *The Development and Scope of Higher Education in the United States*. New York and London: Columbia

References

University Press for the Commission on Financing Higher Education.

Holliman, Jennie. 1931. *American Sports (1785-1835)*. Rpt. Philadelphia: Porcupine Press, 1975.

Howell, Wilbur Samuel. 1971. *Eighteenth-Century British Logic and Rhetoric*. Princeton: Princeton University Press.

Hrdy, Sarah Blaffer, and William Bennett. 1979. "The Fig Connection." *Harvard Magazine* 82, no. 1 (September-October):24-30.

Huizinga, Johan. 1955. *Homo Ludens: A Study of the Play Element in Culture*. Boston: Beacon Press. Translated from the 1944 German edition. Author's Foreword dated 1938.

Hunt, David. 1970. *Parents and Children in History: The Psychology of Family Life in Early Modern France*. New York and London: Basic Books.

Isaacs, Harold R. 1978. "Bringing Up the Father Question." *Daedalus: Journal of the American Academy of Arts and Sciences*, Fall, *Generations*. Issued as vol. 107, no. 4, of *Proceedings of the American Academy of Arts and Sciences*, pp. 188-202.

Jakobson, Roman, C. G. M. Fant, and Morris Halle. 1969. *Preliminaries to Speech Analysis: The Distinctive Features and Their Correlates*. Cambridge, Mass.: M.I.T. Press.

Jencks, Christopher, and David Riesman. 1967. "The War between the Generations." *Teachers College Record* 69:1-21. This article became part of chap. 2 in the authors' book *The Academic Revolution* (Garden City, N.Y.: Doubleday, 1968).

Kahler, Erich. 1973. *The Inward Turn of Narrative*. Translated from the German by Richard and Clara Winston. Princeton: Princeton University Press.

Kierkegaard, Søren. 1968. *Fear and Trembling and The Sickness Unto Death*. Translated with an Introduction and Notes by Walter Lowrie. Princeton: Princeton University Press.

King, W. G. 1970. "Sex Differences in the Perception of Friendly and Unfriendly Interactions." *British Journal of Social and Clinical Psychology* 9:212-15.

Kligerman, Jack. 1978. "'Pigeon Mumblers' of Brooklyn Wage *Guerra* in the Skys," with photographs by Alfred Eisenstaedt. *Smithsonian* 9, no. 2 (May):74-81.

Lakoff, Robin. 1977. "You Say What You Are: Acceptability and Gender-Related Language." In *Acceptability in Language*, ed. Sidney Greenbaum, pp. 73-86. Contributions to the Sociology of Language, vol. 17. The Hague: Mouton.

Larson, Donald R. 1977. *The Honor Plays of Lope de Vega*. Cambridge, Mass., and London: Harvard University Press.

Leo I, Pope St. 1948. *Sermo I de Nativitate Domini*, in *Breviarum romanum*, *pars hiemalis*, pp. 393-94. Rome, Tournai, Paris: Typic Societatis S. Joannis Evangelistae, Desclée et Socii.

Lerner, Harriet E. 1974. "Early Origins of Envy and Devaluation of Women: Implications for Sex Role Stereotypes." *Bulletin of the Menninger Clinic* 38:535-53.

Levenson, Joseph E. 1964-1966. *Confucian China and Its Modern Fate*. 3 vols. Berkeley: University of California Press.

Lévi-Strauss, Claude. 1969. *The Raw and the Cooked: Introduction to a Science of Mythology*, vol. 1. Translated from the French by J. and D. Weightman. New York: Harper & Row.

Liturgia horarum iuxta ritum Romanum. 1975. 4 vols. Rome: Typis Polyglottis Vaticanis. First published 1971. (English version: *Liturgy of the Hours*.)

Lloyd, G[eoffrey] E[dward] R[ichard]. 1966. *Polarity and Analogy: Two Types of Argumentation in Early Greek Thought*. Cambridge, Eng.: Cambridge University Press.

Lockwood, Lee. See Castro, Fidel.

Lorenz, Konrad. 1966. *On Aggression*. Translated from the German by Marjorie Kerr Wilson. New York: Harcourt Brace & World.

Lyman, Stanford M. 1978. "The Acceptance, Rejection, and Reconstruction of Histories: On Some Controversies in the Study of Social and Cultural Change." In *Structure, Consciousness, and History*, ed. Richard Harvey Brown and Stanford M. Lyman, pp. 53-105. Cambridge, Eng., and New York: Cambridge University Press.

Lynn, Robert Wood. 1973. "Civil Catechetics in Mid-Victorian America: Some Notes about American Civil Religion, Past and Present." *Religious Education* 68:5-27.

Mahler, Margaret S. 1965. "On the Significance of the Normal Separation-Individuation Phase: With Reference to Research in Symbiotic Child Psychosis." In *Drives, Affects, Behavior*, vol. 2, *Essays in Memory of Marie Bonaparte*, ed. Max Schur, pp. 161-69. New York: International Universities Press.

———. 1971. "A Study of the Separation-Individuation Process and Its Possible Application to Borderline Phenomena in the Psychoanalytic Situation." In *The Psychoanalytic Study of the Child*, vol. 26, ed. Ruth Eissler. New York: Quadrangle Books.

——— and Manuel Furer. 1963. "Certain Aspects of the Separation-Individuation Phase." *Psychoanalytic Quarterly* 32:1-14.

Manning, Frank E. 1973. *Black Clubs in Bermuda: Ethnography of a Play World*. Ithaca and London: Cornell University Press.

Mark, Hans. 1975. "New Enterprises in Space." *Bulletin of the American Academy of Arts and Sciences* 28, no. 4 (January):14-26.

References

Maspero, Henri. 1928. "Notes sur la logique de Mo-tsen et de son école." *T'oung Pao* 25:1-64.

Mayhew, The Brothers [Henry and Athol]. 1848. *The Image of His Father, or One Boy Is More Trouble than a Dozen Girls, Being a Tale of a "Young Monkey."* London: A. Hurst.

Mead, Margaret. 1967. "A National Service System as a Solution to a Variety of National Problems." In *Draft: A Handbook of Facts and Alternatives*, ed. Sol Tax. Chicago: University of Chicago Press.

Meerlo, Joost A. M. 1961. *The Difficult Peace*. Great Neck, N.Y.: Channel Press.

Meissner, William W. 1971. "Toward a Theology of Human Aggression." *Journal of Religion and Health* 10:324-32.

Merton, Robert K. 1968. "Making It Scientifically," a review of James D. Watson, *The Double Helix: A Personal Account of the Discovery of the Structure of DNA* (New York: Atheneum, 1968). *New York Times Book Review*, February 25, 1968, pp. 1, 42-45.

Midgley, Mary. 1978. *Beast and Man: The Roots of Human Nature*. Ithaca: Cornell University Press.

Mitre Corporation. 1979. *Security and the Small Business Retailer*. A handbook prepared by the Mitre Corporation. Washington, D.C.: Law Enforcement Assistance Administration.

Money, John. 1965. "Psychosexual Differentiation." In *Sex Research: New Developments*, ed. John Money, pp. 3-23. New York: Holt, Rinehart & Winston.

Morison, Samuel Eliot. 1936. *Harvard College in the Seventeenth Century*. Cambridge, Mass.: Harvard University Press.

Muller, Kal. 1970. "Land Diving with the Pentecost Islanders" (with photographs by the author). *National Geographic Magazine* 138:796-811.

Murasaki [Shikibu], Lady. 1935. *The Tale of Genji: A Novel in Four Parts*. Translated from the Japanese by Arthur Waley. New York: Literary Guild. In his Introduction, pp. vii-xvi, Waley quotes from Lady Murasaki's *Diary*, Hakubunkwan text.

Murphy, Robert F. 1959. "Social Structure and Sex Antagonism." *Southwestern Journal of Anthropology* 15:89-98.

Mwindo Epic. See Biebuyck and Mateene.

Neumann, Erich. 1954. *The Origins and History of Consciousness*. With a Foreword by C. G. Jung. Translated from the German by R. F. C. Hull. Bollingen Series, vol. 42. New York: Pantheon Books.

Oliver, Robert T. 1971. *Communication and Culture in Ancient India and China*. Syracuse, N.Y.: Syracuse University Press.

Ong, Walter J. 1954. "Ramus: Rhetoric and the Pre-Newtonian Mind." In *English Institute Essays, 1952*, ed. Alan S. Downer, pp. 138-70. New York: Columbia University Press.

References

---. 1956. "System, Space, and Intellect in Renaissance Symbolism." *Bibliothèque d'Humanisme et Renaissance* (Geneva) 18:222:39.

---. 1958a. *Ramus and Talon Inventory.* Cambridge, Mass.: Harvard University Press.

---. 1958b. *Ramus, Method, and the Decay of Dialogue: From the Art of Discourse to the Art of Reason.* Cambridge, Mass.: Harvard University Press.

---. 1967. *The Presence of the Word: Some Prolegomena for Cultural and Religious History.* The Terry Lectures. New Haven and London: Yale University Press.

---. 1969. "Communications Media and the State of Theology." *Cross Currents* 19:462-80.

---. 1971. *Rhetoric, Romance, and Technology: Studies in the Interaction of Expression and Culture.* Ithaca and London: Cornell University Press.

---. 1974. "Agonistic Structures in Academia: Past to Present." *Interchange: A Journal of Education* 5:1-12. An earlier abridgement of this article appeared under the same title in *Daedalus: Journal of the American Academy of Arts and Sciences,* Fall 1974, issued as vol. 103, no. 4, of the *Proceedings of the American Academy of Arts and Sciences,* pp. 229-38.

---. 1977a. *Interfaces of the Word: Studies in the Evolution of Consciousness and Culture.* Ithaca and London: Cornell University Press.

---. 1977b. "Truth in Conrad's Darkness." *Mosaic: A Journal for the Comparative Study of Literature and Ideas* 11:151-63.

---. 1978. "Technology Outside Us and Inside Us." *Communio* 5:100-121.

Opland, Jeff [Jeffrey]. 1975. "*Imbongi Nezibongo:* The Xhosa Tribal Poet and the Contemporary Poetic Tradition." *PMLA* 90:185-208.

Oppenheim, A. Leo. 1975. "The Position of the Intellectual in Mesopotamian Society." *Daedalus: Journal of the American Academy of Arts and Sciences,* Spring 1975, issued as vol. 104, no. 2, of *Proceedings of the American Academy of Arts and Sciences,* pp. 37-46.

Ortega y Gasset, José. 1956. *The Dehumanization of Art and Other Writings on Art and Culture.* Garden City, N.Y.: Doubleday.

Patai, Raphael. 1973. *The Arab Mind.* New York: Scribner's.

Paton, Alan. 1953. *Too Late the Phalarope.* London: Jonathan Cape.

Peck, George W. 1883. *Peck's Bad Boy and His Pa.* Chicago: Belford Clarke. Enl. ed., Chicago: C. B. Beach, 1883.

Peirce, Charles Sanders. 1931-58. *Collected Papers.* Ed. Charles Hartshorne, Paul Weiss, and A. W. Burks. 8 vols. Cambridge, Mass.: Harvard University Press.

Peristiany, J. G., ed. 1966. *Honour and Shame: The Values of Mediterranean Society.* Chicago: University of Chicago Press.

Pius IX. 1947. "Syllabus complectens praecipuos nostrae aetatis errores." In Denziger et al., 1947.

References

Polanyi, Michael. 1958. *Personal Knowledge*. Chicago: University of Chicago Press.

———. 1966. *The Tacit Dimension*. Garden City, N.Y.: Doubleday.

Rans, Laurel. 1977. *Population Profiles: Iowa Women's Reformatory, 1918-1975*. Pittsburgh: Entropy Limited. A study conducted under Rans's direction by the Pittsburgh consulting firm Entropy Limited and reported on in an article by Lisa Berger, "Profile of the Woman Criminal," *Parade*, July 24, 1977, pp. 7 and 9.

Reik, Theodor. 1957. *Of Love and Lust: On the Psychoanalysis of Romantic and Sexual Emotions*. New York: Farrar, Straus & Cudahy.

Richardson, Lewis F. 1960. *Statistics of Deadly Quarrels*. Pittsburgh and Chicago: Quadrangle Books. See esp. "The Fewness of Wars between Chinese," pp. 240-42.

Robertson, Windham. 1978. "Women M.B.A.'s, Harvard '73—How They're Doing." *Fortune* 76, no. 4 (August 28):50-60.

Rochlin, Gregory. 1973. *Man's Aggression: The Defense of the Self*. Boston: Gambit.

Schneidau, Herbert N. 1977. *Sacred Discontent: The Bible and Western Tradition*. Berkeley: University of California Press.

Scott, John Paul. 1958. *Aggression*. Ed. Peter P. H. DeBruyn. Chicago: University of Chicago Press.

Sebeok, Thomas A., ed. 1977. *How Animals Communicate*. Bloomington: Indiana University Press.

Seigel, Jerrold E. 1968. *Rhetoric and Philosophy in Renaissance Humanism*. Princeton: Princeton University Press.

Shull, A. Franklin. 1965. "Parthenogenesis." *Encyclopaedia Britannica* 17:338-41.

Simon, Rita James. 1975. *Women and Crime*. Lexington, Mass.: Lexington Books.

Smith, Arthur L., ed. 1972. *Language, Communication, and Rhetoric in Black America*. New York: Harper & Row.

Smith, J[oe] W[illiam] Ashley. 1954. *The Birth of Modern Education: The Contribution of the Dissenting Academies, 1660-1800*. London: Independent Press.

Spitzer, Leo. 1968. *Essays in Historical Semantics*. New York: Russell & Russell (rpt. of 1948). See esp. chap. 1, "Muttersprache und Mutterziehung," pp. 15-65. Chaps. i-iii of this book are in German, chaps. iv-vi in English.

Sports Illustrated 50, no. 7 (February 15, 1979; special issue, "The Year in Sports").

Stoller, Robert J., M.D. 1968. *Sex and Gender: On the Development of Masculinity and Femininity*. New York: Science House.

References

Storr, Anthony. 1968. *Human Aggression*. New York: Athenaeum.
Sylvester, D. W., ed. 1970. *Educational Documents, 800-1816*. London: Methuen. See esp. pp. 16, 18, 112 ("Boys should not be struck on the Ears, Noses, Eyes or Faces"—Ruthin Grammar School, 1574).
Talalay, Paul. 1978. "Androgens, Estrogens, and the Mosaic Mouse." *Bulletin of the American Academy of Arts and Sciences* 31, no. 5 (February):9-25.
Teilhard de Chardin, Pierre. 1965a. *Hymn of the Universe*. New York: Harper & Row. First edition published in French in 1961.
———. 1965b. *The Future of Man*. Translated from the French by Norman Denny. New York: Harper & Row. First published in French in 1959.
———. 1969. *Human Energy*. New York: Harper & Row.
Thass-Thienemann, Theodore. 1968. *Symbolic Behavior*. New York: Washington Square Press.
Thomas Aquinas, St. 1941-1945. *Summa theologiae*. 5 vols. Ottawa: Collège Dominicain d'Ottawa; Garden City, N.Y.: Garden City Press.
Tiger, Lionel. 1969. *Men in Groups*. New York: Random House.
Trahim, Betty. 1977. "The Marshall Women's Invitational." *Chess Life and Review* 32, no. 12 (December):639.
U'Ren, Richard C., M.D. 1974. *Ivory Fortress: A Psychiatrist Looks at West Point*. Indianapolis: Bobbs-Merrill.
Van Lawick-Goodall, Jane. 1962. "In the Shadow of Man." *Intellectual Digest* 2, no. 11 (July):57-64.
——— and David A. Hamburg. 1974. "Recent Developments in the Study of Primate Behavior." *Bulletin of the American Academy of Arts and Sciences* 27 (April 7):36-48.
Walther, Fritz A. 1977. "Artiodactyla." Chap. 26 in *How Animals Communicate*, ed. Thomas A. Sebeok, pp. 655-714. Bloomington: Indiana University Press.
Watson, James D. 1968. *The Double Helix: A Personal Account of the Discovery of the Structure of DNA*. New York: Atheneum.
Watts, C. Robert, and Allen W. Stokes. 1971. "The Social Order of Turkeys." *Scientific American* 224, no. 6 (June):112-18.
Wilden, Anthony. 1972. *System and Structure: Essays in Communication and Exchange*. London: Tavistock.
Wiley, R. Haven, Jr. 1978. "The Lek Mating System of the Sage Grouse." *Scientific American* 238, no. 5 (May):114-25.
Wilson, Edward O. 1975. *Sociobiology: The New Synthesis*. Cambridge, Mass.: Belknap Press of Harvard University Press. To avoid multiplication of references to the many and scattered works that Wilson cites and pulls together, in the present work reference is often made simply to Wilson, 1975, through which the various works directly relevant to the matter in hand can readily be traced.

References

———. 1978b. "Altruism." *Harvard Magazine* 81, no. 2 (November-December):21-28.

Wilson, Peter J. 1974. "Oscar: An Inquiry into Madness." *Natural History* 83, no. 1 (February):43-50.

Witkin, H. A. 1967. "Cognitive Styles across Cultures." Extracted from *International Journal of Psychology* 2 in *Culture and Cognition: Readings in Cross-Cultural Psychology*, ed. J. W. Berry and P. R. Dasen (London: Methuen, 1974), pp. 99-117.

Wynne-Edwards, V[ero] C[opner]. 1962. *Animal Dispersion in Relation to Social Behavior*. Edinburgh: Oliver & Boyd.

Index

Abelard, 16
Abrahams, Roger, 35, 108-9, 142
Academia, agonistic structures in, 25-27, 119-48, 186
Achebe, Chinua, 35
Adam, creation of, 98-99
Aggression, 38-41; friendly, 81-82
Agonia, 43-44, 140, 145, 158
Agony, 44
Ali, Muhammed, 108, 152-54
Amadi, Elechi, 35
Anisogamy, 54-55
Antifeminism, 69-70
Arabic, Classical, 133
Ardrey, Robert, 18, 38-39
Ariès, Philippe, 48, 120
Arrowood, Charles Finn, 164
Artes sermocinales, 26
Arthurian stories, 84
Ascham, Roger, 31-32, 132
Asymmetric opposition, 32-34, 100
Augustine of Hippo, St., 120
Austin, Jane, 189

Baader-Meinhof group, 69
Baldick, Robert, 79-80
Balthasar, Hans Urs von, 33
Banyanga. *See* Nyanga people.

Bardwick, Judith M., 61, 64, 66, 68, 77-78, 86, 97-98, 112-13, 115
Barnes, Harry Elmer, 191
Barnett, Samuel Anthony, 59
Barth, E. M., 193
Bateman effect or principle, 55-56
Bearbaiting, 92
Bennett, William, 216
Beowulf, 108, 125
Bereiter, Carl, 146
Bible, interiorizing momentum of, 187, 191; struggle in, 169
Biebuyck, Daniel, 75
Birds as vicarious combatants, 95-96. *See also* Cockfights; Pigeon "mumbling."
Black liberation, 203-5
Bochenski, I. M., 21-22
Bohannan, Paul, 125
Bolgar, R. R., 127
Bombeck, Erma, 67
Bonding, male, 59-60, 81-89, 155-56. *See also* Loners, male.
Bourdieu, Pierre, 109-10, 143
Boxing, 94
"Boy Named Sue, A," 85
Bragging, 110-11, 143, 166
Bruteau, Beatrice, 208

Index

Bryan, William Jennings, 142, 159
Bullbaiting, 92
Bullfighting (*corrida de toros*), 92–93, 185
"Bull session," 82
Bunlap. *See* Pentecost Island, New Hebrides.
Burgess, Anthony (John Anthony Burgess Wilson), 190
Burnett, Carol, 67–68
Byron, George Gordon, 6th baron, 108

Caillois, Roger, 18
Cameron, Kenneth Neill, 191
Camus, Albert, 114
Carmichael, Stokely, 204
Carthy, J. D., 39
Cash, Johnny, 85
Castro, Fidel, 159–62, 192
Celestina, La, 111
Ceremony, 42, 44
Chaplin, Charlie, 67–68
Chapman, Valentine J., 54
Chaucer, Geoffrey, 110
Cheerleaders, 108–9
Chess, 86–89
Children, males' precarious claims to, 74–75
Chinese culture, 22, 34–36, 122
Chinese language, Classical, 133–34
Cicero, Marcus Tullius, 128, 159
Clothing, sex in relation to, 71
Clown, 67–68
Cockfights, 46, 91–92, 94, 96, 185
Coeducation, 139, 145–46
Combat, 42; female, 53, 59–64; male, interspecific, 53; male, intraspecific, 55–64, 96
Communication, human, 196–98, 205
Competition, 43
Competitiveness, 86, 150–51

Computer, hostility toward, 125; mass spectator sports and, 158
Conflict, 42–43
Conrad, Joseph, 115
Conroy, Pat, 84
Consciousness, human: contest affected by, 185–86; evolution of, 25, 28, 140, 149–50, 167–68, 182–83, 184–209; exterior world altered by, 186; reflectiveness of, 186–209. *See also* Self-awareness.
Consciousness of infrahuman animals, 197
Contention, 43
Contest: abstracting effects of, 28–29, 59, 157–58, 191, 202; consciousness and, 28–29; etymology, 45–47; exteriorizing effects of, 201–2; human consciousness affects, 184–87; interiorizing effects of, 201–9; isolating effects of, 201–2; male ceremonial, place of, in evolutionary scale, 51, 193; meaning of, 28–29; socializing effects of, 201. *See also* Distancing by combat.
Corrida de toros. See Bullfighting.
Court, Margaret, 111
Courtly love tradition, 74
Creation, in Genesis, 98–99
Criminals: male and female, 68–69; as vicarious combatants, 93

Dainville, François de, 121
Dakota, 104
Darwin, Charles, 16
Dean, Jerome H. ("Dizzy"), 108
"Dear enemy." *See* Aggression, friendly.
Defense, aggression and, 39
D'Eloia, Sarah, 75–76
Dempsey, Bernard W., 165

Index

Denenberg, Victor H., 41
Dengler, Ralph, 170
Dialectic, as approach to knowledge, 125-26. *See also* Academia, agonistic structures in; Greeks, ancient.
Dialectical structure of thought and knowledge, 29-34
Dialogue, paradigm for, 32-33
Dillard, J. R., 108
Dirksen, Everett, 142
Discovery, competitive basis for, 35-37
Distance, individual or social 38-41, 79-80. *See also* Distancing by combat; Father-son distancing; Territory, aggression and defense in relation to.
Distancing by combat, 59-61, 78-80, 143, 194
Dollard, John, 39
Donne, John, 160
Dostoevski, Fyodor, 189
Douglas, Ann, 166, 208
"Dozens." *See* Fliting.
Dragon, slaying of, 92, 179-80
Dueling, 79-80, 94
Duncan, Otis Dudley, 86, 150
Durand, Gilbert, 22

Ebeling, F. J., 39
Eby, Frederick, 164
Ecology, 186. *See also* Environment.
Eibl-Eibesfeldt, Irenäus, 38, 57, 61, 79, 83
Eleanor of Aquitaine, 189
Eliot, Sir Thomas, 130-31
Eliot, T[homas] S[tearns], 206
Elizabeth I, queen of England, 138
Ellis, Joseph, 112
Ellison, Ralph, 204
Elocution contests, 128
Empedocles, 16

Environment, 77, 82, 102, 145-46. *See also* Ecology.
Erasmus, Desiderius, 153
Erikson, Eric, 16, 19, 85-86, 106
Eucharist, shifting emphasis in interpretation of, 182-83
Euripedes, 97, 106
Eve, creation of, 98-99, 106
Ewer, R. F., 51
Eye gouging, 94

"Fancy talk," 108
Fant, C. G. M., 17
Farrell, Thomas J., 75
Father-son distancing, 85
Faulkner, William, 62-63, 84, 91-92, 190
Featherman, David L., 86, 150
Females: aggressiveness of, 60-61; close affiliation of, in higher animals, 84-85, 90; competitiveness of, 51-52, 60-64; and identity crisis, 147-48, 208; males' pursuit of, 85-86
Feminine, masculine accoutrements appropriated to, 71-74
Femininity as threat to male, 70-76. *See also* Masculinity.
Fey male, 84, 93, 99
Field breaking, 77, 158
Fighting, 42
Fliting (flyting), 108, 125, 142, 154
Foreman, George, 152
Fraternal societies, 89-90
Freedom: Christian faith and, 172-78; human, 10-11, 28, 90, 100-103, 172-78, 181; Mary's virginity and, 172-78
Freilich, Morris, 17
Freud, Sigmund, 65
Friday, Nancy, 84

Index

Frost, Robert, 17
Furer, Manuel, 40, 66, 100

Galloway, K. Bruce, 112
Gambling, 68
Gardner, Howard, 133
Geertz, Clifford, 46, 91, 96, 104, 140
Gender, sex and, 65
Gibson, Bob, 47
Gilbert, Sandra M., 115
Gladiators, 93-94
God: feminity and, 172-78, 183; human response to, 177-78; love of, for human beings, 176-77; masculinity and, 174-77, 183; otherness of, 174-78; as Trinity of Persons, 175-76, 199
Goliath, David and, 108
Goody, Jack [John Rankine], 21
Gothic narrative, 190
Gouldner, Alvin W., 21
Greeks, ancient, 21, 34, 122
Gregg, Richard B., 147, 203-6
Grotjahn, Martin, 67-68, 90, 109

Halle, Morris, 17
Hamburg, David A., 83, 203
Hardships, shared, 81-82
Hardy, C. DeWitt, 120, 131
Hardy, Thomas, 189
Harlow, Harry F., 41
Harlow, Margaret Kuenne, 41
Harvard College, 123
Havelock, Eric A., 21, 161, 188
Heagle, John L., 18
Hebrew, rabbinical, 133
Hediger, H[eine], 57
Hegel, Georg Wilhelm Friedrich, 16, 23, 190
Hennig, Margaret, 62, 85-86
Hero, nonagonistic (antihero), 29, 189-90

Herodotus, 191
Heroic figures (heroes, heroines), 29, 187-90, 192
Heterosexual development, 115
Hibbert, Christopher, 68-69
Hobbes, Thomas, 16
Hofling, Charles K., 114
Hofstadter, Richard, 120, 131
Holliman, Jennie, 94, 152
Homosexuality, 65
Hopkins, Gerard Manley, 10, 177
Horner, Matina, 86
Horse racing, 92
Howell, Wilbur Samuel, 128
Hrdy, Sarah Blaffer, 216
Huizinga, Johan, 18, 25, 33, 44-45, 133, 170
Humor, 67-68
Hunt, David, 48, 134

"I," 194-99, 206-7. *See also* Consciousness, human; Person; Self; Self-awareness.
Iliad, 108, 190
Incest prohibitions, 20
Individuation. *See* Separation of infant from mother.
Intelligence tests, 129
Isaacs, Harold R., 103
Isogamy. *See* Anisogamy.

Jakobson, Roman, 17
Jardim, Anne, 62, 85-86
Jencks, Christopher, 120
Jesus: *agōn* or struggle of, 178-80; diaeretic nature of his mission, 178-80; interiorizing effect of his teaching, 187; as lone male fighter, 180; as nonviolent agonistic figure, 178-80
Johnson, Robert Bowie, Jr., 112
"Joning." *See* Fliting.

Index

Joseph, husband of Mary, 101, 181
Jung, Carl Gustav, 25
Jurisprudence, 17, 28, 43-44. See also Rhetoric.

Kabyle, 64, 109-10, 143, 205
Kafka, Franz, 29
Kahler, Erich, 187
King, Billie Jean, 111
Kligerman, Jack, 94-95
Klingel, H., 83
Knievel, Evel, 67
Knowledge: dialectical structure of, 32-34; polemical nature of, 45; total clarity unrealizable in, 33-34. See also Thought as agonistic activity.
Krabbe, E. C. W., 193

Lacan, Jacques, 47
Lakoff, Robin, 67, 76
Land diving. See Pentecost Island, New Hebrides.
Language: gender forms in, 72; as mother tongue, 36-37; relationship to mother and father, 36-37, 129-39. See also Artes sermocinales; Mother tongues; Speech as combative activity.
Languages, learned, sex-linked, 129-39, 169-70
Latin, Learned, 129-39, 169-70; study of, as puberty rite, 129-33; "toughens the mind," 131
Law. See Jurisprudence.
Lawrence, D. H., 103
Laye, Camara, 35
Legislation, 43-44. See also Jurisprudence; Rhetoric.
Leo I (the Great), pope, 173
Lerner, Harriet E., 70
Levenson, Joseph E., 122

Lévi-Strauss, Claude, 17, 47
Litigation. See Jurisprudence; Rhetoric.
Lloyd, G. E. R., 20-23, 34
Lockwood, Lee, 160-61
Logic: academic study of, 121-22; ancient Greek, 21-23; Indian, 22; not developed in ancient China, 22, 34-36; rhetorical origins of, 21-24, 186
Loners, male, 67-68, 80-83, 155, 180, 201. See also Bonding, male.
Lorenz, Konrad, 18, 38, 40
Ludus (game, school), 132-33, 140
Lyly, John, 108
Lynn, Robert Wood, 128

McGuffey's *Readers*, 127-28
Machismo, 188
Macrocosm. See Microcosm and macrocosm.
McSorley's bar and grill, 89
Mahler, Margaret, 40, 66, 100
Majorettes, 109
Malcolm X, 204
Male: differentiation of, 113; fey (doomed to die), 84, 93, 99; human, dependent on female, 114; insecurity of, 52-56, 64-80, 143-44, 184-85. See also Masculinity.
Male children, preference for, 113-14
Male-female dialectic, 25, 62-64, 100, 103, 140-48, 150, 207-9
Manning, Frank E., 35, 108, 125, 140
"Man of words," 108
Mao Tse-tung, 162
Marie of Champagne, 189
Mark, Hans, 36
Mars's spear, 77, 102
Martyrdom, Christian and Hebrew, 167, 180-82
Marxism, 166-67

227

Index

Mary, mother of Jesus, 100–103, 174–78, 181
Masculinity: differentiation and, 56, 65, 77, 82, 97–98, 112–15; as high-risk condition, 56, 62–70; human, need to prove itself, 70–80, 97–98; relatively small threat to females, 71. *See also* Femininity as threat to male.
Mateene, Kahombo C., 75
Mathematics, 22–23
Matrifocal societies, 83–84
Mayhew, Athol, 66
Mayhew, Henry, 66
Mead, Margaret, 62
Meerlo, Joost A. M., 40
Meissner, William W., 40
Merton, Robert K., 30, 35
Michelangelo Buonarroti, 100
Microcosm and macrocosm, 9–12, 206
Midgley, Mary, 27
Mitre Corporation, 69
Money, John, 112
Moore, Robert, 112
More, Margaret, 138
More, St. Thomas, 138, 182
Mother: aggression absorbed by, 40; deprivation of, 114–15; Great, 92, 100, 188; nurturing (*alma mater*), 40–41; reverence for, 79
Mother tongues, 29, 36–37. *See also* Language.
Muller, Kal, 104–7
Murasaki Shikibu, Lady, 134, 188–89
Murphy, Robert F., 91
Muse, 115

Names, personal, 72–74, 194–95. *See also* Self-awareness.
Native Son (Wright), 190
Nature, Mother, 20, 70, 107, 175

Neumann, Erich, 18–19, 25, 92, 100, 111, 115, 148
New Hebrides. *See* Pentecost Island, New Hebrides.
Noobiology, 11, 27–28, 119, 169
Nyanga people, 75

Oates, Joyce Carol, 190
Odyssey, 108
Oedipus Rex (Sophocles), 190
Oliver, Robert T., 34, 122
Ong, Walter J.: "Agonistic Structures in Academia," 25, 27; "Communications Media and the State of Theology," 138; *Interfaces of the Word*, 29, 133, 187, 189, 199; *Presence of the Word*, 20, 26, 109, 124–25, 127, 166; *Ramus and Talon Inventory*, 25–26; *Ramus, Method, and the Decay of Dialogue*, 21, 24–26, 127; "Ramus: Rhetoric and the Pre-Newtonian Mind," 25; *Rhetoric, Romance, and Technology*, 27, 120, 125, 129, 189; "System, Space, and Intellect in Renaissance Symbolism," 25; "Technology Outside Us and Inside Us," 200; "Truth in Conrad's Darkness," 115
Opland, Jeff [Jeffrey], 109
Oppenheim, A. Leo, 21
Oral cultures, 109, 122–29, 159–63
Orality: academic combat and, 119–44; Afro-American, 108–9, 125; heroic male figures favored by, 187–88, 191; intelligence tests and, 129; machismo favored by, 188; residual, in academia, 27, 125–29; the sexes and, 107–12, 140–44, 187–88; spectator sports and, 153–54

Ortega y Gasset, José, 187, 197
Orwell, George, 136

Parental care, male specialization in, 60
Parthenogenesis, 53–54, 115
Patai, Raphael, 125
Paton, Alan, 97, 106
Paul the Apostle, St., 195–96
Peace, struggle and, 169, 183
Peck, George W., 66
Peirce, Charles Sanders, 17
Pentecost Island, New Hebrides, 104–7, 109, 154
Peristiany, J. G., 109, 124
Person, 199–207; evolution of concept of, 199–201. *See also* Consciousness, human; "I"; Self; Self-awareness
Philosophy, 31–34
Piaget, Jean, 47, 80
Pigeon "mumbling," 94–96
Pius IX, pope, 170
Plato, 16, 131, 161; writing downgraded by, 125
Play, 44–45
Poets, oral and literate, 124
Polanyi, Michael, 23
Polemic, 41–42
Ponca, 104
Praise, 109. *See also* Bragging.
Prizefighting, 94
Protestant Church, 177
Puberty rites, 111–12, 129–33, 148
Public speaking, 140–41

Quietness vs. passivity, 41, 179
Quixote, Don, 63, 99–103

Radcliffe, Ann, 190
Ramus, Peter (Pierre de la Ramée), 24, 127

Rans, Laurel, 69
Reik, Theodor, 69
Rhetoric: academic study of, 121, 126–27; agonistic nature of, 24–26, 121–34, 139–44; oppositions negotiable in, 22; of protest, 203–5; sexuality and, 75–76
Richardson, Lewis F., 122
Riesman, David, 120
Riggs, Bobby, 110–11
Rilke, Rainer Maria, 197
Risk, 56, 62. *See also* Stress.
Robertson, Windham, 62
Rochlin, Gregory, 41
Rojas, Fernando de, 111
Roman Catholic Church: agonistic stance in, 170–71; sexually defined, 172–78
Roman Catholic theology, agonistic structures in, 137–39
Roosevelt, Theodore, 138
"Roots," 112

St. Louis Cardinals, 47
Saint Louis University, 137–39
Sanskrit, 133
Saussure, Ferdinand de, 17
Schneidau, Herbert N., 17
Schnitzler, Arthur, 31
Scott, John Paul, 39, 51
"Screaming." *See* Fliting.
Sebeok, Thomas A., 27
Secret societies, 89–90
Self, 10–11, 20, 196
Self-awareness, 194–99, 206–7. *See also* Consciousness, human; "I"; Person.
Self-fulfillment, 62, 145
Self-giving: female, 100–103; male, 102–3
Separation of infant from mother, 40, 66

Index

Sex: gender and, 65; "weaker," male insecurity regarding, 102, 142. *See also* Unisex.
Sexes, dialectic of, 25, 171–73, 182–83
Sexually determined behavior, culturally conditioned, 51–52, 61, 78
Shakespeare, William, 86, 108, 111, 127
Shelley, Mary, 190
Shull, A. Franklin, 53
Sidney, Mary, countess of Pembroke, 189
"Signifying." *See* Fliting.
Smith, Arthur L., 35, 129
Smith, J. W. Ashley, 164
Sociobiology, 10–11, 19–20, 25, 27, 119. *See also* Noobiology.
Socrates, 125–26
Sophocles, 190
Speech as combative activity, 34–37
Spence, Janet T., 86, 150–51
Spencer, Herbert, 16
Sports, amateur, 42
Sports events: cheering at, 108–9; majorette at, 109; televised, 80, 148
Sterne, Laurence, 153
Stokes, Allen W., 59, 81
Stoller, Robert, 65–66, 115
Storr, Anthony, 40
Strabo, 83
Stress, 75–76; cultivation of, 24–29, 107–12, 115. *See also* Risk.
Structuralism, 47
Struggle, 42
Student protest, 29, 119–22, 145–48, 203–5
Sun Dance, 104
Sylvester, D. W., 120, 127

Talalay, Paul, 65
Teilhard de Chardin, Pierre, 18

Television: and public speaking, 128, 142, 153; and spectator sports, 47, 147–48, 156–58; violence and whodunit on, 190
Territory, aggression and defense in relation to, 39–41, 55–61, 157. *See also* Distance, individual or social; Distancing by combat.
Testes (testicles), as "witnesses," 45–47, 98
Thomas Aquinas, St., 126, 176
Thought as agonistic activity, 34–37, 47. *See also* Knowledge.
Thucidydes, 191
Tiger, Lionel, 79
Tom Brown's Schooldays, 132
Trahim, Betty, 88
Transsexualism, 65–66
Transvestism, 65–66
Truth, dialectical structure of, 32–34

Unisex, 115
Updike, John, 29
U'Ren, Richard C., 112

Van Lawick-Goodall, Jane, 78, 82–83, 203
Vatican Council, Second, 170–71
Venus's mirror, 77
Verbalization, agonistic, 26–27, 34–37, 107–8, 143–44. *See also* Fliting; Orality.
Villalonga, Joachim, 138
Virgil (Publius Virgilius Maro), 81
Virgin birth. *See* Mary, mother of Jesus; Virginity.
Virginity, 90. *See also* Mary, mother of Jesus.

Walther, Fritz A., 58, 61
War as game, 62
War party, 81
War prisoners, 93

Watson, James D., 35
Watts, C. Robert, 59, 81
Western fiction, 190
West Point, U.S. Military Academy at, 112
Whodunit, television, 190
Wilden, Anthony, 20, 80
Wiley, R. Haven, Jr., 56
Wilson, Edward O., 19–20, 25, 27, 38–39, 53–56, 60, 82–83, 90, 201
Wilson, Peter J., 35
Witkin, H. A., 77
Women: education of, 134–39; influence of, on and in literature, 188–90; interiority and self-possession of, 90–91; narrators of folktales, 141
Women's liberation, 203–5
Word, technologizing of, 26, 125, 158
Wrestling, 94
Wright, Richard, 190
Writing, disparities shown up by, 21. *See also* Oral cultures; Orality.
Wynne-Edwards, V[ero] C[opner], 38–39, 59, 107

www.ingramcontent.com/pod-product-compliance
Lightning Source LLC
Chambersburg PA
CBHW070251230426
43664CB00014B/2486